DEVON SHIPWRECKS

Frontispiece: The wreck of HMS *Ramillies* under Bolt Tail, 15 February 1760—*From a painting*

DEVON
SHIPWRECKS

by

RICHARD LARN

DAVID & CHARLES
NEWTON ABBOT   LONDON
NORTH POMFRET (VT)   VANCOUVER

ISBN 0 7153 6337 9

To Maureen,
and my children, Victoria and Tracy

Set in 11 on 13pt Times and printed in
Great Britain by Latimer Trend & Company Ltd
for David & Charles (Holdings) Limited
South Devon House Newton Abbot Devon

Published in the United States of America
by David & Charles Inc North Pomfret
Vermont 05053 USA

Published in Canada by Douglas David & Charles Limited
3645 McKechnie Drive West Vancouver BC

CONTENTS

LIST OF ILLUSTRATIONS

7

LINE DRAWINGS IN THE TEXT

Whilst the small wreck-site charts show almost exact locations, the larger charts illustrating individual chapters show only approximate positions

'Sink, sink, and oh so
gladly like a stone
To the deep dark'

—Hilton Brown, 1936,
from the poem 'Herzogin
Cecilie speaks'

INTRODUCTION

The coast of Devon shares so many of the geographical features of neighbouring Cornwall that a stranger could readily mistake one for the other. Both counties have seaboards facing the English and Bristol Channels, with bleak headlands separating the major ports and an abundance of fishing villages between, all of which have seen more prosperous times.

Wrecks have occurred on the Devon coast in their thousands for the same reasons as in Cornwall and elsewhere, namely stress of weather, fog, or bad navigation. Unfortunately, there has been in Devon less local interest in the subject of wrecks than further west, where shipwrecks are still a byword and are well documented. With virtually no existing records, this history of Devon wrecks has been compiled by original research through countless thousands of newspapers, lifeboat records, State Domestic Papers, Custom House records, Manor Rolls, and other sources. Inevitably, there must be mistakes and a great many wrecks are not mentioned; for these I make no apologies other than to say that every effort has been made to eliminate errors where possible. When three different newspapers spell a ship's name in three different ways, none of which agree with *Lloyds Register*, which in turn differs from the captain's hand-written deposition, it becomes impossible to decide which is correct.

In some earlier volumes in this series the 'index of ships' was limited to those mentioned in the text, so reducing their reference value. Since the profusion of wrecks around Devon prohibits every incident being catalogued in its respective chapter, a comprehensive index has been provided, which offers the reader sufficient information to conduct his own research.

St Austell   RICHARD LARN
January 1974

13

PLYMOUTH SOUND TO
THE EDDYSTONE

It is doubtful if any county in the British Isles can claim a closer hereditary connection with the sea than Devon. Described appropriately as 'the cradle of British seafarers', there was once a time when every leading town was a seaport of considerable standing, many of which had intimate connections with some of the most famous seamen in history. Drake, Hawkins, Raleigh, Frobisher and Gilbert; Grenville, Cavendish, Cook, the Earl of Cumberland, among others, are but some of the many adventurers who left Devon on voyages of discovery or to fight for England. Whilst these names are well known, almost household words to the British in fact, Devon can equally well boast of her thousands, if not tens of thousands, of ordinary, anonymous seamen. Men who manned the king's ships in time of war—even if with reluctance during the dark days of the 'press'—or the inshore fishing fleets, deep water, and coastal trade during peace; men who followed the banners of the Crusaders, voyaged to the ends of the earth to discover new continents or fought and died for principles dear to their nation. Regardless of rank, they all contributed towards an unparalleled maritime history.

The vagaries of nature were partially responsible for the growth of Devon to such an extent that, by the latter half of the sixteenth century, it had become England's foremost county. Had the courses of the rivers Tamar, Tavey, Lynher or Plym been diverted elsewhere, their estuaries would not have combined to slowly scour away the coastline and emerge as the huge, natural anchorage known today as Plymouth Sound; for the Sound and the many anchorages it encloses have been a major contributory factor in the history of the British Isles, and one whose importance

15

in military and economic affairs cannot be over-emphasised. Although the wide sweep of the Sound has probably remained unchanged, apart from natural silting, for thousands of years, sailing-ship masters of the middle ages, naturally reluctant to be caught at anchor within a bay should the wind blow onshore, preferred the estuaries of Salcombe, the Dart, Exe and Teign, with the result that Plymouth was slow to develop.

Although mentioned in the Domesday Book as Sutton or South Town, little is known of the port which was the beginning of Plymouth until the thirteenth century when, for example, a 'fleet of 325 ships assembled in the Sound in 1287, in preparation for an attack on the French coast'.[1] Ten years later, army stores for Gascony were being assembled in the town, awaiting the arrival of the fleet, this time one of even greater proportions. The growth of the town and an ever increasing number of ships in the area soon began to attract pirates and other undesirables. In 1388 it is recorded that '—certaine Pyrates sail about the havens of Cornwall and Devonshire, doing in all places much harme to the fishermen, and such shippes as they find unarmed they fiered. At length they entered Plimmouth Haven where they brent certaine great shippes and a great part of the towne'.[2]

Obviously, ships both large and small were being wrecked on the Devon coast from the earliest times. Of Plymouth itself, in 1794 it was said 'wrecks often happen under Mount Batten and other eminences near the town—',[3] but records of shipwrecks in the area go back to 1362, when, for example, 'Hugo de Courteney and two other commissioners were appointed to hear and determine a case relating to spoil of wreck of a ship called the *Tarrit*. The offence was seizure of wreck at Plymouth belonging to the king'. Cross-Channel raids by the Bretons were frequent, and despite a chain boom across the harbour mouth, the crews of ships and the occupants of Sutton were forced to flee into the countryside on more than one occasion, leaving unattended vessels which were frequently set on fire and lost. Even the Turks ventured as far as Plymouth looking for galley slaves, and in 1640 the bays of Wembury and Cawsand were strewn with abandoned ships, deliberately run ashore and wrecked rather

Page 17: The East Indiaman *Dutton* wrecked under Plymouth Hoe on 26 January 1796—*From an oil painting by T. Lury*

Page 18: (above) Caught by a gale while at anchor in Cawsand Bay, Plymouth, the full-rigged ship *Oregon* was blown ashore and wrecked under Picklecombe Battery, 18 March 1867; (below) an unidentified wreck in Plymouth Sound, probably a hulked warship of about 1850

than be allowed to fall into enemy hands. When eventually gun batteries and defences were erected at Mount Batten, St Nicholas (now Drake's) Isle, and on the Hoe to counter these attacks, it is worth noting that their purpose was not entirely defence of the town and port. In referring to the massive Citadel, whose foundation stone was laid by the Earl of Bath in 1666, Count Magalotti wrote in 1669, '. . . built by the king to be a check on the inhabitants, who showed themselves on former occasions prone to sedition, and that spirit being now fostered by the influx of wealth which a flourishing commerce produces, renders them objects of reasonable suspicion. The Citadel, placed on the top of a mountain, serves as a defence to the port against the sea, hence it equally commands the sea, or the town, and defends or batters, as occasion may require'.[4]

Plymouth was chosen by the Admiralty in 1690 to become the major naval base in the south-west, and with shipping activity increasing in volume right up until the early part of the twentieth century it is not surprising that it has a considerable history of shipwreck. The majority were caused directly by the elements, with collisions, inevitable in a crowded roadstead, a second best. Others were brought about by fire, explosion, accident or enemy action. The earliest wreck incident recorded in any detail was that of the *Lavinia*, a prize vessel captured from the French, which dragged her anchors until she went ashore on St Nicholas Isle in December 1603; whilst the first record of an entire fleet being endangered concerned the Duke of Buckingham, who had recently returned from Ile de Rhe. His ships were caught at anchor during a severe gale on 26 November 1627, and by morning fifteen of them were ashore in the Hamoaze and five more in the Cattewater. How many of these, if any, were saved is not known, but iron cannon have frequently been dragged up from the mud here, several being raised by a dredger during 1972, but were unidentifiable apart from being of typical sixteenth century construction. An interesting reference in the State papers for 1637 gives details of the wreck of an East India Company ship, the *Paulsgrove* of London, which was lost on St Nicholas Isle, and reads:

B

The governor and East India committee sent letters for the ship to come to London. When endeavouring to leave Plymouth, the weather upon the sudden grew exceeding violent, that she could not with safety get out of the Sound. The pilot, purser, and one Thomas Monmouth seeing the danger the ship was in, did entreat the defendant [Captain Cluett] not to proceed, but to return to her former moorings. Defendant being in a fretful mood and passionate humour, threwe downe his staff and stamping said, that 'he would not return'. That the company of the said ship, perceiving the great danger she was in, by prayer committed their souls to God, and after an hour the carpenters were employed about stopping her hawsers to prevent the seas cominge in too faste uppon the deck, and called for hands to bale the water from the gun deck. Afterwards the cable broke, and the ship was driven ashore.

The closing months of 1689 saw a series of severe gales that played havoc with vessels both in and outside the Sound. A six-gun fireship of 120 tons, the *Charles and Henry*, was lost somewhere close to Plymouth on 29 November, and on Christmas Day, HMS *Centurion*, thirty-four guns, 513 tons (bm), built by Pett & Ratcliffe in 1650, was lost on Mount Batten, along with the sixty-two gun *Henrietta*, which had been launched down a Thames slipway in 1654 as the *Langport*, only to be renamed in 1660. Of the many disasters concerning naval ships at Plymouth, the greatest loss of life occurred in the foundering of the 2nd rate, ship-of-the-line, HMS *Coronation*, on 3 September 1691 during a gale which also claimed the sixty-gun, 3rd rate *Harwich*. This incident is best described in the words of Edward Barlow, who writes:

> ... and Admiral Russell being come up as far as Plymouth, and our coast being a lee shore to southerly winds, it then blowing hard and fearing bad weather, Admiral Russell bore up and sailed into Plymouth Sound. A great part of the fleet followed him, and running so hastily one upon another, caused many of them to run on board of one another. Some ran into the Cattewater, and in running into the Hamoaze, three or four ran ashore, one of them of sixty odd guns, named the *Harwich*, which was bilged and lost along with 420 men, the rest getting off much damaged. The *Coronation*, coming into the Sound and her anchor being let go, veered out cable to bring her up. She took a salley and sank down to rightes in about twenty-two fathoms, having on board above 500 men, and not above twenty of them saved, and a ship of ninety guns, a very dreadful accident and a great loss, the cause of which is scarce known.[5]

HMS *Harwich* of 993 tons (bm), built by Deane of Harwich in 1674, was in fact a seventy-gun vessel and not sixty as suggested by Barlow, whilst the *Coronation*, of 1,346 tons (bm), had been launched at Portsmouth dockyard in 1685. Although Barlow makes no mention of the *Coronation* being dismasted before sinking, another report by Burchett suggests that this was the case. He states,

> . . . a violent storm arose, in so much that all which could be done for their preservation was to bear up for so dangerous a port as Plymouth—the ships were so confusedly scattered that the greatest part of them were not seen when the admiral himself came to anchor in the Sound. When it grew somewhat clearer, one of the second rates, the *Coronation*, was discovered at anchor off the Ram Head without anything left standing but the ensign staff, and foundering soon after.

Although a wreck site discovered by divers at Penlee, in which some thirty iron cannon lie scattered on the seabed, has been claimed to be that of the *Coronation*, there is not a scrap of evidence to support this theory. If Barlow's report is true in its detail, then the *Coronation* foundered in 132ft of water, and since this depth can only be found some 2,000yd offshore, it would be more accurate to describe this find at Penlee as being simply, 'an unidentified wreck site'.

As a direct result of the loss of the *Harwich*, the Admiralty stated to buoy the main channel leading into the Hamoaze. These buoys, and others in the Sound, bear the names of famous naval vessels such as *Albermarle, Vanguard, Panther, Melampus* and *Asia*. There may well be some truth in the suggestion that these names refer to particular ships that struck reefs or went ashore in the vicinity, but this is difficult to establish. The reef currently known as *Asia* was, in fact, named *Africa* on charts prior to 1780, and in the preparation of this book no incidents involving naval vessels of the above names could be unearthed. It would be interesting, by the same token, to establish whether or not there is any historical connection between the Shovell rock, now part of the breakwater, and the famous admiral, Sir Cloudesley Shovell, who lost his life in the wreck of HMS *Association* in 1707.

Wrecks around the turn of the eighteenth century included two naval vessels named *Mermaid*. The first of these, a 174 ton fireship, was accidently burnt on 25 February 1693; the other, a

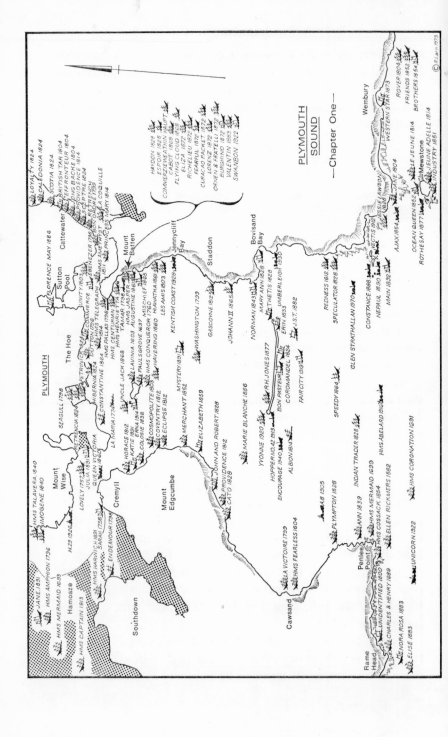

PLYMOUTH SOUND

—Chapter One—

© R.Lenn 1973

HAYDON 1828
ESPOIR 1826
COMMERCE WITHIN HAUFT 1782
CABOT 1869
FLYING CLOUD 1856
ELIZA 1872
RICHELL 1872
FEARFUL 1872
CURACAO PACKET 1872
LORENZ 1872
ORNEN & FRATELLI 1872
BURGHINO 1872
VALENTIN 1883
SWANBON 1922

5th rate, thirty-two gun frigate, foundered with all hands at the mouth of Plymouth Sound on 5 January 1699. Although not strictly wrecks in the accepted terms, the thirty-six gun prize *Saudadoes*, the 6th rate *Dunwich*, and the 4th rate *Moor*, were all deliberately sunk at Mount Batten as breakwaters, or foundations for them, between 1712 and 1716, to be joined by HMS *Vengeance* in October 1766. The sloop *Lovely*, another victim of storm, drove from her moorings in 1757 to sink off the naval victualling yard, and in 1758 the *Sarah* struck a rock in coming down the Tamar after loading coal. She drifted off to sink in deep water near Cremyll Passage, unlike the seventy-gun HMS *Conqueror*, only two years old when she went ashore on the south-east corner of St Nicholas Isle on 26 October 1760 to become a total wreck. At the court martial held aboard the *Barfleur*, the pilot was found to be 'highly blameable in getting the ship underway in such weather as prevailed at the time, and from his want of knowledge as a seaman, did not direct the proper sails to be set, by which neglect the *Conqueror* drove to leeward and was stranded'. The unfortunate pilot, Henry Harris, was confined in Marshalsea prison for eighteen months.

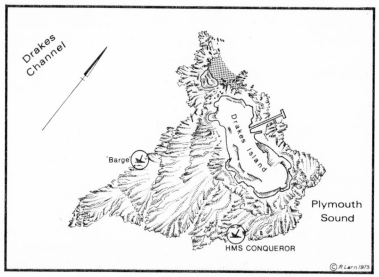

Location of HMS *Conqueror* on Drake's Island

Credit for the first successful submersible craft or submarine must go to the American, David Bushnell (1776), but there were many other experimenters striving for the same goal, although some of them had doubtful motives. Amongst these must be counted Mr Day, who conducted two experiments at Plymouth, the latter proving fatal. It would appear that he had more enthusiasm for making money than technical ability for such a task, since he was described as, '. . . a man, very illiterate and indigent in his circumstances. He was bred with no particular trade, but had been employed as a labourer amongst ships' carpenters at Yarmouth, his native place'.[6] For reasons best known to himself, and almost certainly mercenary, he had pursued this project for many years, and in fact conducted his first 'experiment' in the comparatively shallow Cattewater, where he remained underwater, inside a 'submarine vessel', for the full six hours of an ebb tide, followed by the flood, before unscrewing two pins that retained some ballast, thereby allowing the device to rise to the surface.

In 1774 Mr Day proposed his scheme to a Charles Blake as an affair by which wagers could be won, saying that he was confident he could remain underwater in twenty fathoms for six hours. At the invitation of his sponsor, Mr Day went to London, made a model of his device, then took it back to Plymouth where a shipwright named Hunn accepted the task of converting a suitable vessel. The vessel chosen was a fifty-ton sloop named *The Maria*, purchased from her owner, Mr Sparks, for the sum of £350. She was fitted out according to Mr Day's instructions and must have aroused much interest locally as she lay on the slipway. With a keel length of 31ft, a 16ft beam, and 9ft in the hold, she was an old ship but still in good condition. Her conversion required her to be completely recaulked, then sheathed overall, after which a wooden chamber was built inside the hull, measuring $12 \times 9 \times 8$ft deep and having a capacity of 'seventy-five hogsheads'. This chamber was scarfed, bolted and secured with knees and cross supports inside, then sheathed with 2in planks at right angles to the main timbers, the whole then being liberally coated with pitch from the outside. These requirements severely taxed the imagination of the shipwright, who had to overcome many difficulties in building a wooden box capable of holding sufficient air to keep a man alive for a whole day if necessary at a depth of 130ft.

Access to the interior of the chamber was gained by means of a hatch, suitably wedge-shaped in cross section, so that the increasing pressure as the vessel sank would improve the efficiency of the flannel-lined seal. So heavy was this hatch, in fact, that it required a large counterbalance on the inside. Considerable ingenuity went into the method of signalling the surface once the vessel was under water. Three coloured buoys were attached to the outside of the chamber, secured by plugs which could be forced out from inside, the release of which allowed them to float to the surface. If a white buoy appeared, it indicated that the occupant was 'very well'; a red buoy showed that he was 'indifferent'; and black, 'very ill'. To achieve some positive buoyancy in order to get back to the surface, the release of stone ballast was arranged. Four lead pipes through the floor of the chamber and hull held four iron bolts, which in turn were secured into shaped granite blocks. It was envisaged by the designer that he had only to take off four large nuts and the ballast would be released. The sheer impossibility of undoing nuts, each holding back some five tons of rock, seems to have been completely overlooked, as was the method of resealing the holes left open to the sea once the ballast bolts had been withdrawn. The diver—since this is how Mr Day saw himself—intended to take a mallet and a number of wooden plugs which would be hammered into the open ends of the pipes, but this would have been against the external water pressure of approximately sixty pounds per square inch, and difficult to accomplish.

On the day of the experiment, 20 June 1774, the vessel was taken round to Millbay and there Mr Day entered the chamber, taking with him, 'a hammock, watch, small wax taper, a bottle of water, and two ship's biscuits'. Once the hatch had been sealed, *The Maria* was towed to a position described as 150 fathoms offshore from Firestone Bay, due north of St Nicholas Isle. Under the supervision of the sponsor, the vessel's flooding plugs were withdrawn, but she refused to sink! Despite ten tons of stone ballast inside the hull, plus a further twenty tons hanging on the release bolts, a further twenty had to be added before she finally began to sink, and at 8 am touched bottom in roughly 100ft of water. A few minutes later there was a violent ebullition of air and the surface boats watched carefully for a signal, but none came. The appointed time for the vessel to return to the surface was 2 pm, and as the hour approached the Hoe and other high areas became crowded with spectators, a great many of whom had wagers on the outcome. By late afternoon it was obvious that something had gone wrong, but for reasons completely inexplicable the whole night was allowed to pass before assistance was sought of Lord Sandwich, superintendent of the dockyard. He offered full use of the facilities available, and for three days hundreds of men were employed in sweeping for the wreck. Unfortunately, in the sloop's conversion, all projections had been removed, which along with Mr Day's insistence that she carried no attachments to aid salvage, made it almost impossible to snag the hull with grapples. Located finally in twenty-two fathoms, it took until 3 August before ropes were successfully swept beneath the vessel and hauled taut from the surface. *The Maria* was then lifted on the tide and moved 300ft nearer to St Nicholas Isle, only to slip from her cradle and disappear again. Her re-location and re-slinging wasted another month, and just as everything was ready for a second lift into shallow water on 21 October, a gale sprang up and work had to be abandoned. Mr Blake then returned to London, unable to neglect his business further, and the wreck with the presumably drowned occupant was abandoned. Many were the theories put forward as to the cause of the accident, whereas it is now obvious that the experiment was doomed to failure from the outset. It was even seriously suggested that the changing air temperature as the vessel sank caused an almost perfect vacuum inside the chamber, and that Mr Day was asphyxiated. The author of the lengthy report concerning the affair suggested that 'the air pressure does not depend on the depth but the coldness of the air. Mr Day's blood must have been chilled into an immediate coagulation'.

This minor tragedy was followed by a long succession of wrecks on the Hoe, Mount Batten, St Nicholas Isle, and unspecified locations in the Sound, but none was of any great consequence until 1796, when two major losses occurred, the East Indiaman *Dutton* and HMS *Amphion*. Bound for the West Indies with part of the Queen's 2nd Regiment aboard, the *Dutton* had already been at sea for seven weeks when her condition forced her captain to turn back for Plymouth. Whilst making for the Cattewater, since the open Sound offered little shelter, she struck the Mount Batten shoal, its warning buoy having gone adrift in a recent gale. Rudderless, the *Dutton* was swept helpless on to the rocks beneath the Hoe and within minutes all three masts fell, the entire wreck becoming a tangled mass of rigging and canvas. Panic broke out on board due to lack of leadership, the ship's officers having already abandoned their charge, leaving the remaining crew and passengers to their fate. Despite large numbers of spectators on the Hoe, not one of them made any attempt to effect a rescue, and it was not until Sir Edward Pellew, captain of HMS *Indefatigable*, appeared on the scene that anything was done. He risked his life by climbing aboard the *Dutton*, using the same rope by which her officers had escaped, but before leaving the shore he sent a message to his own ship calling for assistance and offering money to any local who would put a boat alongside the wreck.

In reaching the *Dutton*, Sir Edward injured his back when climbing round the fallen mainmast but, undaunted, assumed command and supervised her abandonment. Two boats from the *Indefatigable* arrived alongside, plus another from a schooner, and were instrumental in saving almost 600 lives, thanks to Sir Edward's intervention. The citizens of Plymouth showed their appreciation by awarding him the freedom of the city. The wreck of the *Dutton* made sufficient impression to inspire him to adopt a stranded ship in his crest when he was made a baronet the following year (Picture, p 17).

Until the end of the eighteenth century, warship losses continued to predominate in the Plymouth area, and whilst the *Coronation* was the most tragic in terms of lives lost, the most spectacular was that of the *Amphion*, in the Hamoaze. A 5th rate vessel of 680 tons (bm), carrying thirty-two guns, the *Amphion* had been launched at the royal Chatham yard on 21 December 1780. In September 1796 she was away cruising in the North Sea, on the lookout for signs of Napoleon's threatened invasion, when a gale sprang her foremast, forcing her to return to Plymouth. Under new orders to join a squadron of frigates commanded by Sir Edward Pellew, brother of Lord Exmouth and the *Amphion*'s captain, it was imperative that no time be wasted in stepping the new mast; for these were uneasy days, with war on the horizon and troopships leaving for Ireland every day to counter the French threat. The *Amphion* was brought into the Hamoaze on 14 September, placed alongside a sheer hulk, and work began on the removal of her bowsprit and damaged mast. The task was completed by the 21st of the month and orders came aboard for her to sail on the morning of the 23rd. As was the custom, a farewell party was held aboard and wives, children and sweethearts swarmed aboard the frigate, crowding her lower deck. Meanwhile, the ship's officers were dressing for the evening meal, having been invited to dinner by Capt Israel Pellew, who had also asked Capt Swaffield of the Dutch man o' war *Overryssel*, a sixty-four gun ship at anchor in the Sound. A massive explosion occurred at 4.30 pm on Tuesday 22 September, which was felt as a violent shock throughout Stonehouse and neighbouring Plymouth. Even at considerable distances from the dockyard, the sky was seen to be bright red and people thronged the streets in a state of panic, thinking the town was under attack.

When the confusion had died down it was ascertained that the *Amphion* had blown up, fortunately without serious damage to nearby ships. Remarkably, the old receiving hulk, HMS *Yarmouth*, only yards away, survived the blast but was found to be well splattered with human remains. Amongst the few eyewitnesses to the incident was the signal lieutenant aboard the flagship, moored a short distance down stream. At the inquiry he stated, 'she rose out of the water till part of her keel was visible, and the strangeness of the sight made me feel I was giddy. Almost as quick as the thought passed through my mind, she blew up'.

So violent was the explosion that the entire forepart of the *Amphion* disintegrated, while the remainder fell back into the harbour and sank instantly in ten fathoms. It was never established with any accuracy how many people were aboard at the time, but certainly there were not less than 100 visitors, in addition to her crew of some 215 officers and men. According to contemporary accounts, 300 out of the 312 aboard were killed, only ten men, one woman and a child surviving, some of whom received fearful injuries. The surface of the Hamoaze was strewn with broken timbers, spars and rigging, and 'the deck of the sheer hulk, to which the frigate was lashed, was red with blood and covered with mangled limbs and lifeless trunks, all blackened with powder'.[7] Complete corpses and severed limbs alike were collected and taken to Stonehouse naval hospital so that relatives could identify the dead, the majority of whom were local men.

In all probability there were two explosions in quick succession. The first of these had the effect of throwing both ships' captains, plus the 1st lieutenant, against the carlings of the cabin deckhead, leaving them partially stunned. Capt Pellew had the presence of mind to leap for the stern windows, whereupon the second explosion hurled him clear of the vessel and into the harbour where he was later found injured, but alive. Similarly, the 1st lieutenant saved his life by diving headlong through the window, but the unfortunate Dutchman was killed. When his body was eventually recovered, one month later, severe fracturing of his skull suggested he had been crushed to death between the side of the *Amphion* and the sheer hulk. Only four officers survived the disaster, the dead including Mr Hearle, 3rd lieutenant; Mitchell, master; McGowan, surgeon; Lieut Campbell, Royal Marines; the gunner, carpenter, and several midshipmen. Some remarkable escapes were recorded; the sentry at the door of the captain's cabin remembered glancing at his pocket watch at the instant of the explosion, but when found ashore, wandering aimlessly, uninjured and in dry clothes, he had no recollection as to how he had got there. The bo'sun, who was standing on the starboard cathead supervising the re-rigging of the jib boom, was directly over the first explosion but suffered only a broken arm, whilst every man in the working party was blown to pieces. Amongst the few civilian survivors was a female child, well and alive, clutched in the arms of her mother who was already dead, having had the entire lower portion of her body blown off. The accident resulting in the loss of the frigate was blamed on a gunner, said to be stealing powder, who ignited some spilt explosive when drunk, so detonating the forward magazine. During salvage of the shattered forepart, a sack was recovered containing gunpowder concealed beneath a layer of ship's biscuit, which tended to support the allegation. Only a few of the ship's guns were recovered from the deep mud of the harbour and many weeks passed before the stern portion was dragged into the shallows alongside the dockyard wall, where the decomposed corpse of a female floated out from below decks.

Sheltered though Plymouth Sound might be from prevailing winds, it was open and unprotected from southerly gales and scarcely a month went by without some vessel beating her bottom out in the shallows. On 24 February 1798 a culm-laden schooner, the *Ebenezer*, was wrecked on Batten rocks, and less than two months later the thirty-two gun frigate *Pallas* was lost in exactly the same place. Commanded by the Hon H. Curzon, she parted her cables and went ashore, huge seas sweeping clean over the wreck. Despite the fact that the *Pallas* was on her beam ends, only one member of her crew lost his life. Three days later her already shattered timbers were joined by those of a large dockyard lighter, the *Tamar*, also put ashore by a gale. Bad weather brought the sloop *Seagull*, carrying coal from Liverpool, scurrying into Plymouth Sound for shelter, only to be driven into Millbay and lost on 17 September of that same year. Before Christmas there was a repetition of the *Amphion* incident, fortunately with little loss of life, involving the French prize *La Coquille* of forty-four guns, taken by Sir Warren off Ireland. One of many such prizes that filled the Cattewater, she blew up while at anchor at the foot of Millbrook Lake. The explosion blew out her entire quarterdeck and sent the mizzen mast 300ft into the air. Flames spread quickly to both remaining masts and in less than half an hour she had to be abandoned. Grapples were thrown aboard and the blazing vessel was then towed clear of the anchorage and run ashore on the mudbank north-east of Southdown. But not before she had brushed against the coal-laden brig *Endeavour*, of Scarborough, setting her ablaze. Both vessels burnt to the waterline and became total losses.

The gale of February 1799 was described by the *Gentleman's Magazine* as being, 'the most severe hurricane ever remembered at Plymouth'.[8] The privateer *Bon Orde* was stranded and wrecked in the Cattewater, and *La Victoire* went ashore and was lost in Cawsand Bay shortly after, in addition to others. In complete contrast, the Liverpool cotton ship *Washington* was lost by fire on 23 October, following the visit of a naval press gang. Her crew took to a specially prepared hiding-place deep down in the hold when the press boat appeared. While hiding, the cook dropped his knife and, in searching for it with a naked light, accidently set some cotton alight. She burnt all that day and half the night, and out of the 3,000 bales aboard valued at £30,000 only 350 were saved. As storm after storm swept through the Sound, so they left behind an increasing trail of wrecked ships, drowned seamen, and impoverished owners. On Christmas Day 1803, a French prize named *Les Amis*, an unidentified brig, the privateer *Cosmopolite*, the *Unity* and several smaller craft were all wrecked. The larger of these, the twenty-year-old prize, had been on passage from Martinique to Bordeaux with 178 hogsheads of sugar and 38 of coffee when she was captured by HMS *Malta*. After being blown ashore, her stern fell completely off and it became necessary to call on Col Longnead's battalion of Plymouth volunteers to mount guard over the cargo that scattered over the shore. A captain, two subalterns, and forty rank and file remained on duty all night, during which time they fired several shots at water pirates who attempted to come in from seaward to plunder. The *Unity*, a brig carrying coal and pipe staves from Liverpool to Jersey, went down in Deadman's Bay with a sick member of her crew still in his bunk. By some remarkable act of providence, he floated up from the wreck long after she sank and was picked up alive.

Another gale on 19–20 January 1804 was particularly severe

and ten vessels were lost in the area. In the *Sherborne Mercury*, a reporter commented:

> ... the storm of the 19th was dreadful, and its effects much felt at this port as well as to both eastward and westward of Plymouth. A whirlwind frequently carried water in sheets over the town of Cawsand, and deluged the fleet in a sluice. A large brig without a soul on board was found wrecked, all standing, near Wembury. She soon went to pieces and her cargo floated ashore, being boxes of stationery and chests of valuable books, especially some fine editions of the Latin classics, elegantly bound but sadly damaged, which with other articles supposes she was bound for some foreign port.

Although the name of that particular vessel is not known for sure, others that were recorded during the same gale include the brig o' war *Fearless* in Cawsand; the *British Tar*; *L'Effronteur*, a captured French privateer; the *Jong Backe*, and two fishing sloops, all of which sank in the Cattewater alone, whilst the *Jane* foundered close to the Mewstone. Still blowing hard, the wind swung from south-west to south-east on the 25th, causing many vessels to slip their cables and capsizing a large pinnace belonging to HMS *Prince* between St Nicholas Isle and Redding Point. Of the eleven men aboard, only one survived, the accident taking place in exactly the same place and in the same manner as that in which Capt Drew of HMS *Cerebus* and Capt Pulling of the *Kangaroo* had been drowned a few years earlier. Such accidents amongst store and prison boats from the fleet were commonplace. On 17 January 1805 a launch from the 110-gun *Hibernia* was upset and sunk on the Rannies, between the Shagstone and the mainland, with a midshipman and twenty-three seamen drowned. Several of the men in this particular incident were survivors from HMS *Venerable*, wrecked the previous year in Torbay.

In one respect, the first decade of the nineteenth century was dramatic and exciting for Plymouth, for during this period literally thousands of prize vessels were brought into the Sound, where they were either taken into the king's service or else stripped of their valuables and auctioned. These prizes brought wealth to just about everyone in some measure; the crews of the capturing ships enjoyed prize money; the monarch or government took any treasure aboard; the navy acquired a number of additional ships; and the people of Plymouth welcomed the extra money that passed into their hands via traders. Some of these captured vessels were exceptionally wealthy. On 17 January 1805 HMS *Phoenix*, of forty-four guns, Capt Halsted, brought in the Spanish *El Mercurio*, whose hold contained 20,000 silver dollars, 300 ounces of gold dust, 80,000 animal horns, 140 barrels of tallow, 150 bales of wool, plus beef, copper, hides and cocoa. Later that month, the Spanish frigate *Santa Gertruda* was escorted in by the *Polyhemus*, and swelled the national coffers by over one and a half million silver dollars. It took seven carts, each drawn by four horses, to transfer the specie from the vessel to the Citadel, and later to London, but this was by no means the richest prize of them all. In March 1805, the 'Flying' *Pallas* as she was known, later wrecked on the east coast of Scotland, brought in a Spaniard with diamonds, gold and silver bullion, in addition to over £1m in coin.

It is said that Admiral Earl St Vincent first proposed the building of a breakwater at Plymouth in 1806, since the continuing stream of naval and merchant vessels wrecked annually were more than an embarrassment to those in authority. They needed no reminder that something must be done to make Plymouth a better anchorage. Several proposals as to the form the breakwater should take were investigated, and eventually a central breakwater, with piers jutting out from each shore, was chosen. This was the decision of the Master Attendants of the Woolwich and Plymouth dockyards, Joseph Whidby and Samuel Hemans respectively, in conjunction with John Rennie, who carried out the actual survey. For five years the plan lay dormant, then formal approval was granted by an Order in Council dated 22 June 1811, and fourteen months later the massive foundation stone was laid on Shovell rock. Perhaps the final decision to start work was accelerated by the heavy loss of life in the wreck of HMS *Amethyst*, which occurred at Mount Batten on 16 February 1811. A thirty-eight gun frigate of the 5th rate, built at Deptford in 1799, she drove from her anchorage in a heavy west-south-west gale and went ashore shortly after midnight. Her masts were cut down, but she filled so quickly that her crew were obliged to take to the boats immediately. All six of these were swamped within minutes and their occupants drowned. Other men o' war and transports in the vicinity sent boats to assist, but these, too, capsized and were lost. Exactly how many men died that night is uncertain, since a number of seamen from the *Amethyst* are known to have reached shore and promptly deserted; contemporary accounts of the incident suggest that some 300 corpses were buried locally.

Progress on such a vast undertaking as the new breakwater was naturally slow, the centre section alone being over 1,000yd long, which does not include the canted arms at each end, roughly 350yd each, so that when a particularly severe gale struck Plymouth on 18 October 1812 it offered no protection whatsoever. Next morning, the brand new West Indiaman *Coventry* was found ashore and wrecked, as were the *Eclipse*, *Gascoyne*, *Horace*, *Providence* and *Redness*, plus a detained American ship, the *General Gates*. By the end of 1813 the breakwater showed above the surface at low tide over its entire length, and there were official prophecies that no more vessels would be lost in the Sound, but during that year, and for many more to come, there was no marked reduction in the annual total. On 23 March of that same year HMS *Captain*, previously a 3rd rate, seventy-four gun ship converted to a hulk, caught fire in the Hamoaze and was completely destroyed. Over 200 cannon shots were fired into her waterline by guns hastily removed from the decks of other ships and mounted in launches, but it took three hours to send her to the bottom, by which time there was very little of value remaining. A Fowey-owned lighter, carrying sand for use on the breakwater, sank when overwhelmed by rough seas on 3 September, and a Portsmouth hoy went down on 1 December after striking the Shagstone. She left Plymouth with fifty-two persons aboard, under the command of Capt John Davis. The apprentice was at the helm when, mistaking the outline of the Shagstone for a sail, he luffed up and caused the vessel to strike the rock. Those below decks were drowned in their bunks, and the few who managed to climb into the shrouds were thrown into the sea when she fell over on her starboard side. Thirty-six lives were lost, including

Page 35: (*above*) Built as a trawler, converted into a yacht and then a training vessel, the *Glen Strathallan* is deliberately sunk off the Shagstone, Plymouth, on 27 April 1970; (*below*) the Brazilian river steamer *Goyaz* ashore near Jennycliff Bay, Plymouth, during the Christmas hurricane of 1912, was later refloated and saved

Page 36: (*above*) The Elder Dempster liner *Jebba*, wrecked beneath the high cliffs of Bolt Tail, 18 March 1907; (*below*) seen here in her pre-war colours, the *Persier* (ex-*War Buffalo*) was torpedoed off the Eddystone on 11 February 1945 and later sank in Bigbury Bay, where she remained un-detected until found by divers in 1969

ten marines, sixteen women, three children and a number of Cornish miners.

A sharp fall in barometric pressure on 12 December 1814 forecast bad weather, and during the subsequent gale the *Providence* went ashore in the Cattewater, the *Jeune Adelle* became a total wreck on the Mewstone, and many other vessels suffered damage or lost their anchors. But this was a minor storm compared with that of 18 January 1817 which, coinciding with exceptionally high tides, caused damage that was nothing short of appalling. As if intent on wreaking as much havoc as possible among shipping in the Sound, the strong wind from the south-east swung round to south-west and continued to oscillate between these points, steadily increasing in strength until by 4 pm it had reached hurricane force. According to the editor of a local newspaper, 'the weather bore a very portentious appearance, as if the elements were preparing a terrific mischief'. Late that afternoon, three vessels were wrecked in close proximity to each other at Batten, and 200yd of the still unfinished structure across the mouth of the Sound was torn up by the sea. Individual granite blocks, weighing five tons and over, were thrown completely over the breakwater, and a survey showed that at least 1,000 tons of stonework had been disturbed. HMS *Jasper*, a brig o' war carrying sixty-seven persons, of whom fifteen were females, was wrecked on Bears Head, Mount Batten, and all but two lost their lives. One of the survivors, able seaman John Bere, was on the forecastle when she struck. He grasped a rope hanging from the main yard and swung himself outboard, intending to drop into the sea and swim ashore. To his astonishment, he landed squarely in a small boat adrift in the Sound, which was then washed on to some rocks from which he was able to wade to safety.

Another warship, HMS *Telegraph*, previously the American privateer *Vengeance*, dragged three anchors clean across the Sound, finally going beam-on to the rocks under the eastern Hoe. William Kells was the only member of her crew to lose his life, being crushed to death between decks while trying to recover some personal property. Mr Dick, the ship's surgeon, despite a fractured leg, not only saved his wife from drowning but managed

C

to get a line ashore, by which means the crew were saved. Another victim of this storm was the packet ship *Princess Mary*, from Jamaica. She went down in Deadman's Bay with the loss of her master, Capt Gidley, his wife and son, brother-in-law, and two crew. The Gidleys had been married shortly before the vessel left England, and on its return, learning that it had overshot Falmouth and entered Plymouth, Mrs Gidley, her newborn son and brother, journeyed by road from Cornwall and embarked for the short passage back to Penryn. All six bodies were later recovered from the sea and laid side by side in the back room of the King's Arms before burial in a common grave. The *Western Daily Mercury* gave a graphic insight into what followed: 'The three wrecks filled the lower classes of the port with rejoicing, their sole object being pillage. Hundreds, if not thousands of them are to be viewed in all directions, bearing off portions of the wrecks not merely by hand, but in buckets, barrows, by hand carts, and all are heard to be congratulating each other on what they jocularly call God-sends. An amicable contrast were the ladies of the Plymouth Soup Association, who distributed a quart of excellent soup, a pound of beef, and a two penny loaf, to each of the sailors from the *Telegraph*'.[9] That same gale also brought about the loss of the collier *Deptford* in Whitesands Bay and the sloop *Albion* near the breakwater, both with their entire crews.

Further damage to the seaward face of the breakwater occurred in 1824, on 23 November, when something like twenty-two vessels went down in the Cattewater. A total of 796yd of stone-work was thrown out of position, most of it rolling over to the northern side and reducing the gradient of the seaward slope from three to five in one. For some time Rennie had recommended that the authorities take a lesson from nature and let the sea dictate the best slope. Although he never lived to see the change, the 1824 hurricane convinced the government and brought about a permanent alteration in the breakwater's gradient. A large West Indies trader from London, the *Colonist*, and the *City of Rochester*, were both blown ashore at Teats Hill, and amongst the sixteen others wrecked in Deadman's Bay were the ships *Scotia* and *Caledonia*; a fruit-laden schooner from Alicent; the brigs

Loyalty and *Sceptre*, plus the *Retrencia, Petrinick* and *Hibernia*. The most remarkable incident that night concerned the ketch *Coromandel*, whose crew experienced an ordeal only matched in later years by that of the *Nerina*, off Scilly, in 1840.[10] Bound from Portugal to the Downs with cork, for orders, the *Coromandel* was capsized by heavy seas when close to the Eddystone. Only two of her crew were on deck at the time, the helmsman and lookout, both of whom disappeared and presumably drowned, leaving Capt Renton, the two remaining crew, and a passenger in the unenviable position of being trapped in the cabin of an inverted vessel. In complete darkness, with the water level rising by the minute, the four terrified men crept inside part of the bilge used to store coal, remaining there with water up to their chins for over six hours. Fortunately, the ketch drifted towards Plymouth instead of out to sea and eventually impaled itself on a sunken projection on the breakwater, allowing the trapped men to escape at low tide.

What part, if any, the Plymouth lifeboat played in all this drama is uncertain, since no mention of it can be found in local newspapers or lifeboat reports. That one originally existed is in no doubt, since a Greathead boat, built at South Shields, had been installed on 20 July 1803, but appears to have rotted away in its boathouse. A second lifeboat appeared in service here in April 1826, but this, too, appears to have remained unused and was eventually transferred to the Isles of Scilly.

As the nineteenth century progressed, so the annual total of wreck incidents around the Plymouth area increased, and never a winter went by without the Sound being strewn with ships' timbers and rigging. In 1828, the *Cato, Plympton, Speculator, Jessie Lawson, Indian Trader, John and Robert*, and the *Haydon*, all went on the rocks, the majority becoming complete wrecks. These were followed by the *Mary Ann*, lost in Bovisand Bay, also the *Erin* and *Thetis*, wrecked on the breakwater, which was now near to completion. At the height of a heavy easterly gale on 5 December 1838, the Boston schooner *Commerce* left the Hamoaze for the Cattewater to take in ballast. When off the Hoe, the wind veered and she was forced to anchor, but later dragged and went ashore under the Citadel. No sooner had she been refloated at high water than the gale swung southerly and she went ashore for a second time, eventually going to pieces. That same afternoon the French brig *Colosie* entered the Sound, anchoring between St Nicholas Isle and the shore, but parted her cables and was wrecked in Sandy Bay. Her mate gallantly attempted to swim a rope ashore but was drowned in the attempt, the remaining crew eventually being rescued by the revenue cutter *Harly*.

It is interesting to note at this stage that although the number of merchant vessels lost was on the increase, incidents involving naval ships had taken a sharp, inexplicable decline. Only three warships were lost during a ten-year period, and two of these, the seventy-four gun, 3rd rate *Talavera*, and the twenty-six gun *Imogene*, were the result of a severe dockyard fire. In September 1840 a blaze, thought to have started in one of the saw pits, spread to the old Adelaide gallery and in addition to causing the loss of two warships was a national calamity, since it destroyed some of the most historic and valuable relics of the Royal Navy. In the Adelaide gallery were stored the mementoes of many a hard-won battle and famous men; in addition to literally scores of figureheads, there was the flag under which Nelson had fought and died at Trafalgar, the banner carried by the *Queen Charlotte* at the bombardment of Algiers, and other irreplaceable items. The flames which devastated almost half the dockyard soon set fire to the heavy coating of tar on the *Talavera*, *Imogene* and *Minden*, only the last being saved by the efforts of twelve fire engines.

At the south-eastern corner of Plymouth Sound, where the high cliffs of Wembury sweep towards the Yealm estuary, lies the Great Mewstone, a tall rocky island, some half a mile off-shore. Already mentioned in connection with previous wrecks, the island has been the scene of several others. The Jersey-owned smack *Industry* was lost here on 16 January 1851, and on 26 December 1852, a 206 ton brig from London with a general cargo, the *Ocean Queen*, went down on the Little Mewstone with the loss of fourteen of her fifteen crew. It was here, too, that the first steamer wreck in the vicinity of Plymouth occurred, on 13 October

1854, despite a calm sea and perfect visibility. The London-registered *Ajax*, with a general cargo and almost 300 passengers, hit the rock in broad daylight and became a total loss. In the report rendered by the local coastguards, the duty officer wrote, 'it was either done purposely, or else from sheer culpable negligence'. Perhaps he was influenced by the knowledge that the same captain had lost another steamer, the *Minerva*, in August. Twelve years later the fishing vessel *Matilda* was passing the Mewstone on 1 March 1866 when she struck the engines of the *Ajax* which still lay just awash, and sank. From the crew of three, only a boy, William Bunce, survived. Evidence of an early wreck on the Mewstone comes from a number of iron cannon on the seabed, and currently an underwater archaeological survey is being carried out to determine its identity; a task made difficult by the presence of pieces of the *Ajax* in the area, plus the remains of another steamer, the *Rothesay*, which sank on 15 October 1877. This 332 ton coasting vessel, built at Hull in 1874, became a total wreck while on passage from Caen to Cardiff in ballast. She had called at Dartmouth for bunkers and, rather foolishly, her captain took her to sea in the teeth of a gale. Unable to weather the force eleven wind, she was blown inshore, struck a rock and sank. At low water, a dozen or more holes were to be seen in her hull; in addition, both stem and stern posts had been broken off and the propellor shaft snapped.

It hardly seems credible today that anyone could make a home on the Mewstone, but it is a fact that, in 1774, a local man guilty of some petty misdemeanour was sentenced by a magistrate to be 'transported' to the island for seven years. He remained there quietly with his family for the entire period without once setting foot on the mainland. His daughter, known as 'Black Bess', elected to remain behind when the time came for the family to leave. She eventually married and had three children on the Mewstone before her husband was drowned after falling off a rock.

Some eight miles offshore lies the Eddystone reef, which scarcely needs an introduction since its infamous reputation is well known. It was Walter Whitfeld who first proposed a light house here in 1691. It was to be built at his own expense provided certain patent rights were granted in return, but the government declined his offer. Already the scene of numerous wrecks, in 1696 the *Snowdrop* hit the rocks and disappeared with her crew of sixty, followed by the brig *Constant* on Christmas Eve of the same year. The latter had belonged to a London mercer named Henry Winstanley, who was merrymaking at his home with fellow aldermen when two survivors from the wreck arrived and demanded admittance, having walked from Plymouth. This was the second vessel Winstanley had lost to the Eddystone and he vowed 'that no vessel of mine will cross the Channel whilst this menace to life and property remains without a beacon'.[11] Patents were sought, building began in 1696, and for four years the tarred timber and stone construction rose above the surface, the first light being displayed on 14 November 1698. During a routine visit, Winstanley was marooned in the lighthouse by bad weather and forced to stay the night. During the hours of darkness of 27 November 1703, huge seas toppled the entire structure into the boiling cauldron around the reef, taking its keepers and builder to their death. The gale that raged along the entire south coast that night was of exceptional violence, wrecking a great many ships, including almost an entire fleet of men o' war on the Goodwin Sands. An unidentified journalist who witnessed the fury of the sea that night wrote, '. . . the great mad waves were rolling graves'.

That the Eddystone light was missed is in no doubt, for only days after its destruction a richly laden Virginian, the *Winchelsea*, was wrecked with few survivors. For three years the Eddystone remained unmarked, then, in 1706, the Trinity Brethren obtained permission from parliament to build, or grant a lease to have built, a second beacon, the latter option being taken up by Capt Lovet for a period of ninety-nine years. Just why Lovet chose John Rudyerd, the proprietor of a silk shop on Ludgate Hill, to design his lighthouse is uncertain. Nevertheless, this son of a Cornish labourer produced a design, the beacon was built, lit in July 1706, completed in 1709, and lasted for forty-six years. During the early hours of 2 December 1755 the tower was found to be on fire, and one can well imagine the awful predicament in which the keepers found themselves as they retreated from the flames. Red-hot sections of iron, blazing timbers and molten lead poured down on them, and one keeper died after ingesting the liquid metal, a 7oz piece of lead being found in his stomach. The lighthouse was again completely destroyed and, Capt Lovet having since died, his interest was acquired by Robert Weston who, through the president of the Royal Society, the Earl of Macclesfield, obtained the services of John Smeaton for the next attempt to tame the rock.

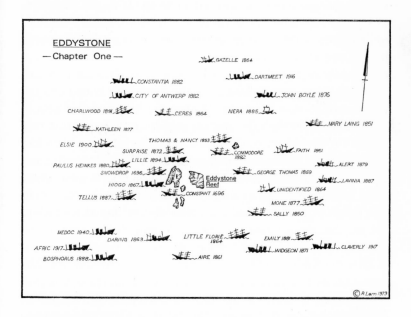

EDDYSTONE
— Chapter One —

GAZELLE 1864
CONSTANTIA 1882
DARTMEET 1916
CITY OF ANTWERP 1882
JOHN BOYLE 1876
CHARLWOOD 1851
CERES 1864
NERA 1885
KATHLEEN 1877
MARY LAING 1851
ELSIE 1900
THOMAS & NANCY 1853
SURPRISE 1872
COMMODORE 1882
FAITH 1861
PAULUS HEINKES 1880
LILLIE 1894
SNOWDROP 1696
GEORGE THOMAS 1869
ALERT 1879
HIOGO 1867
Eddystone Reef
LAVINIA 1887
TELLUS 1887
CONSTANT 1696
UNIDENTIFIED 1864
MONE 1877
SALLY 1850
MEDOC 1940
DARING 1863
LITTLE FLORIE 1864
EMILY 1881
AFRIC 1917
WIDGEON 1871
CLAVERLY 1917
BOSPHORUS 1898
AIRE 1861

© R.Larn 1973

Neither of the previous builders had had an easy time working on the Eddystone, Winstanley having once been marooned on the reef for eleven miserable days, while Rudyerd and his work-men were all taken prisoner by a French privateer and carried over to the continent. When news of their capture reached the ears of Louis XIV, he ordered their immediate release and return to Plymouth, saying, 'although I am at war with England, I am not so with mankind'.[12] Smeaton's worst experience during the rebuilding of the lighthouse occurred in November 1756, when he and a working party left the rock for Plymouth, but in the face of a full gale and huge seas were forced to run for Fowey. They missed the harbour and almost went ashore on the Gribben, after which they cleared the land and were blown part way to Biscay. Their next sight of land was the extreme tip of Cornwall, and it took them a further four days' sailing to reach home, during which time they suffered greatly from thirst, having no water on board. Of the three attempts to tame the Eddystone reef, Smeaton's tower was the only one to withstand gale after gale without damage, and it continued to do so for the better part of 125 years, when it was replaced by the existing building. The old lighthouse was dismantled and re-erected on the Hoe, where it still stands today.

If the record of vessels actually lost on the reef itself is sparse, it is well compensated for by the hundreds that have been lost in the vicinity, vessels such as the *Mary Laing*, carrying coal from Newcastle to Quebec. She sprang a leak on 30 April 1851 and attempted to reach the lighthouse, but when within a few miles, her pumps choked and she sank. Similarly, the Brixham schooner *Faith*, also coal-laden, sank close at hand on 6 September of the same year after collision with the Plymouth-owned sloop *Fear Not*. In 1853, on 21 February, the emigrant ship *Bolton*, Capt Darby, on passage from Plymouth to Sydney, ran down and sank the pollacca *Thomas and Nancy* within sight of the reef, whilst the brig *Aire*, of Goole, foundered when overwhelmed by a gale on New Year's Day 1861. She carried a consignment of government stores from Woolwich, destined for Malta and intended to replace the uniforms, cannon, and shot lost on the Lizard when the steamer *Czar* was wrecked in 1859. Although the Yankee ship *Bostonian* managed to rescue every member of the brig's crew, the majority lost their lives the following day when this vessel hit the Le Hanios reef, in the Channel Isles, and went to pieces with only three survivors. Spars, cabin furniture, twelve casks of flour, a keg of brandy and a complete bulwark from the *Aire* came ashore on Looe Bar, in Cornwall; later, a medicine chest from the *Bostonian*, several handspikes and a boat's yoke, all marked, were found on south Devon beaches and as far away as the Manacles.

Risk of collision, even today, is an occupational hazard for fishing vessels which choose to work the grounds south of the Eddystone, and a great many local boats have been lost with all hands. The *Little Florie*, a London brigantine built at Little-hampton in 1862, was on passage from her home port to Nassau on 26 January 1864 when she struck and sank an unlit trawler three miles off the lighthouse, and to this day the vessel remains unidentified. Similarly, the Glasgow-registered *Haiti* and the Plymouth trawler *Gazelle* collided on 3 March 1864, and the Norwegian *Ceres* was run down and sunk by a ship that failed to stop on 18 August 1864. Two years later, the locally owned wooden sloop *Constantine* had picked up her cargo of pigs at Treginier and was south-south-west of the Eddystone when the smack *Spring*, of Faversham, ran into her. The larger vessel's bowsprit, main boom, and several sails were carried away, in addition to starting a serious leak. With distress signals flying, the *Constantine* limped into Plymouth, settling lower by the minute, until off Drake's Island she filled and sank on 3 March.

Only one steamer has been lost on the reef itself, this being the 501 ton *Hiogo* of Sunderland. She left London for Japan on 28 September 1867 and all went well until off Start Point. It was during the second mate's watch that the Eddystone light was sighted, but when informed, in accordance with his orders, Capt Bainton refused to go on deck or to allow any alteration of course. Incredible though it may sound, the second mate continued to plead for instructions for a further hour and, even when the steamer was within yards of the reef, would not order a change of course himself, with the result that the *Hiogo* struck on the north side and became a total loss. At the subsequent Board of Trade enquiry the certificates of both master and second mate Johnson were suspended for twelve months, for having by joint default contributed to the loss of their ship.

Meanwhile the Sound continued to claim ship after ship, despite the completion of the breakwater. The 80 ton sloop *Ocean*, of Boston, hit the new stone structure on 2 February 1853

and literally fell apart, fortunately without loss of life, while the
British ironclad HMS *Cossack*, of twenty-nine guns, had a narrow
escape in October 1854 when she went ashore at Penlee Point.
Under orders to proceed to Sheerness for repairs prior to joining
the North American station, she hit the Draystone when leaving
the Sound, stove in her forward bilges, broke off all her forefoot
and false keel, and badly damaged her engines. That same day,
Admiralty tugs pulled her off and she managed to reach the
dockyard without further assistance. Only a short distance away
the Looe-owned *Mary Ann* was involved in a collision with the
steamer *Nile* on 24 November 1854, the former sinking with the
loss of one life. Ironically, the *Nile* was lost on the Stones reef,
near Hayle, only a week later.

Probably the most unusual wreck of the century at Plymouth
was the 906 ton ship *Havering*, of London, lost as a direct result
of mutiny. Built on the Tyne in 1849, the *Havering* left London
on 8 March 1860 under the command of Thomas Rickaby,
bound for Hong Kong with government stores. By 30 March she
was well out into the Atlantic but already in severe trouble,
having repeatedly been swept by gales which had started several
leaks. Her crew then refused to obey any orders which would
take the vessel further from home, demanding that they put
back in order to stop the leaks and allow the crew's quarters and
bedding to dry out. Capt Rickaby attempted to compromise by
saying that he would order the carpenter to do his utmost to make
the accommodation more habitable, but the men still refused to
work. A pilot was taken aboard from a passing cutter to act as
an independent witness while the ship's articles were read out,
part of which refers to the punishment for mutiny. But as even
this had no effect, the *Havering* put back to Plymouth with its
refractory crew. On arrival in the Sound the vessel was inspected
by the company surveyor, who declared that nothing was wrong
with the ship, but still the men would not change their attitude.
The unfortunate master then had no alternative but to seek legal
aid ashore, but while he was in Devonport seeking a warrant
for the crew's arrest he was informed that his ship was ashore on
Batten reef. Returning on board by means of a pilot boat, Capt

Rickaby learnt that the crew had just stood around and done nothing as the *Havering* dragged her anchors and eventually finished up on the rocks. A few of the men were persuaded to man the main pump, but gave up after half an hour, went below with the remainder to collect their belongings, and walked off, leaving the ship to become a total wreck.

The majority of steamship wrecks in the Plymouth Sound area have occurred in the vicinity of the Shag rock, or the Mewstone. The *Ajax* and *Rothesay* have already received a mention, but only a short distance from their remains can be found those of the Bristol Steam Navigation Co's *Constance*, lost on 21 January 1888, and the *Nepaul*, wrecked on 10 December 1890. Registered at Bristol, the 563 tons net *Constance* went ashore in calm conditions, but even then three of her crew died, unlike the more fortunate individuals aboard the P & O liner *Nepaul*, all 147 of whom were saved. She was by far the largest steamship loss at Plymouth, being 3,550 tons gross, carrying passengers and a general cargo from Calcutta and Marseilles to Plymouth. *The Times*, reporting the contents of a Reuter telegram, had this to say: 'The P. and O. Company's steamer *Nepaul* will be a total wreck. All the watertight compartments have burst, and also parts of the deck. The cargo is washing out, and large quantities of tea are floating about. The government, steam tugs, and coastguards, are maintaining order and endeavouring to protect the property. The steamer's valuables, furniture, and stores are salved for conveyance to London.' This was followed in the same newspaper by two letters to the editor, both emphatically contradicting the rumour that the lascars among the crew had rushed the ship's boats. Shortly after the *Nepaul* struck, the trawler *Baroda*, which had been following in her wake, also grounded on the Shagstone, less than 100yd clear of the steamer, and became a total loss.

Only the steamer *Queen Victoria*, of Newcastle, can claim to have been wrecked right inside Plymouth Sound. Owned by Palmer Brothers, this 1,434 tons net steamship was carrying a cargo of telegraph cable, shipped by Glass Elliott of Greenwich for the post office authority at Rangoon. The *Queen Victoria* put

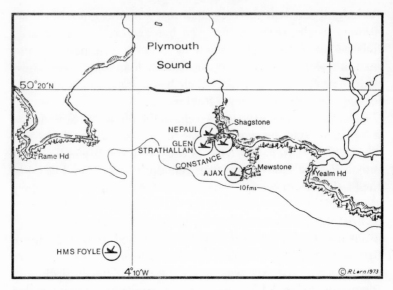

Locations of the steamers *Glen Strathallan*, *Constance*, *Nepaul* and *Ajax*

into Plymouth in early December 1860 for orders, and in accordance with her instructions proceeded on 2 January 1861 to Keyham dockyard to coal ship. A dockyard pilot, Robert William, was taken aboard for the short journey and all went well until she reached the Vanguard buoy. Here she refused to answer her helm and went aground on Wilderness Point, in Barn Pool. Hawsers were secured to mooring buoys and tugs passed ropes, but despite every assistance she still refused to move. The Master Attendant of the dockyard was put in charge of salvage and for several days lighters, gangs of riggers, and sailors from HMS *Impregnable* were employed in pumping out fresh water and landing the cable, but still she refused to be refloated. Even with huge cables rove beneath her hull and secured to lifting lighters to establish the maximum benefit of the tide, the steamer remained fast. Shortly after this attempt to save her, she was found to have sprung several leaks and water rose inside to her orlop-deck level. Divers reported that she had bilged and was cracked in several places, so with no further hopes of salvage possible, all her stores and cargo were removed and the vessel was broken up where she lay.

Amongst the long succession of south-westerly gales which have created such havoc at Plymouth, the great storm of 20 February 1861 deserves special mention. The first victim of the elements was the French brig *Augustine*, which entered the Sound during the afternoon and anchored. At 10.45 pm, at the height of the gale, her cables parted and she began to drift towards Mount Batten reef at an alarming rate. Just before she struck the shore a boat was lowered, into which her master and five men clambered, but they hardly had time to get the oars out before the *Augustine*'s mainmast fell on top of them with a terrific crash. The small boat was smashed to pieces and its occupants would all have drowned but for the timely intervention of a Brixham fishing sloop which saved the master and two men. By three o'clock the following afternoon, with the wind still literally howling in from off the sea after having blown unabated for twenty-four hours, Plymouth Sound was a fearful spectacle. The entire breakwater was often completely buried beneath massive breakers while over forty merchant or government vessels heaved and snatched at their cables. Meanwhile, on shore, the scene was watched by thousands of people who had never previously witnessed such a gale. The next vessel to be lost was an American brig named *Hiawatha*, Capt Hall, bound for New Orleans in ballast. She dragged her anchors, collided with three other ships, then went ashore surrounded by the broken timbers of the *Augustine* which had already gone to pieces. Only a short while later, four other vessels were on the rocks in the same location. A local reporter who witnessed some of the local men engaged in the so-called 'time honoured custom of wrecking', had this to say of them in the *Western Daily Mercury*:

> . . . we had thought that the trade of wrecking had long since ceased to exist, but we found one branch of that disreputable mode of obtaining a livelihood being openly practised. Large numbers of men of the worst description were making good use of the time in taking off all the moveables which had been washed ashore upon the rocks. Loitering about in every available crevice were gangs of men, well known drunkards, poachers and thieves, surrounded by sundry heaps of spoil,

but the arrival of Mr Freeman, of the Devon County Constabulary,
by his boldness and decision, cleared the rocks of every person who
had no business there.[13]

There was a considerable public outcry following these wrecks,
directed at the so-called Plymouth lifeboat. Local newspapers
commented:

> We are sorry to say that there is no lifeboat at Plymouth. The case
> is rather worse than that, since we have one for show but not for use.
> This mockery is placed upon the eastern pier, near Teats Hill. There
> is no means of launching it in emergencies, and should the lifeboat be
> required and a crew be ready to man her, it is necessary to first knock
> up, or look for the harbour master—then to see his man—get the
> key of the boathouse, and then the crew from the Barbican to the
> eastern pier. This mockery of a lifeboat is nothing more than a former
> ship's lifeboat, and since newly christened has been in the water but
> twice.

The 1860s and '80s were eventful years as regards local shipwrecks, for with an ever increasing number of vessels using the
English Channel, losses by collision and amongst the coasting
trade were all too frequent. The *Speedy*, a Waterford schooner of
sixty-six tons, and carrying coal, was forced into Plymouth with
bad leaks, but sailed again two days later, on 10 July 1864. The
Sound was barely three miles astern when her foretopmast
carried away, she became unmanageable and was struck by an
unidentified brig close at hand. Cut down to the waterline just
abaft of her main chains the *Speedy* began to settle, her crew
being rescued by HMS *Geyser*. A desperate attempt was made to
save the schooner, and under tow she reached the breakwater,
only to founder with the Hoe in sight. Storm damage also brought
in the Swedish brig *Johann II* which was lying quietly at anchor
as her crew carried out essential repairs when, on 22 November
1865, a sudden blow from the south-west parted her from her
cables and she was driven ashore. During the same gale, the
Penzance schooner *Mischief*, along with the *Espoir*, a Belgian
brig, and the *Commerzieweathin Haupt*, were all wrecked on
Mount Batten. A November gale in 1868 saw the Brixham sloop
Uncle Jack lost on Drake's Island with all five crew drowned, and
a month later the *Cabot* dragged her cables until she fouled the
Bideford brig *Flying Cloud*, when both ships stranded on Batten
reef.

During the building of the breakwater it could not possibly have been envisaged that the crane erected at the eastern end would literally be the saving of three lives. Caught at sea on 26 January 1884 in the most violent gale for ten years, the French lugger *Bon Pasteur*, of Noirmontier, carrying phosphate from Havre to Bristol, rolled so heavily when close to the Eddystone that her mainmast snapped clean off. She put about and headed for the Sound, but was so difficult to steer, yawing back and forth, that she could not be navigated through the western channel and struck the breakwater. A succession of huge waves flung the lugger against the stone blocks, battering great holes in her starboard side; meanwhile the wind continued to drive her along the breakwater towards the east. Then, one particularly large wave lifted her high in the air and she would have gone clean over the top and into the Sound had not the iron crane impeded her progress. Her four-man crew had been washed overboard when the *Bon Pasteur* first struck and, like the wreck, they too were slowly swept east along the breakwater. The same wave that flung the remains of the vessel into the air also flung the men up the seaward slope, from where they managed to climb the jib of the crane. They remained on their lofty perch for four hours, exposed to all the fury of wind and sea, watching the slow disintegration of their ship until it finally fell back into the shallows and went to pieces. By 10 pm conditions had improved sufficiently for the four men to leave the crane and reach the safety of the lighthouse, whereupon the keepers, who were unaware of the wreck, fired the standard distress signal of three rockets in succession. A dockyard tug came out in response but, seeing no further signals, her master assumed the rockets had come from some vessel passing Plymouth and returned to harbour. Next day, a flag hoist on the lighthouse indicating 'assistance is required' had the desired effect, and the Frenchmen were taken ashore by the tug *Perseverance*.

Although gales continued to sweep the Sound, inflicting yet more damage and suffering, it was Batten reef that was the actual cause of so many wrecks and which, in consequence, acquired a somewhat infamous reputation. In one twenty-four hour period during 8/9 December 1872, the *Eliza, Richelieu, Fearful, Curacao Packet, Lorenz, Ornen & Fratelli*, and the *Burghino*, all finished up on the reef. Another notorious gale, which began on 14 October 1877 and lasted two whole days, not only put four vessels ashore in Deadman's Bay but also sank two others near the Hoe and wrecked the steamer *Rothesay* near the Mewstone. This was the last occasion on which a vessel was washed clean over the top of the breakwater, the victim this time being the Newport barque *R. H. Jones*, of 726 tons register, on passage from Bremerhaven to Newport in ballast. Presumably, she had tried to reach the dubious shelter of the Sound, but exactly what happened will never be known for certain since all that was found were her anchor cables draped across the stonework of the breakwater like garlands. Seventeen of the eighteen crew aboard lost their lives, as well as Capt Roberts, his wife and young son. The only survivor was a German seaman, Alfred Blom, who would certainly have lost his life as well but for the prompt and unselfish action of a naval petty officer named Barnes, who heard cries for help while on the upper deck of HMS *Turquoise*, leapt overboard in pitch darkness, and swam to the man's assistance. A vast amount of wreckage from the *R. H. Jones* was strewn around the Sound and in Jennycliff Bay, including lifebuoys, the ship's nameboard, a boat, cabin furniture, personal effects, and the corpse of her master. Two days after the wreck, her anchors and cable were recovered and, along with other items, sold locally by public auction.

Less than a month later, more evidence of wreck was floating around the entrance to Plymouth and the Wembury coastline. This time it was currants, the cargo of the unfortunate *Western Star*, wrecked near the Yealm estuary on New Year's Day 1873. She was a Bideford schooner of seventy-four tons, built at Appledore in 1869 and on passage from Zante to Plymouth. When close to the Eddystone and enshrouded in thick fog, her master, Silvanus Williams, spoke to the skipper of a sailing trawler who assured him that Plymouth lay to the north-east. When land was eventually sighted, Williams incorrectly identified it as Rame Head, altered course accordingly, and went ashore.

Exactly how many steamers have gone down within a fifteen-mile radius of the Eddystone will never be known for certain, but the number must be astronomical. Thick fog on 4 April 1876 saw the 633 tons gross Cardiff steamship *John Boyle* creeping down Channel, her steam siren mournfully warning of her presence. From out of the murk another steamer loomed up, the *Emma Lawson* of Whitby, carrying cotton seed from Alexandria to Hull. She struck the *John Boyle* a terrific blow, cutting a 6ft wide gash in her side forward of the poop. Capt Lewis of the *Emma Lawson* had the presence of mind to keep his engines at 'full-ahead', which effectively sealed off the hole and gave the twenty-man crew of the sinking vessel time to clamber aboard over his forecastle. As he backed away, so the *John Boyle* commenced to settle and twenty minutes later she sank like a stone. In this instance no lives were lost but on 16 October 1882 a more serious collision between the steamers *City of Antwerp* and *Constantia* resulted in the loss of both ships, with only the captain and three survivors from the former and none from the *Constantia*.

As the nineteenth century drew to a close, vessels continued to be wrecked at Plymouth with such alarming regularity that it would be impossible to detail each and every incident. An inshore collision close to Penlee Point on 29 November 1882 ended the career of the 307 ton barque *Ellen Rickmers*, a member of the once famous Bremerhaven fleet of Rickmers. The fifteen-year-old wooden vessel, Seghorn master, carrying coconuts and ivory, with ten crew and one passenger, took a pilot aboard and was about to enter the Sound when she struck the Weymouth brigantine *Guide* and sank in the fairway. One month later the fishing lugger *J.S.T.* of Looe sank in similar circumstances at the eastern entrance, after colliding with the *Agenoria* on 22 December. Batten breakwater, which served to protect the entrance to the Cattewater, claimed the 123 ton German brigantine *Valentin*, which anchored close at hand on 12 February 1883, only to drag her anchor until she went ashore and broke up, while Rame Head saw the end of the schooner *Nora Rosa* on 10 May the same year.

Not many vessels have been so fortunate as to have struck the
D

Shagstone and got clear, but such was the luck of the Brixham ketch *Florence May* on New Year's Day 1886. Her crew abandoned ship thinking she would sink any minute, but when she continued to remain afloat they reboarded her and sailed into Sutton harbour, only to have her sink beneath their feet. The *Florence May* was successfully refloated and eventually returned to service, unlike the French *Marie Blanche* which foundered in seven fathoms between the breakwater and Picklecombe Fort on 16 September 1886. Her wreck constituted such a hazard to navigation that Capt Sutton, the Queen's Harbourmaster, ordered her destruction by explosives, the cargo of flints not being considered worth salvaging. On 8 October, after naval divers from the torpedo school had packed several hundreds of pounds of explosive inside the hull, she was blown to pieces. The final gale of the century proved to be the worst for over a hundred years. It reached its height within twenty-four hours, by which time the wind, accompanied by blinding snow, had reached hurricane force. This was the holocaust of early March 1891 now known as the 'great blizzard', which raged from the 9th of the month until the 13th, cutting off the West Country almost completely. Ships of all sizes were lost along the length of the south coast, but remarkably few in the Sound. The Admiralty sailing cutter *Julia* broke from her moorings and foundered near Stonehouse; the *Jane*, a ten-year-old fishing dandy, and the pilot cutter *Mystery*, were both sunk, whilst the Falmouth ketch *Katie* was blown from Batten quay across to Drake's Island and then ashore at Mount Edgcumbe.

All the royal dockyards at some time or another have experienced a submarine disaster, the first at Plymouth being the *A.8*. In company with Torpedo Boat *No 80*, the submarines *A.7* and *A.8* left their parent ship HMS *Forth* at 8 am on 8 June 1905 and proceeded towards the mouth of the Sound for exercises. Both submarines were of 320 tons displacement, 150ft in length, capable of sixteen knots on the surface and ten submerged, and were in the same class as the ill-fated *A.1*, sunk near the Nab Tower, off the Isle of Wight, in February 1904. On board the *A.8* were fourteen officers and ratings, plus five men from the depot ship, additional to complement and under instruction. In near perfect sea conditions, both submarines passed through the western entrance and began manoeuvres and diving drills in the vicinity of their escort. At about 10 am the *A.8* went missing and, almost simultaneously, signals were received from the breakwater lighthouse and Picklecombe Fort to the effect that the submarine had been seen to sink in distress. How the witnesses to the incident were able to differentiate between the submarine carrying out a normal dive and sinking in distress is uncertain; nevertheless the *A.8* was in trouble. Fortunately, a local fishing boat in the vicinity lowered a boat and rescued Lieut Algernon Candy, the submarine's commanding officer; Petty Officer 1st class Waller, and acting Leading Stoker Watt. The officer was in fact responsible for saving Waller's life when he became exhausted through treading water in heavy seaboots. The only information the survivors could offer was that the *A.8* had been on the surface, 'running light' as it was called, when an explosion occurred inside the hull. She at once began to go down rapidly, after which a second explosion hurled all three men off her deck and into the sea.

Vice-Admiral Henderson, superintendent of the dockyard, assumed command of rescue operations and ordered the tugs *Assurance* and *Perseverence* to the scene, accompanied by divers from HMS *Defiance*. The submarine's commander confirmed that the *A.8* had sunk with her main hatch still open, but it was hoped that at least some of the crew might be alive behind a watertight door, either in the bow or engine-room compartments, although the explosions greatly reduced their chances. Sweep wires passed over the hull caught in the special lifting hooks fitted to all 'A Class' boats following the *A.1* incident, and by 1 pm, in a remarkably short time, the vessel was ready to be lifted. As the winches of the tugs began to lift the wreck the deep rumble of a third explosion came from the seabed and the sea round the salvage vessels boiled, after which a great deal of loose gear and two wooden gratings floated up. In view of the risk, no more diving was allowed and the entire fleet, apart from a guard boat, returned to the dockyard. For reasons best known only to the authorities, the Admiralty were very reticent about the disaster and neither newspapers nor relatives were able to glean any official details. That same evening a diving party did, in fact, return to the site, but it was found inexpedient to let them go down, so the special service vessel *Jackal* placed a wreck buoy in the vicinity and anchored nearby for the night.

At dawn on the 9th salvage work was resumed and two mooring lighters, divers, and a great many riggers were put to work, the exact location of the wreck being midway between the breakwater light and Penlee Point, near the Knap buoy, in 60ft of water. Diver Phillips was the first man to reach the submarine and reported over his telephone that she was on an even keel, lying on hard shingle, and that the body of a drowned seaman, caught by its clothing, was swaying about the deck in the tide. A closer inspection of the hull showed no obvious signs of an explosion, but several newspapers at the time made reference to 'thick glass scuttles having been blown out', so presumably she was flooded. By 5 pm on the 10th, the *A.8* was off the bottom and about to be towed away when a strongback snapped and she plunged back to the bottom, breaking every one of the lifting wires. Having managed to sling and lift the *A.8* in such a remarkably short time, it is difficult to imagine why the Navy then sought the advice of a civilian, when they seemingly had the ability to complete the salvage themselves. However, at the request of the Admiralty, Capt Anderson, of the famous Western Marine Salvage Co, was called in and sailed from Penzance to Plymouth in the company's salvage vessel, *Lady of the Isles*. Capt Anderson had already distinguished himself locally in the commercial salvage field, having worked on almost every known wreck in Devon and Cornwall, and only the previous year he had raised the special service vessel *Traveller*, sunk in the Hamoaze.

On 12 June the *A.8* was brought directly to the surface and moved to a more sheltered part of the Sound, and on the following day into No 2 Dock. Capt Lees of HMS *Forth* undertook the unpleasant task of searching the interior of the submarine. In full 'standard' diving dress, but without front and back weights, he entered the *A.8* through the forward hatch and, after determining the position of every control and examining the damage caused by the three explosions, brought out all fourteen corpses. An Admiralty enquiry held on board the battleship HMS *Empress of India* found 'that whilst running on the surface at ten knots, with a starting buoyancy of six tons, trimmed 4° by the stern, the *A.8* foundered due to water getting inside the submarine via the conning tower, her buoyancy and trim having altered for some inexplicable reason'. One loose rivet found in the forepart of the submarine during her examination, when simulated under test conditions, let in one ton of water in ten minutes and almost certainly was the cause of this tragic accident. Following a complete refit and overhaul, the *A.8* was returned to service, survived World War I, and was eventually sold to Phillips of Dartmouth for scrapping.

It was 1912 before another steamer was lost in the Plymouth area. This was the 907 tons gross, two-masted *Vectis*, owned by John Hill of Sunderland, which went on the Rennies on 5 February to become a total wreck. Later the same year, during the notorious 'Christmas hurricane', the schooners *Ottawa* and *Guild Mayor*, the Amazon river steamer *Goyaz*, ketch *Johnny Toole*, and the Plymouth lifeboat itself, all went ashore, but none was lost (Picture, p 35). The 62 tons net *Johnny Toole*, of Newport, built at Bideford in 1886, survived until 29 April 1918, when a German submarine sank her off Carnsore Point. Another wreck attributable to the breakwater was the self-propelled hopper barge *No 42*, which sank first on 13 September 1913 and again the following day. This 150 ton vessel, on passage from Cadiz to Southampton and having recently completed a dredging contract in Spain, arrived off Plymouth in the dark. Flares were burnt for a pilot to come out, but when they met with no response her master attempted to enter the Sound without assistance. From his position aft, Capt Bun saw a dark shape loom up ahead and called to the lookout, 'What is that black ahead?' The lookout had no sooner turned to ask, 'What black?', than the barge hit the breakwater, filled and sank. Next day, with engine room and accommodation flooded, she was pumped out and refloated, then taken in tow by the tugs *Stag*, *Boarhound* and *Deerhound*, but quickly became low in the water and finally sank for the second and last time.

With memories of a spate of submarine disasters between 1903 and 1912 still fresh in the public mind, the nation was shocked to hear of yet another on 16 January 1914, off Plymouth. Previously, there had been a severe explosion aboard the *A.1*, and one year later, in 1904, the same submarine was rammed and sunk at Spithead by the Union Castle Steamer *Berwick Castle* with the loss of all hands. This was followed by the *A.8* incident, then the *A.3* near Portsmouth in 1912, with all fourteen crew drowned; the *A.4* went down in Portsmouth harbour with her entire crew in 1905; and the *C.11* and *B.2* were both run down and sunk off Cromer and Dover respectively. This latest disaster off the Devon coast concerned the *A.7*, lost whilst carrying out dummy torpedo runs against HMS *Pigmy*. For five long days the Navy swept the area for the missing craft, finally locating her on 21 January in twenty-three fathoms four miles west-north-west of Rame Head; or, more exactly, two miles offshore from Fort Tregantle. Divers reported that her stern was already embedded at least 22ft into thick mud and that no response had been made to signals tapped on her pressure hull. Wires were swept under the hull by the tugs *Alliance* and *Firm*, then passed to the Sheerness salvage lighter *No YC94*, but the submarine refused to move as much as an inch. Bad weather prevented any further work on the wreck and by the 28th of the month the Navy was smarting from newspaper taunts. The 14,000 ton battleship HMS *Exmouth* was then taken to the scene and her powerful capstans took the strain on the lifting wires, keeping them as taut as bowstrings for over half an hour in the hope of breaking the suction, but she only succeeded in ripping off a great deal of the *A.7*'s casing. For the last time the salvage crews went through the routine of passing wires under the hull, a task made none the easier by the submarine having sunk into the seabed to conning tower level. Once again the *Exmouth* took the strain, lifting first on one wire, then another, attempting to ease the *A.7* from her grave. Suddenly the wires went slack and hopes ran high for success until divers reported that the hull had only been torn wide open. So, reluctantly, the submarine and its occupants were abandoned. The *Western Morning News* opened a fund for the dependents of the drowned crew, and when it was finally closed the citizens of Plymouth were proud to announce they had collected £1,024 12s 6d.

Only one wreck of any consequence occurred at Plymouth before the outbreak of World War I, this being that of the 91 ton schooner *Erna* of Bremen. It had been Capt Kuhlke's intention to enter the port of Charlestown, in Cornwall, to load china clay, but a severe south-easterly gale forced him to seek the shelter of Jennycliff Bay, where the vessel was anchored. Next day, 21 February 1914, the *Erna* began to drag and eventually struck the south-western edge of the rocks at Drake's Island. Huge breakers and near gale force winds prevented the Plymouth lifeboat from getting alongside, but when its coxswain realised the *Erna* was sinking, he anchored and then dropped back as close to the wreck as he dared. By this means all six crew were saved, leaving the schooner, valued at £1,750, to go to pieces where she lay.

Naturally, the outbreak of hostilities during 1914 saw a tremendous increase in shipping activity around Plymouth, but there were remarkably few wreck incidents and the only inshore loss was that of the requisitioned trawler HMS *Abelard*, lost near the breakwater on Christmas Eve 1916. A number of ships were torpedoed offshore, near the Eddystone, and there were also several collisions, in one of which, on 30 November 1916, the Teignmouth steamer *Dartmeet* was lost after having been struck by the steamer *Swazi*. Within twelve months of the armistice there were two wrecks on the breakwater, the first being the Grimsby schooner *Fair City*, carrying fifty tons of stone and clay ballast from Fowey. Her master, Frederick Allison, in his deposition stated, 'at 7.35 pm on 8 January 1919 we were swept at a huge pace broadside onto the breakwater, where we struck at 7.45 at a point 100 yards east of the fort, our mainmast going overboard immediately'. The *Fair City* became a total loss, along with all her gear, stores and cargo, since the stone was in the form of partly dressed blocks. It is interesting to note that the Board of Trade record shows her as still carrying two naval gunners in addition to her normal complement, despite peace having been declared more than one month previously. The *Fair City* was a relatively small vessel of only seventy-two tons gross, but the next sailing ship lost on the breakwater was a large four-masted barquentine of over 1,000 tons. This was the French-owned *Yvonne*, built at Fairhaven, in California, in 1900 and carrying 419 tons of selected logwood from Savannah le Mer to Havre. On 3 October 1920 she was caught by a severe gale close to the Eddystone and but for the prompt action of her deck watch in reducing canvas down to two small topsails and jib she would almost certainly have been wrecked on the reef. As it was, she missed the rocks by less than a ship's length, drove straight in towards the Sound, and headlong into the breakwater. The sea pounded her unmercifully as she lay on her side, with waves going over her crosstrees. Fortunately, she carried radio equipment and her distress signals were soon answered by the arrival of the Plymouth lifeboat and several tugs, but none of them was able to get close to the wreck. The nineteen crew aboard the *Yvonne* were instructed to put on lifejackets and jump into the sea; seventeen of them were picked up by the lifeboat, one by the tug *Rover*, and one drowned.

In 1926 there was yet another submarine accident, this time in the heart of Devonport dockyard, but in the years between the Cardiff-owned steamer *Swanston*, carrying 450 tons of zinc plate, had stranded at Queen's Battery on 8 March 1922 and been refloated, only to sink off Start Point on 20 December. The submarine was the *H.29*, which sank in less than one minute, drowning seven men. She was alongside a jetty taking in water ballast on 9 August when, due to negligence in overfilling, she sank low enough for the sea to enter a hatch and went to the bottom in 35ft of water.

From then until the outbreak of World War II the majority of incidents were confined to strandings, such as that of the steamer *Kentish Coast* in Jennycliff Bay on 16 November 1928. She was refloated and towed away, but was found to be so badly damaged that she was scrapped. The *Umberleigh*, another steamer, went ashore in Bovisand Bay in 1930 but got off, and it was not until

Page 61: The last of the many 'tall ships' wrecked in the West Country, the Finnish four-masted barque *Herzogin Cecilie* struck the Hamstone on 25 April 1936 and finally sank in Starehole Bay, Salcombe

Page 62: The tug *Joffre* stranded under Bolberry Down on 27 May 1925.
Nearby is a boiler from the wreck of the *Jane Rowe* and, closer inshore,
another from the drifter *Charter*

Page 63: (*above*) The steamer *Liberta* of Genoa, wrecked and broken in two at Bolt Head, 15 February 1926; (*below*) the French trawler *Amelie Suzanne* breaking up near Salcombe on 1 April 1972

Page 64: (*above*) The Belgian steamer *Louis Sheid* stranded at Beacon Cove, Thurlestone, on 7 December 1939 with 62 survivors from a torpedoed Dutch liner in addition to her own crew of 46; (*below*) a total wreck and almost under water, the steamer *Cantabria* in Steeple Cove, near Bolt Head, 13 December 1932

the German U-Boat campaign was felt for a second time that the wreck incidents again began to increase. An Admiralty motor-fishing vessel, the *Encourage*, was sunk by a mine on 5 October 1940, close to the breakwater, followed by the requisitioned trawler *Lord Inchcape* only twenty days later. The *Kingston Alalite* was lost in the same manner, but these were small losses compared to ships like the steamer *Medoc*, torpedoed near the Eddystone on 26 November 1940 with the loss of thirty-nine of her crew.

It is fitting that this chapter, which has recorded so much loss of life and property, should close with a wreck incident which was deliberately planned. It is one in which no lives were lost because the vessel had no crew, neither was there any cargo or ship's stores aboard; it represented no financial loss and was done with the owner's full consent. The vessel involved was the *Glen Strathallan*, best described as a steam pleasure yacht although she had been built in 1928 as a trawler. Her owner, the multi-millionaire, Colby Cubbin, bought and converted her at a cost of over £30,000, yet sailed in her less than a dozen times before he died. In his will, he decreed that she should be used as a boys' training ship until of no further service, after which she was to be scuttled in deep water. For many years she served as a floating school, then the cost of repairs and upkeep became prohibitive and it was announced she would be sunk in the Hurd Deep, at the mouth of the Channel. The Science Museum requested permission to remove her steam engine complete for public exhibition in London, after which Plymouth Ocean Projects, who run the Fort Bovisand Underwater Centre, requested that the ship be sunk at the entrance to Plymouth Sound for the benefit of student divers. On Monday, 27 April 1970, Capt Clucus of the Plymouth School of Navigation opened three seacocks in her engine room and the *Glen Strathallan* sank close to the Shagstone in a position 50° 18′56″ N, 04° 07′34″ W. (Picture, p 35.) She became an immediate embarrassment to her new owners and local fishermen alike and following a representation to the authorities that she constituted a hazard to navigation and trawlers, her position was for a time marked by a buoy. During the first months of winter, however, the wreck went completely to pieces, so that the main object in scuttling her—to serve as a 'classroom' and obtain a record of her gradual collapse—was never realised.

CHAPTER TWO

STOKE TO PRAWLE POINT

Stoke Point, situated four miles east of the Great Mewstone at Plymouth, marks the western extremity of Bigbury Bay; a bay which bears a striking but unfortunate resemblance from seaward to Whitesands Bay. Unfortunate since, over the years, countless numbers of sailing masters and captains have mistaken one for the other and sailed towards what they fondly imagined was Rame Head, only to find themselves embayed. Once confronted by the sheer cliffs of Bolt Tail, and with an onshore wind, there was no escape. The ten mile sweep of Bigbury Bay, followed by the formidable five miles of rock between Bolt Tail and the Salcombe estuary, has been a graveyard for ships since time immemorial. Comparable only with Mounts Bay and the Lizard headland in Cornwall, this short stretch of coastline has been the most tragic in the whole of Devon.

The most interesting of the early wrecks in the area was the *San Pedro Mayor*, or *St Peter the Great*, a twenty-nine gun vessel of the Spanish Armada. After successfully evading the British ships in the Channel, she navigated round Scotland and down the west coast of Ireland, only to be blown east and go ashore near Hope Cove on 28 October 1588. She has been described by various authors and authorities as a 'hulk', a 'hospital ship', or a 'galleon', even a 'treasure ship', but it would appear from evidence in the state papers of England and Spain that she should be correctly described as a 'hospital hulk'. She was part of a small fleet of hulks, led by Juan Gomez de Medina on board the *Gran Griffon*, which lost their leader when his ship was also wrecked, on Fair Isle, to the north of Scotland, and as a result became confused and lost. Cary, in a letter to the government, wrote:

> . . . and during my abode at Plymouth, having understanding that one of the Spanish fleet was cast on shore at a place called Hope, and

the great pilfering and spoils that the country people made, I rode thither and took order for the restoring and rehaving again of all such things as either by search or industry I could find out, and have put the same in inventory, and took order for the orderly saving of the rest, as weather would give leave, to have the same on land, appointing two head constables to attend that service. The ship is a hulk and called *St Peter the Great*, one of those two ships appointed for the hospital to the whole army.

She is in burden as they say, 550 tons, but I think not so much [she was, in fact, the equivalent of about 581 tons gross by our modern reckoning]. The ship is said not to be recovered, she lieth on a rock, and full of water to her upper deck. They confess that there were put into her, at her coming out of Spain, thirty marines, one hundred soldiers and fifty appertaining to the hospital, there now remaining about 140 or thereabouts, also drugs and pothecary stuff as come to 6,000 ducats, of which I think little good will come of the same, being in the water this sennight, the weather such as none could get aboard. There hath been some plate and certain ducats rifled, and spoiled at their first landing both from their persons and their chests. The ship I think, is of no value, the ordnance is all iron and no brass, the ground tackle all spent, save one new cable.[1]

This was not the only Spanish vessel of the period to be lost in Bigbury Bay. According to John Leyland,[2] 'two of Philip, King of Castelle's shippes felle to wrack in this haven, when he was driven into England by tempeste'. The haven in question was either Ayrmer Cove or the mouth of the river Erme, neither of which was exactly suitable as an anchorage for a ship of any size, since even in those days Leyland described it as follows, '—the mouth where is no haven, lyith full of flattes and periculus rokkes, and no shippe cummeth in tempest hither, but in desperation'. Both of these wrecks offered the locals rich pickings, as did an unnamed Dutch galliot of about 100 tons, which was lost on Thurlestone Sands in January 1750. Laden with wine, brandy, coffee and indigo, from Zante to Hamburg, the vessel went ashore late one evening, and, '—it was with difficulty that the country people were kept from plundering it. On the Saturday evening, as many as ten thousand people congregated around this wreck, coming from all parts of the county for the sole purpose of stealing what they could of the remainder of the cargo, and were only kept at bay by the arrival of soldiers from Plymouth. The ringleader of the mob got killed, being drunk and falling on a soldier's bayonet, and got fixed to it.'[3]

Prior to this, a valuable wreck occurred at Bantham, in the

mouth of the river Avon, where the *Dagger* went ashore in 1736. At a manor court held at Hope during April the following year, the steward recorded in the court roll, 'George Hamblin of Orford Jefford, took up a graper, about 50 weight, at the place the *Dagger* was cast away; also, one John Piles, another small gun'.[4] This particular court was composed of thirteen respectable men who had the task of settling all disputes respecting salvage, or preserving property until claimed by the owner. As in other counties, the right of wreck, originally vested in the Crown, was in certain cases made over by special grant to the lords of local manors. The Courtenay family, whose claim existed from as early as 1416, had their right to wreck confirmed by Edward VI and Elizabeth, and it was later re-established by Lord Devon, after a bitter dispute, shortly before the first Merchant Shipping Act was passed in 1854. The rights of this particular family extended from Dartmouth Castle to the eastern shore of the Avon, below Aveton Gifford, and 'as far out to sea as a man on horse-back could see an umber barrel'.

In 1757, on 8 October, a particularly valuable hoy was driven ashore in Bigbury Bay and lost with all hands. Her entire cargo of brandy, 6,000 gallons in barrels, was saved, unlike the rich cargo from the *Chantiloupe*, which was stolen when she stranded in the bay in 1772. Homeward bound from the West Indies, the only survivors to reach shore were a seaman and a wealthy female passenger named Burke, said to be related to the famous Edward Burke. She was wearing a great deal of valuable jewellery which attracted the attention of the wreckers, '. . . the savage people from the adjacent villages, who were anxiously waiting for the wreck, seized and stript her of her clothes, even cutting off some of her fingers, and mangling her ears in their impatience to secure the jewels, and left her miserably to perish.'[5] Who buried her body on the foreshore is not known, but her corpse was later uncovered by a dog and exhumed, when it was proven that the unfortunate woman had been alive when cast ashore and deliberately murdered. Two years after the event Henry Hingeston, a prominent local Quaker, disgusted by the behaviour of his fellow men at the scene of wrecks, wrote to a local newspaper:

I have been deeply affected to see and feel how sweet the report of a shipwreck is to the inhabitants of this county, as well professors as profane, and what running there is on such occasions, all other business thrown aside and away to the wreck. I am verily persuaded that it hath been more sweet to hear that all the men drowned and so a 'proper wreck' than that any were saved, and by that means hinder their more public appearance on that stage for getting money . . . remember the broadcloth slupe stranded in Bigbury Bay, richly laden, O! for shame for shame, I am really vext that ever my countrymen should be guilty of such devilish actions.[6]

A relatively recent and macabre reminder of the loss of the *Chantiloupe* came to light in 1900, when some children digging in the sand turned up a skull and several bones from a shallow grave. They were pronounced the remains of a Negro, almost certainly one of the crew of this tragic wreck.

Other eighteenth-century wrecks in Bigbury Bay include the caravel *St John Baptista* which, '. . . in 1795, sailed from Brest in company with the *Ekinbcom*, but has since been driven ashore on Mothecombe beach, fifteen miles east of Plymouth, where she suffered the loss of her anchors and cables, and received great damage.'[7] The reference adds that the *Ekinbcom* was totally lost in this harbour, which presumably refers to Brest, but since no specific mention is made to the *St John Baptista* suffering the same fate, it may be assumed that she was refloated and saved. An unidentified Danish sloop o' war went down with all but seven of her crew during a tremendous south-south-west gale on 31 October 1798 and, two months later, the Plymouth brig *Rofe* sank while carrying a general cargo from Bristol to her home port on 27 December. Another Danish vessel, the *Frederick Julins*, of Kaffe, which had left Plymouth in ballast for Frederickstadt that very morning, became a total loss when blown ashore and wrecked on 10 November 1799.

Reminiscent of the *Marlborough* incident on the Manacles reef,[8] also in the early 1800s, was the stranding of the *George and Ann* of Exeter, near Ayrmer Cove, on 23 October 1808. Chased inshore by a French privateer which had been lurking around the Plymouth area for weeks, the British vessel stood in for the mouth of the Avon and reduced sail. As the enemy vessel drew closer, the helm of the *George and Ann* was put hard over, giving the crew the satisfaction of seeing the privateer strike a shallow rock and founder, until they, in turn, found themselves stranded close at hand. Less than one month later the military transport vessel *Selina* foundered in deep water, on 21 November, to be followed by the *Ann*, a West Indiaman, bound for London from St Kitts, lost on 30 April 1811, and the *Betsey* on 11 January 1816. The last of these was carrying sixty-five French prisoners of war, twenty-three of whom drowned. Information concerning yet another early wreck of September 1812 has come down to us via Charlotte Brontë. Her mother, Maria Branwell of Penzance, prior to her marriage, put all her possessions aboard a small sailing ship which was lost in Bigbury. In a letter dated 18 November 1812, she wrote, 'my box was dashed to pieces by the sea, and all my property except a few articles were swallowed up'.

During the next fifty years, Bigbury was the setting for a great many shipwrecks. In 1838 the brig *Barbara* was lost; *John*, a Bideford-registered snow, stranded on the Blackstone rock in November 1824; the Exeter-owned *Caroline* was wrecked near Challaborough on 20 December 1851, and on 11 December 1869 the French brig *Commerce de Paris*, Charles Chibourg master, drove ashore midway between the Erme and the Yealm. Homeward bound from Rio de Janeiro with coffee, cotton, tapioca and dye wood, the 618 ton vessel anchored in Bigbury Bay during a gale, which was followed by thick fog. During the early hours of the morning she began to drag, and at high water went beam-on to the beach and was bilged. Several bales of cotton and a large number of hides were salvaged, and the threat of plunder by the Devon wreckers was sufficiently strong to justify the eight policemen brought in by the French consul, all of whom were armed with pistols. The *Commerce de Paris* was, in fact, the sister-ship to the *Paulista*, wrecked under Jennycliff only a year previously. With the law guarding the only worthwhile wreck, the locals were obliged to look elsewhere for their 'God sends', and were soon attracted east to Blackpool Sands, in Start Bay, where newspapers were excitedly reporting the finding of valuable gold coins of Edward III, Henry IV, and Charles and Louis of

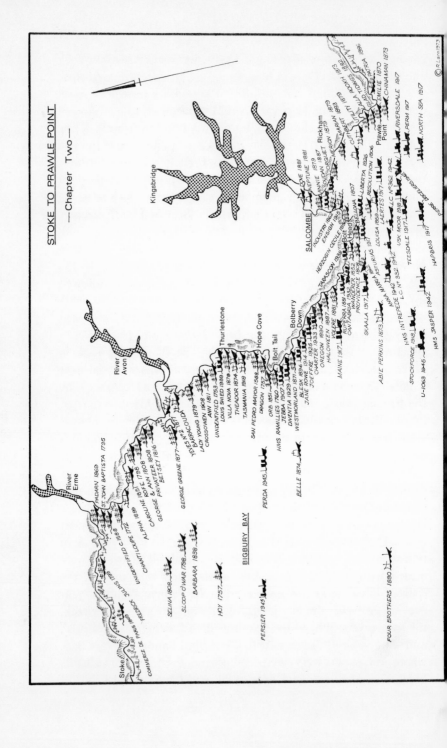

STOKE TO PRAWLE POINT

— Chapter Two —

Kingsbridge

River Avon

River Erme

Stoke

Thurlestone

Hope Cove

Bolberry Down

Bolt Tail

SALCOMBE

Prawle Point

BIGBURY BAY

© R. Larn 1973

JULIUS 1755
COMMERCE DE PARIS 1788
FREDRICK
FADARN 1869
UNIDENTIFIED C. 1588
ST JOHN BAPTISTA 1795
CHANTILOUPE 1699
ALPHA 1851 1796
CAROLINE ROFE 1796
CAROLINE & ANTFER 1808
GEORGE PRIV BETSEY 1816
GEORGE GREENE 1877
YVES N°2 1871
BARRACOUDA 1879
LADY YOUNG 1908
CROSSOWEN 1811
UNIDENTIFIED 1753
LOUIS SHIED 1939
VILLA NOVA 1879
THEADOR 1874
TASMANIA 1918
SAN PEDRO MAYOR 1588
DRAGON 1757
ORB 1851
HMS RAMILLIES 1760
JEBBA 1907
DIWENTIA 1929
WESTMORLAND 1871
BLESK 1896
JANE ROWE 1914
FRE 1926
JOE CHARTER 1933
HALOWEEN 1887
OREGON 1890
KOLERE 1881
MAINE 1917
PEDRA 1891
CANTABRIA 1932
WAINGAR 1852
PROVIDENCE 1858
SKAALA 1917
ABIE PERKINS 1873
ANNA MARIA 1942
ASTURIAS 1917
LOUISA 1859
LAERTES 1917
U-1063 1946
STOCKFORCE 1918
HMS INTREPEDE
LC N° 332 1942
USK MOOR 1981
LC N°362 1942
TEESDALE 1917
HMS JASPER 1942
HAPBRIS 1917
NORTH SEA 1917
PERM 1917
RIVERSDALE 1917
CHINAMAN 1873
EMILIE 1870
PATRA 1886
GLAD TIDINGS 1876
UTILITY ROOKH 1873
CUTTLEFISH 1879
TORQUETON 1873
ARIAN 1883
RICKHAM
DYAN 1887
ANNIE 1879
NEPTUNE 1881
COVE 1881
INDUSTRI 1852
ENSIGN 1918
HERZOGIN CECILE 1936
TARANSON 1938
HEAD
BELLOWA 1907
LIBERTA 1859
RESOLUTION 1806

SELINA 1808
SLOOP O'WAR 1798
BARBARA 1836
HOY 1757
PERSIER 1945
BELLE 1874
FOUR BROTHERS 1880
PERDA 1945

France; no doubt the specie from some long-forgotten wreck of the 1400s.

A January gale in 1877 saw the loss of the *George Green* at Challaborough, and on 14 October of the same year the Santander schooner *Yves No 2*, Capt Pedro Albano, was smashed to pieces in the breakers of Ayrmer Cove. When still a mile from shore, a huge wave swept Capt Albano to his death, and before mate Rosende could take charge of the situation the schooner struck the shore. The breakers made short work of the wreck and the beach was strewn with timbers and ruined casks of flour, but not before the local rocket brigade had saved the remaining six crew. The next wreck was considerably bigger, being the Liverpool barque *Lady Young* of 598 tons. She had left Cardiff for Hamburg on 20 October 1879 but, six days later, lost her foretopmast and a great deal of canvas when off Devon. Realising that his ship had been blown into Bigbury and embayed, Capt Watkins ordered distress rockets to be fired. These were sighted and answered by the Hope Cove coastguards, who hurried with their apparatus to West Down Point, near Bantham. The entire crew were taken off by breeches buoy, but all lost their belongings. Next day, John Nabsly, the ship's steward, volunteered to return aboard to gather up anything of value. He got aboard via the buoy but, on his return, fell out of the chair and met his death on the rocks below.

Very few wrecks have no survivors at all, and the fact that there were none in the case of the brigantine *Crossowen*, led to much speculation. Registered in Glasgow but owned in St Austell, the *Crossowen* was found on the beach on 7 May 1908 with all sail set and less than 3ft of water in the hold, yet completely abandoned. She had embarked a cargo of china clay at Par the previous day and it can only be assumed that shortly after sailing she encountered a dense bank of fog which blanketed the south-west. None of her crew of seven was seen alive again, their drowned corpses being found in, or close to the mouth of the Avon. A possible explanation is that she struck Burgh Island, whereupon her crew, thinking that she was sinking, abandoned her, only to be overwhelmed in the breakers on Bantham Bar. Six bodies

E

were buried together in Thurlestone churchyard, together with that of a boy who, although not part of the official crew, was presumed to have been aboard.

It is a strange fact that the largest of the wrecks in Bigbury Bay went unidentified until 1969, twenty-four years after it had foundered. This was the steamer *Persier*, built in Newcastle in 1918 by the Northumberland Ship Building Co as the *War Buffalo*, a World War I 'Standard B class ship' of 5,030 tons gross. As far as the official records of World War II are concerned, the *Persier* ended her days near the Eddystone, after being torpedoed on 11 February 1945, but in fact she sank close inshore, bringing to a close a chequered career that was dramatic to the end. On completion in 1919 as the *War Buffalo*, she was sold to the Belgian Maritime Co, which had evolved from the defunct Lloyd Royal Belge, who renamed the ship *Persier*. Between the wars she traded throughout the world, completing seventy-four voyages before being ordered to Dunkirk in May 1940. Voyage No 76 found her homeward bound from New York, with 6,833 tons of steel on board, and the convoy in which she sailed might well have been completely destroyed but for the heroic action of HMAC *Jervis Bay*, which held off the German battleship *Admiral Scheer*. Christmas Eve 1940 found the *Persier* anchored near Oban, where she was attacked by enemy aircraft. Two bombs exploded close astern and damaged her hull, but this went unnoticed until after she had sailed on voyage No 77 to Baltimore and back. Several leaks were discovered on the outward passage, but it was not until she was loaded down to her marks in the USA with cast iron, steel, and dismantled vehicles that they became serious. Again she sailed in convoy, but after frequent stops to seal leaks, and handicapped by fog and snow, she was soon on her own in the Atlantic.

On 27 February her cargo shifted, then a huge wave brought down the foremast, which smashed open No 2 hatch cover and allowed the sea to enter. To add to her troubles, her steering gear broke down, three lifeboats were smashed in their chocks and shortly after her electrical system had failed completely she went ashore on the snow-covered coast of Iceland, near Halvidru.

The *Persier* sat on the beach, partially flooded, for the whole of March, lashed by gales and settling further into the sand with each passing day. During April, salvage work began, and on 15 May she was refloated and beached again at Gufunes for examination. Her No 1 hold was found to be open to the sea, two blades of her propellor had broken off, her rudder and stern post were missing, and the double-bottom tanks were stove in. During July she was moved again, this time to a site opposite Kleppsvik, so that a new rudder which was being hand-forged ashore could be fitted. This work was completed by January 1942 and the vessel refloated yet again, only for it to be found that she was leaking so badly that she had to be beached for a fourth time, and yet again in February. Finally, on 21 May 1942, after being stranded for fourteen months, she left for England in tow of the *Empire Larch* and *Bascobel* and arrived at Yarrow on 18 June to be dry-docked directly opposite the yard where she had been built.

Early the following year she was back in service and completed a further five voyages before being selected to be sunk as a block-ship on the Normandy beaches. She was hastily prepared for the sacrifice on the Clyde, all winches, derricks, and other usable fittings being removed. Six-foot square openings were cut in every bulkhead and certain sections were packed with high explosive, but these were never needed for a change in orders brought her a reprieve. Back went all the fittings, the openings were sealed, and on 8 February 1945 the *Persier* left Cardiff, loaded with foodstuffs for Belgium, on what was to be her last voyage. Chosen to be the convoy commodore's ship, she sailed with sixty-three persons aboard, some of whom were survivors from the steamer *Leopold-ville*, torpedoed and sunk off Cherbourg on Christmas Eve and now returning home. Designated convoy BTC 65, the ships were forced by rough weather to shelter at Lundy, then Clovelly, and it was 11 February before they reached the Eddystone.

An alert lookout spotted the periscope, but the torpedo was already on its way towards them. An immense column of water indicated a premature explosion, several hundred yards away, and a second torpedo went astern of the *Persier*, but at 5.25 pm a third struck No 2 hold, exploded, and the vessel began to list heavily. With his ship's engines now stopped, Capt Mathieu ordered the boats lowered, during which time he inspected the damage, only to find the forward holds completely flooded and some 1,500 tons of soap mixed up with tinned meat and dried egg powder. The evacuation of the *Persier* can only be described as disastrous, since by now her engines had started themselves, due to a defective valve, and could not be stopped. Both Capt Mathieu and Commodore Wood boarded No 1 lifeboat which, in lowering, became unhooked from its falls at one end and hung vertically, throwing its occupants into the sea. A liferaft was released but became entangled with some obstruction and was dragged along, half in and half out of the sea. Lifeboat No 3 got away full of men, but drifted into the still turning propellor and was smashed. Number 4 boat, with no plug fitted and filling rapidly, was lifted by a wave clear of its hooks, leaving two men clinging to the fall blocks, and also went into the propellor.

One boat that did manage to get away went to the rescue of the men swinging on the empty falls; both were rescued safely, but a stoker sliding down from the boat deck caught his foot, fell head downward and drowned. In going to his assistance, the same boat drifted astern and was cut clean in two by the propellor. Only one lifeboat now remained afloat and of the many rafts and Carley floats released, every one either drifted off empty, or else sank. The defective engine control valve which had caused so much loss of life now appeared to be functioning correctly and the engines were stopped, but not for long. HMS *Cornelian* began to depth charge a sonar contact close at hand and the violent explosions started the steamer off again. Several escort vessels, seeing the *Persier*'s predicament, closed in on her, took off the remaining crew and left her to sink, or else go ashore somewhere in the night. Back at Plymouth, the *Gem* landed twenty survivors, a motor patrol boat a further seventeen, and the *Birker Force* another seven men. HMS *Ellesmore* (ex-*Kos XXIV*), herself torpedoed in the area twelve days later, brought ashore the bodies of four men and one woman. The body of the 1st officer was found on Thurlestone sands; that of the steward near Hemmick Bay,

Gorran Haven; the radio officer at Marazion, the last of these being buried in war grave no 11N7 at Penzance. During the hours of darkness, the *Persier* must have continued to steam towards the shore, sinking slowly as she went, until she foundered in Bigbury Bay. She could well have waited a further quarter century before discovery had not fishermen located her on their echo-sounding equipment and passed the information to a local diver. In May 1970 her bell was brought to the surface, confirming her identity, and the Hydrographic Department of the Admiralty was informed that she lay on her side, a 4in gun still mounted on the stern and two machine-guns on the bridge (Picture, p 36).

At the extreme eastern end of Bigbury Bay, where the cliffs climb towards Bolt Tail, lie Thurlestone sands and Hope Cove, both of which have a long association with wrecks. A large German brigantine, the *Theador*, registered at Blankensee and carrying timber and cotton from the West Indies, was blown ashore and lost at Thurlestone on 14 February 1874, simply because her remaining crew were unable to manage the ship. She had encountered severe weather conditions for three days prior to entering Bigbury Bay, during which time her deckhouse galley had been washed overboard, along with both master and mate, leaving a crew depleted to the point where they were virtually helpless.

The similarity between Bigbury and Whitesands Bay has already been mentioned and the confusion is understandable, but to mistake Bolt Tail for Lands End is not so excusable, as was the case with the *Villa Nova* in 1879. Capt Little was in command of the Ardrossan brigantine, in ballast from St Malo to Cardiff, when a choked pump forced her to seek the shelter of land, and in attempting to round what was assumed to be Lands End, she went ashore and broke in two.

The closing days of World War I saw another wreck in the area, the sixty-three year old Dublin schooner *Tasmania*, carrying china clay, which stranded on 4 November 1918. Twenty-one years later the Belgian steamer *Louis Sheid* (ex-*Kendal Castle*, ex-*Ultor*) was also lost in Beacon Cove. This 6,057 tons gross steamer built in 1920 for the Rickmers Line, was on hand when the Dutch *Tajandoen* was torpedoed in the Atlantic and stopped long enough to rescue sixty-two crew, mostly coloured men, from a sea of blazing oil in which six died. The *Louis Sheid* was making for Antwerp with a cargo of grain when she stranded in Bigbury Bay on 7 December 1939. Refloated and beached at Thurlestone she broke in two and became a total loss, but was later so heavily salvaged that today only her double bottoms remain recognisable (Picture, p 64).

From this part of Bigbury Bay the coastline gives way to stark, rugged cliffs and the ancient fishing village of Hope which nestles in the lee of the great headland known as Bolt Tail. Hope Cove is aptly named, for hope is what it offered the generations of seamen shipwrecked on or around this notorious promontory. It has been said of the area that there is 'scarce a cove but holding stout timbers, legends of silver ingots, pieces of eight, moidores, doubloons and dollars'. Certainly, if any coins remain buried in the foreshore, they are more likely to be found on this stretch of coast than any other in Devon. The occupants of Hope Cove have witnessed many a tragedy over the centuries, but none to compare with the loss of the *Ramillies* in 1760. A king's ship of the 1st rate armed with ninety guns and carrying a crew of 720, she had been launched at Woolwich dockyard on 26 October 1664 as the 2nd rate *Katherine* of eighty-two guns and 1,003 tons (bm). From 1696 until she was completely rebuilt in 1702, she became known as the *Royal Katherine*, after which she was renamed the *Ramillies*. Rebuilt for a second time at Portsmouth in 1749, her tonnage was increased by additional armament and fittings to 1,698 (bm). During her service, which was to last ninety-six years, a remarkable record in itself, she was in almost every major battle of the time and consequently earned herself a reputation in the fleet. At Minorca, she was Admiral Byng's flagship in an incident that cost the nation its base at Port Mahon and the admiral his life, and at Quiberon Bay, with Admiral Hawke aboard, great things were expected of her. Unfortunately, she leaked so badly that the flag was transferred to the *Royal George* and the *Ramillies* was sent home for repairs.

It was January 1760 before she was again fit for service, and

she was then ordered to join Boscawen on Channel blockade
duty. In company with the flagship *Royal William*, the *St George*,
Sandwich, *Princess Amelia*, *Venus* and cutter *Hawke*, the *Ramillies*
left Plymouth on 6 February to join the fleet. By 11 February a
south-westerly gale, accompanied by driving rain and sleet,
caught Boscawen's ships in the open sea; so fearful was the gale
that the admiral recorded in his log, 'we could seldom carry even
a topsail'. On the 14th the *Royal William*, caught in a squall, lost
the lashings and gaskets from every sail, which were torn to
ribbons, as well as her lower quarter stern galleries, and leaked
so badly that her crew had to be kept pumping around the
clock. Not surprisingly, the seven vessels were scattered far
and wide, each receiving its share of storm damage. On board
the *Sandwich* several men, hurled from the main topsail yard
by the wind were killed as they struck the deck below and,
along with the *Royal William* and *Princess Amelia*, all three
ships narrowly escaped being wrecked in Mounts Bay, Cornwall.
By late afternoon on the 15th the wind had reached hurricane
force, its effect being felt as far away as London where a huge
sheet of lead, 27ft wide, covering part of the Admiralty roof, was
torn up and rolled back like a carpet. It was 16 February before
the whereabouts of the individual ships became known. The
St George turned up at Spithead with every mast sprung; the
Venus at Portland with her upper deck swept clean and her hull
full of water; the flagship at Plymouth, being 'much shattered',
followed by the *Sandwich* which had lost her mainyard. Only
then was it known that the *Hawke* had foundered in mid-Channel
with all hands, and that the *Ramillies* had gone to pieces on Bolt
Tail with less than twenty-four survivors.

The *Ramillies* had become detached from the rest on the 14th,
when severe leaks had forced her to heave-to. She lumbered away
to the east before the wind until her sailing master estimated
they were off Plymouth, when the ship was stood in towards
land which lay somewhere ahead over an indistinct, heaving
horizon. When eventually the blurred outline of an island appeared ahead, it was mistakenly identified as Looe island and
the warship was steered further east, seemingly towards Rame

Head. Only then was it discovered that the island had been that of Burgh, in Bigbury Bay, and that the *Ramillies* was now hopelessly embayed. Her captain and officers expressed their fears at even attempting to weather the great headland of Bolt Tail, but the sailing master insisted that all was well and ordered all canvas set in an attempt to stay ship. Under the tremendous strain, the mainsail gave way and split from top to bottom; the main sheets had to be let go and then the whole mainmast came crashing down. Shortly afterwards, the mizzenmast also went overboard and the order was given to anchor and take in all remaining sail, followed shortly after by instructions to cut down the foremast and bowsprit.

With no top hamper remaining, the *Ramillies* rode easily to her best and second bower anchors, half a cable's length from the rocks, but the weather was so thick that the ship's presence went unnoticed by those ashore. She remained in this position until 6 pm when both cables parted and she drove towards the shore. Her passage was briefly checked with a sheet anchor, which served only to bring her stern even closer to the shore, after which it also parted and the *Ramillies* went on the rocks. Mountainous seas broke clean over the wreck, sweeping all before them and throwing men helplessly into the sea to drown, or else dashing them to death amongst the rocks. Some of the scenes on deck before the wreck went to pieces were pitiful. The captain of marines went completely off his head and marched up and down the poop deck, singing and exclaiming, while the ship's bo'sun, who had taken his small son to sea with him, attempted to save the child's life by throwing him towards the shore, only to see his brains dashed out on the rocks. Midshipman Harrold was the only commissioned officer to survive the wreck; he escaped over the stern, taking with him a party of eight seamen. The last man to reach safety was William Wise, who literally threw himself off the deck as the ship went to pieces beneath his feet (see frontispiece).

More than 700 men and women died at the foot of Bolt Tail that night, and next day Bigbury Bay was a mass of floating wreckage and bodies. The stern of the *Ramillies* was jammed

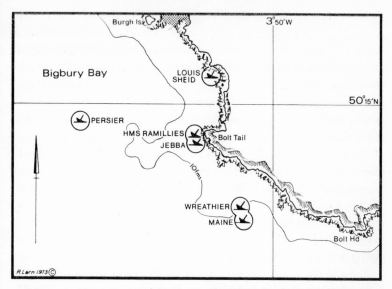

Locations of the steamers *Persier, Louis Sheid, Jebba, Maine* and *Wreathier,*
also of HMS *Ramillies*

into an inlet to the east of Bolt Tail, in a cove which today bears
the name of the wreck, while the rest of her hull lay offshore,
completely submerged. 'I can't see any part of her hull, masts,
sails or yards', wrote the Master Attendant of Plymouth dockyard to the Admiralty, when he visited the site next day. So
scattered was the wreckage that the revenue men were hard
pressed to prevent the locals from plundering. It would appear
that apart from some initial salvage work, when a great many of
her guns were recovered, the wreck remained virtually untouched
until 18 May 1906, when Stephen Chapman, a diver resident at
Hope Cove, agreed to visit the site. The villagers had recently
purchased the wreck of the Brixham trawler *Ibis*, and when
unfavourable weather or tide prevented work in the Thurlestone
area, they agreed they would salvage the *Ramillies'* remains. On
his very first dive Chapman found several iron cannon; a large
brass wheel, marked with a broad arrow, and weighing some 60lb;
a brass belt buckle bearing the name Turner; solid shot and several
shells; the brass trigger guards of several muskets; the handle of

a sword; a brass weight with the number 14 stamped on it, and a large iron hook used to fish the anchor. Subsequent dives revealed many other items of interest and work continued on the site all that season, so that it must have proved a profitable venture.

In later years other wrecks were to occur in almost the same cove, but these were steamers of a more modern age. In the meantime, the small sailing vessel *Orb*, Davey master, with granite from Falmouth for Hull, filled and sank two miles west of Bolt Tail on 26 September 1851. A 275 ton wooden brig, the *Ricardo*, with 2,000 quarters of oats aboard, went ashore in Ramillies Cove on Sunday 26 December 1869, and might well have joined the bones of the old warship had she not been refloated and saved by the Hope Cove coastguards. Another total wreck was the London barque *Westmoreland*, on 14 July two years later, which went ashore in dense fog one and a half miles east of the tail. This 456 ton vessel, built at Sunderland in 1858, was carrying a valuable cargo of sugar, rum, coconuts, fustic and logwood worth £12,000, most of which was lost.

The first of a long succession of steamers to go ashore on this part of the Devon coast was the Russian oil tanker *Blesk*, carrying petroleum from Odessa to Hamburg. On 1 December 1896 she hit the Graystone rock in fog and settled down until the sea lapped over her upper deck, spreading oil over the immediate coastline and well up into the Kingsbridge estuary. Fog also caused the loss of the steam collier *Jane Rowe* of Gelfe, in Sweden. Built by Palmers of Newcastle in 1889 and launched as the *Mary Thomas*, she was renamed *Barto* when first she changed hands, and later, when sold yet again, she became the *Jane Rowe*. As such she went ashore three-quarters of a mile west of the Lantern rock, under Bolberry golf links, at 5.45 am on 28 February 1914. Loaded with 3,000 tons of burnt ore, loaded at Oran for Rotterdam, the wreck was first sighted by the *Kingsbridge Packet* which plied between Plymouth and Salcombe. A hawser was passed between the two vessels but all efforts to pull the *Jane Rowe* clear failed. Meanwhile, news of the wreck had been passed to the Hope coastguard and lifeboat by some rabbit trappers on the clifftop, but despite a speedy launch the lifeboat could be of no assistance. The steamer had gone ashore on the only stretch of sandy beach hereabouts and hopes ran high that she would be saved, but even the combined efforts of the tugs *Boarhound*, *Dencaba*, *Venture*, *Totnes* and *Dragon* all proved futile. By evening, having been driven high up the beach and on top of rock, the *Jane Rowe* was found to be leaking badly and it was obvious she was finished. Many hundreds of spectators crowded the clifftops all night, one of whom, fifteen-year-old John Moses, fell over the edge. His employer, a Mr Stidston, in going to his assistance also fell over the cliffs, but neither suffered severe injuries.

Next morning, the rocket brigade fired a line across the wreck —now only 150yd offshore—which was secured high in the foremast and a breeches buoy rigged. The entire crew were then taken off, the first to come ashore being the ship's cabin boy, who brought with him a kitten; the second was a seaman carrying the ship's cat, and the third struggled across with a large dog.

The wreck of the *Jane Rowe* was followed by an unprecedented shipping disaster in the early hours of Monday 18 March 1907, when two large liners went ashore in the West Country, one in Cornwall, the other in Devon. The incident was unprecedented, not only because of the extraordinary coincidence of time and place, but also because the vessels concerned carried between them 611 passengers and crew, yet not a single life was lost. The Cornish wreck was the *Suevic*, which stranded on the outer Cledges rocks, at the Lizard. Her stern section was subsequently saved by cutting the wreck in two, but no reprieve was possible for the Elder Dempster West African mail steamer *Jebba*. She overshot the Eddystone in fog and stranded near Bolt Tail, only yards from where the *Ramillies* and *Blesk* had been lost. Carrying specie, ivory, palm oil, fruit and mail to a total value of £200,000 and with seventy-nine passengers from Nigeria and the Gold Coast, plus a crew of seventy-six, mostly Kroo boys, the *Jebba* ended up beam-on to the cliffs less than 30yd offshore. Her distress rockets were sighted almost simultaneously by members of the Hope Cove lifeboat and the coastguard, and within minutes the maroons brought men tumbling from their beds. On board the liner, the boiler fires had been drawn to prevent any explosions, since there was already several feet of water inside, and everyone went to their lifeboat stations. There was no trace of panic or disorder among either passengers or crew, and all calmly awaited the captain's instructions. Although the Hope Cove lifeboat had already been launched, two local fishermen, Isaac Jarvis and John Argeat, risked their lives by climbing down the 200ft sheer cliff face in the dark to help rig two bosun's chairs. Many a ghost must have stirred that night, for the rescuers were great-grandsons of the men who had hauled survivors from the *Ramillies* up those selfsame cliffs some hundred and forty-seven years earlier.

Everyone from the wreck reached safety without serious injury, thirty-eight by means of the official rocket apparatus, and 117 by the lines rigged by the two fishermen, both of whom later received the Albert Medal for bravery. There was much interest ashore in the pets brought off the wreck by the crew. First came the ship's cat, then two chimpanzees and several parrots, while the last three coloured seamen each carried a monkey wrapped in a blanket. Although the Hope lifeboat stood by until the last person was safely ashore, its services were not required; in fact, no use was made of the ship's boats either, although one was lowered until just clear of the sea. For days following the incident the sea was too rough for boats to get alongside the *Jebba*, and what little salvage of fittings and personal baggage took place was by way of the cliff face. In due course the Liverpool Salvage Co sent divers to inspect the hull, but there was never any real hope of saving the vessel. Over one hundred bags of mail were salvaged from the holds, but a number were lost on their way to the shore when they spilled from a cargo net. The 2nd officer dived in after the bags and managed to secure several but at the expense of his health, since he collapsed afterwards from exposure and shock and had to be taken to hospital. Much of her cargo, especially the tomatoes on deck, were saved, but the local beaches were littered with bananas and pineapples. Some of the cargo drifted down Channel as far as the

Lizard, where it became mixed with wreckage from the *Suevic*. By 5 April the *Jebba* was starting to break up, and by summer she had gone to pieces completely (Picture, p 36). When the two local heroes proudly stood before Edward VII to receive their awards, it did not escape the king's notice that this was the second and third such awards made to Devon men, Samuel Popplestone, of Start farm, having received the very first Albert Medal from Queen Victoria in 1866, for gallantry at the wreck of the *Spirit of the Ocean*.

The loss of the *Jebba* was by no means the end of an era; the small steam tug *Joffre* stranded close to the remains of the steamer *Jane Rowe* on 27 May 1925, and remained ashore for three months before being refloated (Picture, p 62). Four years later, on 12 February 1929, the British steamer *Deventia*, carrying soda from Fleetwood to London, went ashore during an east-south-east gale, was refloated, but was later scrapped.

Between Bolt Tail and Bolt Head lie five miles of the most stark, beautiful and inaccessible cliffs on the south coast of Devon. A particularly tragic five miles, since they have brought a premature end to at least three dozen recorded wrecks, and probably a great many others of which no record remains. A memorial in the churchyard at Malborough is a reminder of one such wreck, the homeward-bound British East Indiaman *Dragon*, Capt Gleast, from Jamaica to London, lost at Cathole on 22 August 1757. Three boys and a girl, all from the same family, in addition to four of the crew, were drowned. The *Lintor Ken* is reputed to be the rather unusual name of another early loss, but no details survive, not even the year. She is said to have carried a cargo of walnut wood and marble statues which provided many a local manor with decorative materials, and for years fishermen maintained that, in favourable conditions, marble blocks could be seen on the seabed. Another London-owned West Indiaman, the *Bellona*, from Surinam with a valuable cargo, was lost on Bolt Head during September 1807, and on 19 November 1808 the transport *Providence*, homeward-bound from Corunna with troops and stores. Others during the years following include the *Nelly* on 27 July 1852; the *Wanderer*, a 91 ton schooner; the

Anna Maria, offshore from Bolt Head on 23 July 1862, and an unidentified French brig in 1869. A fearful south-westerly gale put the brig ashore and only the corpses of her crew, barrel staves, and a claret-stained area of sea marked her passing. So strong was the wind that night that spray went clean over Bolt Head and contaminated fresh water in a cart standing outside the coastguard station, half a mile inland. Although the Nova Scotian schooner *Abie Perkins* was lost by fire ten miles south of the head on 3 April 1873, her crew were landed at Salcombe, so giving the wreck a local connection. Bound from New York to London with a cargo of naptha, benzole and gas oil, all went well with the ship until she was off Devon when, without warning, there was a violent explosion in the hold which blew out her entire main deck. The schooner was abandoned with her captain and one seaman, both badly burned, still aboard, and presumably drowned when she finally sank.

One of the dozen or more steamers to be wrecked between Bolt Head and Tail was the *Ruperra*. Owned by John Cory & Sons of Cardiff, she was carrying 1,529 tons of cotton seed from Alexandria to Hull when she went ashore to the east of the Hamstone at 5.15 am on 27 January 1881. Within minutes, the level of water in the forward hold had reached 3ft, and increased to 5 by the time both ship's boats had been lowered. One of these was rowed round to Hope Cove; the other, with the captain and 1st mate aboard, stood by the wreck for over an hour until it was obvious that the ship could not be saved. Her loss was attributed to an inexplicable deviation in her master compass. Although the first of the four lifeboats to be stationed at Hope, all of which were named *Alexandra*, was in service at the time, it played no part in the *Ruperra* incident, nor any other, from the time of its installation on 28 February 1878 until the morning of 18 January 1887.

At 7.30 the previous evening, the full-rigged ship *Halloween* of London had gone ashore in Sewer Mill cove. She had left Foochow on 15 August with 1,600 tons of tea aboard, her owners anticipating that this would be on the market by the end of November 1886 at the very latest. Despite the *Halloween* being one of the fastest sailing ships afloat, having reached Sydney in sixty-nine days on her maiden voyage in 1870, bad weather slowed her down and 155 days passed before the Eddystone light was sighted on her starboard bow. A course of south-east was set, which should have allowed her to clear the Start by some eight miles, yet two hours later she struck midway between Bolt Head and Tail, inside of the Hamstone rock. Heavy seas broke over the wreck, quickly gutting both cabin and forecastle and forcing the crew to take to the rigging. They remained there, in relative safety for some time, then a stay parted, making the mizzenmast unsafe, and the men returned to the deck. Flares were burnt, rockets and hand guns fired, even a bonfire lit on the poop, but no one ashore became aware of the wreck until morning.

John Ford, of Southdown farm, was the first to sight the wreck, and it was his messenger who roused the Lloyds agent at Salcombe and escorted him back along the cliffs to the scene. Meanwhile, 2nd officer McLean and able seamen Wigil and Gorse, volunteered to swim ashore to get help, but the latter drowned in the attempt. It was 10 am before the Hope Cove lifeboat arrived, when nineteen numbed and exhausted men, more dead than alive, were taken off and landed safely. At high water, the deck of the *Halloween* was completely submerged, and three days later local newspapers reported that her back had broken, all three masts had gone overboard, and that her valuable cargo now lay on the beach as a massive barrier, some 12ft high in places. Although the underwriters compensated the owners for the loss of cargo, valued at £40,000, the ship itself was uninsured and represented a severe loss to Messrs John Willis & Co, of Leadenhall Street, London. A man came down to Devon from the capital and arranged for a considerable quantity of the damaged tea to be carted to Kingsbridge, from whence it was taken to London by train, but the locals were never paid for their efforts and it is even doubtful if the stranger had the owners' permission to salvage the tea in the first place.

Mention has already been made of a wreck carrying walnut and marble, the *Lintor Ken*, lost hereabouts. There is no reason to doubt the authenticity of this information, but at the same time there is a remarkable similarity between the cargo mentioned and that of the Italian barque *Volere*, of 464 tons, blown ashore and wrecked by a south-westerly gale on 6 March 1881. The *Volere*, whose master, Gavagnin, was also part owner, carried marble and selected timbers from Genoa for London, and went ashore in Sewer Mill Cove with the loss of five crew and one passenger.

Although visited by dozens of divers each year, few of them know the identity of the steamer whose remains lie close to the bar, at the entrance to Salcombe. The 844 ton French steamer *Soudan*, with twenty-four crew, eight passengers, and a cargo of pig nuts from Senegal, was only a few hours from her destination of Dunkirk, when she struck the Hamstone rock in thick fog on 27 June 1887. Tugs attempted to get her into the harbour, but she foundered at the entrance. Two Belgian salvage steamers, the *Berger Wilheim* and *Newa*, were engaged to raise the vessel and for two whole months worked on the wreck. Air was blown into her ballast tanks, air bags were placed inside the hold, huge chains were passed under her hull and secured to lifting lighters, but every attempt to refloat her failed and she became a total loss. The wreck of the *Soudan* heralded a number of incidents involving steamers between Bolt Head and Tail, and of the next seven shipwreck incidents, six were steamers of considerable tonnage.

Dense fog, which blanketed the south coast from Lands End to Portsmouth, saw the *City of Hamburg* go ashore half a mile to the west of Sewer Mill, beneath South Down cliffs, on 7 August 1888. After establishing that his ship was well and truly stranded, Capt Lamont was firing off a distress signal when the gun burst, inflicting fearful injuries which later necessitated amputation of his right arm. The first lifeboat lowered from the *City of Hamburg* was swamped and lost; the second, with the injured captain and five others aboard, managed to reach Salcombe; the third boat landed at Mothecombe, and a fourth was taken in tow by the Salcombe rowing lifeboat *Lesty*. At 4 pm the following day the steamer was successfully refloated by the tug *Power* and towed away to Plymouth. Also refloated and

Page 89: (*above*) The steamer *Betsy Anna* stranded inside of the 'island' at Prawle Point on 17 August 1926; (*below*) the French trawler *Tarascon*, wedged under cliffs near Salcombe, was refloated by hand, using blocks and tackle

Page 90: (*above*) Stranded in fog on Gara Rock, between Salcombe and Prawle, on 11 April 1934, the trawler *Touquet* was refloated three days later; (*below*) the 15,000 ton battleship HMS *Formidable*, torpedoed and sunk off Start Point by the *U-24* on New Year's Day 1915

saved was the 12,000 tons gross hospital ship *Asturias*, which had been deliberately run ashore on 20 March 1917 after being hit by a German torpedo, which killed forty-five crew and nurses. Prior to the outbreak of war, the *Asturias* had been a Royal Mail liner and was one of the first merchant vessels to be requisitioned by the Admiralty. Fortunately, she had already disembarked a large number of wounded troops from Salonika at Avonmouth and was on passage up-Channel when attacked. Her identity could have been in no doubt, since every light on deck was burning and huge red cross emblems on either side of her hull were floodlit.

Other losses or incidents included the 4,073 ton Barclay Curle-built *Liberta* (Picture, p 63), ashore and wrecked on Bolt Head during fog on 15 February 1926; followed by the *Cantabria* of Spain (Picture, p 64), in Steeple Cove on 13 December 1932, with a cargo of iron ore from Bilbao to Newcastle and, only twenty-five days later, the steam drifter *Charter*, under Cathole cliff. The *Charter* went ashore between the remains of the *Jane Rowe* and the site of the *Joffre*'s stranding, and at low water her boiler can still be seen. These rusting plates might well have been joined by those of another trawler, the *Tarascon*, ashore in Steeple Cove on 22 March 1938, had she not literally been winched clear by hand. Wire strops were passed around some offshore rocks and threefold tackles rigged, and at high water, with a dozen men sweating on the falls, the trawler was inched off into deep water and saved (Picture, p 89). The last wreck in the area to date was also a trawler, the *Amelie Suzanne*, which stranded on 1 April 1972 and was smashed to pieces (Picture, p 63).

Between Bolt Head and Prawle Point lies the entrance to Salcombe, a sheltered port and anchorage downstream from Kingsbridge. A census in 1791 showed that the inhabitants of Salcombe numbered 271, who lived in exactly fifty houses, and a further ten years were to pass before the population reached 500. The port, besides its lawful and more general commercial activities, was at one time a centre for smuggling and saw a phenomenal traffic in contraband between France, the Channel Isles and Devon. In common with other ports, the coastguard

F

and revenue system brought it under control, and the locals were forced to turn to the more lawful occupations of pilotage, fishing and shipbuilding, with the result that the district prospered. In Leyland's time, he saw fit to describe Salcombe as, 'Saultecumbe haven, sumwhat barrid and having a rok at the entering into it, a Fisshar Towne'. Presumably, the rock in question was the Mewstone, and it is strange that Leyland should have made special mention of that and not the Salcombe sandbar, which is well known and respected by the seafaring community. At normal low spring tides there is generally 6ft of water over the bar, but there are records of it drying out completely and of people crossing dry-shod from one bank to the other.

On 13 December 1806, the American ship *Resolution*, London to St Lucion, was wrecked near Salcombe in an unspecified location, as was the Helford-built cutter *Louisa* in March 1859, while the *Industry* was lost on the sandbar there on 20 October 1862. The *Western Daily Mercury* of 16 October 1877 reported that on the previous day a vessel, believed to be French, had come ashore near the Rickham coastguard station, but that no bodies had been found, nor the identity of the vessel as yet established. Later, she proved to be the *Pauline*, and local fishermen recovered a total of seven bodies out at sea. Two years later, on 16 January, the 242 ton wooden barquentine *Annie* was stranded and lost on the bar; an unfortunate end to this Salcombe-owned and manned vessel, en route from Bahia with 390 tons of sugar in bags. She attempted to enter port in a deplorable, storm-damaged condition, after having lost her bulwarks, longboat, figurehead, cutwater and topmast. After striking the bar she anchored, but had insufficient water under her keel and went to pieces as she pounded on the bottom. The Salcombe lifeboat rescued the master, Edward Patey, and his mate, the remaining six crew being taken off by a local boat.

Other incidents in the harbour itself include the Salcombe-registered *Neptune*, which caught fire while at anchor on 31 January 1881. Her mate cut her cable, allowing her to drift ashore where she burnt to the waterline and then sank, taking with her some nine tons of beer and traut. A fouled anchor chain and a strong southerly wind combined to drive the 23 ton sloop *Brothers* ashore at Cove Point on 29 March 1881. She soon filled and sank along with her cargo of limestone, and similar circumstances caused the loss of the two-year-old cutter *Dove* which was last seen at anchor on 16 May 1881, then disappeared and presumably sank. Two years later, at the end of January, the Blackstone rock almost claimed the Liverpool barquentine *Chittagong* which put into Salcombe after losing her deckhouse and two hands in an Atlantic gale. She struck the bar and leaked so badly that it became necessary to run her ashore. Similarly, the *Amy*, a Dartmouth schooner carrying devi-devi from Riohacha, also went ashore on the eastern side of the harbour entrance on 8 November 1883. The paddle-steamer *Reindeer* attempted to pull her off, but fouled the wreck and would herself have stranded but for a flooding tide which allowed her to drift clear. There were few incidents following the *Amy*, the Plymouth schooner *Ensign* becoming one of the few total wrecks after striking the Blackstone on 30 January 1915.

There followed, in 1916, the worst lifeboat disaster Devon has experienced, when the Salcombe boat overturned on the bar, drowning thirteen of her fifteen crew. Launched on her sixth and last service on 27 October 1916, the *William and Emma*, which had been on station since 1904, was called out by the Prawle coastguards to attend the wreck of the Plymouth schooner *Western Lass*, ashore in Lannacombe Bay, near Start Point. Sea conditions were bad when the lifeboat left and no doubt Coxswain Distin had some anxious moments before they reached deep water. The lifeboat was still within sight of Salcombe estuary when a message arrived to say that the Prawle rocket brigade had already saved the schooner's crew. Apparently there was no means of communicating with the lifeboat once it had left, and so it continued all the way to the scene of the wreck on a fruitless and wasted journey. It seems strange that it could pass close to both the Prawle coastguard lookout and the signal station without some attempt being made to turn the crew back, but such was the case. By the time the *William and Emma* arrived back at the entrance to Salcombe her crew were wet through and exhausted, and their condition probably influenced the coxswain to attempt the bar when, in different circumstances, he might well have waited another hour. As the lifeboat approached the line of breakers, a huge wave overtook it, lifting the stern high in the air, and lookouts on the cliffs saw the boat slew sideways down the slope, fall beam-on to the sea and capsize. Unfortunately the tide was on the ebb and the overturned boat and its crew were swept seawards. Edward Distin, brother of the coxswain and one of the only two survivors, regained the boat by hauling himself along the sea anchor rope, followed by William Johnson. Eventually they managed to reach an offshore rock, to which they clung until a weighted cane, attached to a line, was thrown to them from the shore. They were by then so weak that brandy had to be lowered to them before they could summon up strength enough to pull down a heavier rope. By this means they were dragged ashore and saved, but spent many weeks in hospital recovering from the ordeal. It was a major disaster for the town to lose thirteen of its men in this tragic manner, yet within two months a new volunteer lifeboat crew had been found, and by April 1917 a new boat, the *Sarah Ann Holden*, was on station.

One of several ships sunk by enemy action off Salcombe in World War I was the West Hartlepool steamer *Teesdale*, of 2,470 tons gross, torpedoed when three miles south of Salcombe on 15 June 1917. Bound for Gibraltar with Tyneside coal aboard, she was beached and refloated after repairs, but eventually foundered three miles north of Saltburn, Yorkshire, while on passage to the Tees for permanent repairs. Another World War I victim, which has since received a great deal of publicity, was the Atlantic Transport Co's steamer *Maine*, torpedoed and sunk off Salcombe on 23 March 1917. Built in 1904 by Hendersons as the *Sierra Blanca* (ship No 440), the war risk insurance fund paid out £19,429 for her loss, a sharp contrast to the £38,000 purchase money paid to the Sierra Shipping Co in 1913, and the £100 which the Torbay sub-aqua club paid for ownership of the wreck in 1961. The prize these amateur divers sought was not her cargo of chalk, cow and horsehair, goatskins or seeds, but her $6\frac{1}{2}$ ton bronze propellor, which was eventually brought to the surface by the naval boom defence vessel *Barbastel* in April 1963. During 1969, several champagne bottles, still tightly corked and full, were salvaged by divers, their contents still drinkable, despite fifty-two years under water.

Although the famous *Herzogin Cecilie* was not the last of the 'tall-ships', she was certainly amongst the last half-dozen and the last big sailing ship wrecked in the south-west of England. Built by the German firm of Rickmers, she was the winner of many a long-distance grain race and the crack cadet ship of Norddeutscher Lloyd until the outbreak of World War I, at the end of which, following a long period of voluntary internment in Chili, she was handed over to the French. They refused German offers to repurchase her, and eventually the *Herzogin Cecilie* passed to a Finnish owner, under whose flag she tramped the world. Her career was not without incidents, particularly in 1935, when she lost nineteen sails during a gale off the Lizard. In June, only a month later, her donkey boiler exploded, killing two members of the crew, and in October she was in collision off Anholt with the German steam trawler *Rastede*.

Her last passage was the unofficial grain race from Australia in 1936, when she reached Falmouth in eighty-six days, seven whole days ahead of her nearest rival, the *Pommern*. Two days after she had reached Cornwall the grand 'old Duchess', as she was affectionately known—her figurehead being that of the Duchess Cecilie, daughter of the Duke of Oldenbourg—struck the Hamstone rock and eventually became a total wreck. The great four-masted barque had left Falmouth for Ipswich at 8.20 pm on Friday 24 April, clearing the Manacles, before setting course up Channel. It was almost as if Capt Sven Eriksson and his wife Pamela had had some premonition of the disaster, for on her passage home from Australia he had woken from a nightmare shouting, 'She's on the rocks; look, look, she's on the rocks!' And right up until the moment she had left Falmouth, Mrs Eriksson had pleaded with her husband not to sail, so strong was her foreboding. The 'Duchess' struck just before 4 am when at least ten miles north of her intended track; how she came to be there will never be known. In his deposition to the Receiver of

Wreck, Eriksson wrote, '. . . loss due to fog and possible magnetic attraction, plus the presence of sufficient tidal impulse to set the vessel right off course'. There was a great deal of newspaper talk and correspondence suggesting that the cliffs had a high iron content which had caused this and many other wrecks in the area, but the same has been said of every cliff from North Foreland to Lands End at some time or another.

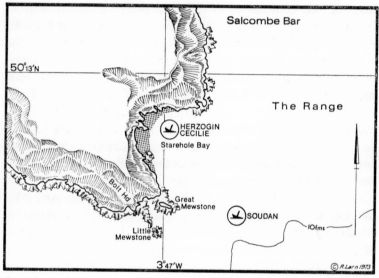

Locations of the wrecks of the *Herzogin Cecilie* and the steamship *Soudan*

As soon as she struck, her anchors were let go but failed to hold, and the 3,111 ton ship swung round, crashing her stern against other rocks, very close to the spot where the tea clipper *Halloween* had ended her days. Capt Eriksson fired off distress rockets which were sighted by the local coastguard, who in turn alerted the Salcombe lifeboat, but the first person to see the wreck from ashore was Jack Jarvis, a resident of Hope Cove, who spotted her outline through the now thinning murk. He hailed the vessel, but the crew only shouted back, 'Get some tugs!' Dawn on the 25th brought out everyone who could find an excuse to attend the wreck, most of them mere sightseers.

Customs officers, the Receiver of Wreck, Lloyds' agents, salvage men, reporters, photographers, corporation and health officials, local police and doctors, they all attempted to get aboard or else just hung about getting in the way of everyone, especially the lifeboat. A breeches buoy was rigged from the clifftop and used to land personal belongings and baggage, which was promptly rifled by members of the public and everything of value stolen. Twenty-two members of the crew were then taken off by the Salcombe lifeboat, leaving only the captain, his wife, both mates, and four seamen aboard. The Customs officers, on learning that these eight intended to stand by the wreck, impounded every drop of spirit and every cigarette, and in a bout of over-zealous officialdom even slaughtered the pet piglet whose corpse was flung overboard and floated around the vessel for days. They then boxed up and took away the ship's cats, but lost some of their enthusiasm when faced by the captain's Alsatian dog, Paik, who took an instant and obvious dislike to the intruders.

For seven long weeks the *Herzogin Cecilie* lay on the rocks while from the clifftops tens of thousands of spectators stared down at her, the last sailing-ship wreck most of them would ever see. Local farmers made a good thing out of the incident by charging people to cross their land, and the coastline between Bolt Head and Tail was visited by more people than at any previous time in its history. Salvage was technically possible, even after seven weeks, and various authorities were approached for funds and assistance. Lady Houston offered to foot the bill if the Royal Navy would take the vessel into service as a sail training ship, but the Admiralty declined the offer. Finally, it was agreed that the cost of salvage would be offset if the owner, Gustaf Eriksson, would give British deck-officer cadets and apprentices the opportunity to serve aboard, and a general appeal was launched, headed by a donation of £500 from Canada. The question then arose as to what should be done with the barque once she was refloated, and local officials began to show concern. A great deal of the grain cargo had been discharged from the wreck in good condition, but more than half still lay rotting and fermenting in the hold, its stench quite appalling. Capt Eriksson naturally wanted to get his ship into Salcombe harbour, where she would have complete shelter while temporary repairs were carried out, but fearing wholesale pollution of local beaches with the holiday season on hand, the local council insisted that she be beached in Starehole Bay at the mouth of the estuary.

On 19 June she was successfully refloated amidst great cheering from the watching crowds, taken to the supposedly sandy cove, and run ashore. University students on vacation volunteered to assist in clearing the rotting grain, and by 27 June had reduced the original 4,242 tons to less than 1,500. It was a close-run thing, and had the ship not worked herself 12ft into the sand and settled down on a hidden reef, she might well have survived the south-east gale of 18 July which caused her to break her back. Similarly, had the Salcombe authorities allowed her inside the harbour a month previously, she would have been able to have discharged her cargo in half the time, completed repairs and sailed. As it was, her beaching at Starehole was no improvement on the original plan to bring her into the estuary, since grain washed out of the wreck and smothered the beaches, where in any case it was quickly devoured by seabirds. Assisted by work gangs from ashore, the remaining crew helped strip the wreck of all her fittings. Her figurehead and her saloon, complete with upholstery, curtains, lamps, clock and barometer, were donated to the Maritime Museum at Alands, Finland, and on 24 September the wreck was sold to Messrs Noyce, a Kingsbridge scrap metal dealer for £225. By January 1939, the *Torquay Times* reported that all four masts had gone overboard and that the wreck had broken into four separate pieces (Picture, p 61).

East of Salcombe, on Rickham sands, is where the Liverpool full-rigged ship *Meirion* went ashore in thick weather during the early hours of 7 September 1879. An iron ship built at Sunderland only the previous year, she had left Rangoon for London, commanded by Capt William Williams, on 13 March. With her holds full of rice and cutch, she was flying round the Cape of Good Hope in the teeth of a gale when she was flung on to her beam ends and suffered considerable damage. Her cabin was completely flooded and just about all the furniture and provisions aboard were destroyed, while able seaman Taylor was washed from off the upper deck and lost overboard. As she passed the Eddystone on her way up Channel, the wind swung from the south-west to south-east, forcing her inshore, and she was unable to weather the Prawle. The local rocket apparatus was used to save her entire crew, and the tug *Heron* made two attempts to pull her off, but failed.

From this point the cliffs run out towards Prawle Point, the southernmost extremity of Devon and the eastern boundary of this chapter. A German barque, the *Emilie*, went on the rocks here in dense fog at 8 pm on 29 May 1870 and eventually went to pieces. Bound from Iquique to Falmouth for orders, the 290 ton vessel, carrying saltpetre and a crew of thirteen, refused to go about after she had been sailed too close to the shore in making a landfall. An anchor with fifteen fathoms of chain was dropped, but the cable parted and the barque went ashore. The following day the crew returned to the scene intending to re-board her at low water and collect their belongings, but it was a wasted trip; the *Emilie* had already broken up and little remained above water. Close at hand, on Gammon Head, are the remains of another victim of fog and the second tea clipper lost in the vicinity of Salcombe. This was the famous *Lalla Rookh*, lost on 3 March 1873. She was on passage from Shanghai to London with the first of a new season's leaf tea, 1,200 tons in all, plus a further twelve tons of tobacco, one passenger, a crew of twenty and a stowaway. They had left China on 22 October and made good time to the mouth of the English Channel, but were then slowed down by fog so dense that the helmsman could not even see the forecastle. They ploughed on past Cornwall and the Eddystone, completely blind to anything ahead, and her lookouts neither saw nor heard anything until Prawle Point loomed up only yards ahead. The *Lalla Rookh* struck just once, then drifted into a small cove where the mizzenmast fell clean through her bottom plates and she quickly filled. Thomas Groves, the mate, lost his life when the first of the ship's boats to be launched was swamped; the only other victim was the stowaway, who was thought to have died from dysentry in his bunk before the ship went ashore. Prawle Point coastguards rescued fifteen of the crew by breeches buoy, the remainder saving themselves by jumping onto the rocks and scaling the cliffs.

Other losses around Prawle Point include the Fleetwood schooner *Utility*, wrecked between Black Cove and Pigs Nose on 3 January 1879; the 1,292 ton ship *Glad Tidings*, and the barque *Patria*. Registered at St Johns, New Brunswick, the *Glad Tidings* had some 1,900 tons of raw linseed on board from Calcutta. Charles McMillan, her master, calling at Falmouth for orders, was redirected to Amsterdam and was passing Salcombe when he mistook a light there for the Start. Thinking he was at least five miles offshore, he altered course towards the shore and soon afterwards, without warning, the ship crashed on to the rocks a quarter of a mile west of Prawle. Some sparks from a distress flare fell into the lazarette and fire quickly spread throughout the ship. Nineteen of her crew were saved, but two drowned when they tried to swim ashore. Nine years later, on 22 March 1888, the Porsgrunn barque *Patria* also went aground here to become a total loss, the victim of incorrect information given by a pilot vessel. The *Patria*'s master, Willhelm Wright, went alongside Falmouth *Pilot Cutter No 2* in the Channel to ask for a bearing of the Lizard and was informed, 'Due east, about sixty miles'. This did not agree with Capt Wright's own calculations, but he accepted the information as correct and set course accordingly. Five hours later, breakers were sighted ahead and the *Patria*, laden with pitch pine boards, hit the rocks and was wrecked. She was later sold, as she lay, for £22.

During World War I, the steamer *Riversdale* of Sunderland, 2,805 tons gross, was torpedoed and sunk off Salcombe, followed by the Ocean Steamship Co's *Laertes*, of 4,541 tons gross, on 1 August 1917 one and a quarter miles south-west of Prawle. The only war-time stranding in the area was that of the Norwegian, coal-laden *Nosted V* on 2 November of the same year. Other strandings in the 1930s were the French trawler *Touquet*, which went on the Gara rock on 11 April 1934 (Picture, p 90), and the large steamer *Benmohr*, three years previously, on 25 February

1931. Since then, the extent of the toll has been limited to four small warships, all lost during 1942; the *Pierre Desceliers*, a requisitioned trawler; the *Intrepede*, of the same category; and Landing Craft Nos *332* and *362*, lost in a gale.

CHAPTER THREE

PRAWLE POINT TO
SCABBACOMBE HEAD

Prawle Point occupies the same position in Devon as does the Lizard in Cornwall, since both mark the southernmost extremity of their respective counties and were both renowned for their Lloyds' signal station. Ships passing up or down Channel reported their progress to first one and then the other of these squat, white-painted buildings, whose telegraph link with Leadenhall Street in London played such an important part in seaborne trade.

As with the Lizard station, which has a phenomenal number of wrecks in its immediate vicinity, so Prawle Point has seen a quite remarkable number of incidents, both to the west and on the formidable stretch of coast reaching east to Start Point. Fittingly, one of the most famous shipwreck rescues in the whole of Devon took place here, a quarter of a mile west of the Start, on 23 March 1866, and led to the introduction by Queen Victoria of the Albert Medal for gallantry. The London barque, *Spirit of the Ocean*, 578 tons, built by Jones & Co, was running down Channel in bad weather, bound for Halifax, Nova Scotia, when an attempt was made to reach the shelter of Dartmouth harbour. An offshore wind from the north-east caused the barque to fall off and she drifted away across Start Bay, in great danger of becoming embayed should the wind change. She did just manage to scrape past Start Point itself, but then a submerged rock brought her to a shuddering halt and, shortly afterwards, the *Spirit of the Ocean* broke in two. On board were twenty-four passengers, eighteen crew, and a valuable general cargo, including a large quantity of tea. The wreck occurred in such an inaccessible location that it is doubtful if anyone on board would have survived had not Samuel Popplestone, a Start Point farmer, actually seen her go ashore. He was instrumental in not only informing the Hallsands coastguard of the wreck, but risked his own life by climbing down the sheer face of the cliffs to save two men. It has often been stated that these were the only survivors, but in point of fact four men escaped alive, the mate, the bo'sun, and two seamen. A memorial to the thirty-eight dead was erected in the form of a stained glass window in the south transept of the church at Stokenham.

Two and a half years later, on 10 December 1868, another disastrous shipwreck involving a sailing vessel took place, midway between the remains of the *Spirit of the Ocean* and Prawle Point, with a heavy loss of life. This was the 734 ton Liverpool-registered *Gossamer*, a full-rigged ship of considerable fame. She also had taken part in the annual tea races from Shanghai to London, and only two months before her loss had been the second vessel home from China. Now outward bound for Australia, the *Gossamer* left London for Adelaide with a general cargo, twenty-four crew, four passengers, and the master's wife aboard. Her passage west from the Downs was very stormy and Capt Thompson was obliged to remain on deck for one day and two whole nights without sleep. Whether or not this was over-zealous devotion to duty or distrust of the Channel pilot's ability is uncertain. Pilot Grant had joined the vessel at Gravesend and was to remain on board until the ship reached Plymouth, where additional passengers would be embarked.

In great need of rest, the captain finally went below to his cabin when the *Gossamer* was off Dartmouth, but had his sleep disturbed twice within the hour by the chief mate, who informed him that the pilot refused to set topsails. Much later, at the Board of Trade inquiry held at the Seven Stars inn at Chivelstone, a village about eight miles from Prawle, there was indisputable evidence that the pilot was not only under the influence of drink, but also negligent in refusing to set more canvas. Capt Sladen, of the Salcombe schooner *Astrea*, passed the *Gossamer* when off Start Point and confirmed that she had been too close inshore and was carrying insufficient sail. Other witnesses to the wreck were the Prawle coastguards, who saw the *Gossamer* attempting to tack half a mile offshore, miss stays, and then lower or reef most of her canvas. Meanwhile, on board, the sound of chain in the hawsepipes was the first knowledge Capt Thompson had of the danger facing his command. For a full twenty minutes the *Gossamer* held to her anchors, then, simultaneously, both cables parted and she went ashore. Unfortunately she missed a shingle beach by less than 150yd, hit some rocks and went to pieces, drowning fourteen persons. In a desperate attempt to save his bride of only two weeks, the captain lashed his wife to a spar and was seen by watchers on the clifftop to be supporting her in the water. Neither survived, and it was assumed that they had been struck by falling wreckage and killed.

By Sunday 13 December, eight bodies, including those of the captain and his wife, had been recovered and laid out in the belfry of Chivelstone church. Many relatives of those aboard visited the scene to recover property or identify the dead, but literally thousands of pounds worth of goods found their way into the hands of the wreckers. In many instances, they broke open chests or parcels to steal the most trifling articles, allowing the sea to spoil the remainder. A detachment of police and troops had to be sent for and, under the leadership of Superintendent Vaughan and Captain Mauthom of the coastguard service, attempted to save as much cargo as possible and prevent further looting. But it was already scattered far and wide, giving spectators ample time to help themselves. It was said at the time, 'The inhabitants of Prawle, Salcombe, Torcross, and adjacent villages around, will not need to purchase any drapery goods for a very long time.'[1] Shop goods, clothes, boots, books and toys, a great many patented Howard ploughshares, salt meat, cloth, and ingots of iron, all lay scattered on the rocks and foreshore. William Edmonds, a respectable farmer of High House, East Portlemouth, was apprehended for plundering the wreck by night. Not only did he visit the wreck to steal himself, but brought all his labourers along as well to help, all of whom were sent for trial at the Kingsbridge Town Hall. Pilot Grant, who caused the wreck in the first place, was found guilty of manslaughter at the local sessions, remanded on bail of £350, and sent for trial at the local assize the following March. The outcome of this trial is, unfortunately, unknown.

If the *Gossamer* provided the locals with clothing, then the next wreck, that of an Italian brig, gave them fuel at a time of year when it was most appreciated. The *Marie Theresa* of Genoa, Nicola Bozza master, left Newcastle for her home port with 850 tons of coal in late November 1872. On 4 December, when fifteen miles west of the Start, a green light appeared on her starboard bow. This vessel then altered course directly towards the Italian until both sidelights were clearly visible. Shortly afterwards, she struck the *Marie Theresa* a terrific blow on her port side, cutting her planking down to the waterline, then backed off and sailed away. In imminent danger of foundering, the brig was headed inshore and beached one mile east of the signal station, where she broke up very quickly. Fortunately, no lives were lost amongst the crew of twelve, all of whom landed at Lannacombe Bay in their own boat. A few sails were all that was officially recovered from the wreck itself.

Seemingly, that was the end of the incident, but what was to follow must surely be unique in wreck history. The Italian crew of the brig were quartered overnight at an East Prawle inn and gave no trouble until next morning, when, for reasons unknown, they began to quarrel amongst themselves. One of the seamen then went beserk and stabbed three of his shipmates. With no policeman in the village, the only authority to whom the landlord could look was the coastguard. When eventually one of them appeared in uniform, the half-crazed seaman mistook him for the law and fled towards the coastguard station and houses. The duty officer in the station opened the door in answer to his knock, only to be violently assaulted and stabbed five times in the chest. His wife, attracted by her husband's shouts, was also stabbed three times, and another officer and his wife fourteen times between them. As the assailant left the building, he was confronted by the chief boatman and another officer, both of them armed with cutlasses. They, too, were attacked, whereupon the senior of them drew his cutlass and, choosing his moment, felled the Italian with a single blow from which he later died.

Such incidents were, of course, exceptional and the majority of wrecks received little publicity in nineteenth-century newspapers, especially if their cargo was as singularly unattractive as the seventy tons of boulders on board the Fleetwood schooner *Utility*, which went ashore near Prawle during a south-easterly gale on 3 January 1879. Capt Sumner and his crew of five managed to get away in the ship's boat when the twenty-year-old vessel broke up, but had to abandon all their possessions. More fortunate in this respect were the men aboard the trawling ketch *Florinda* (DH191). She foundered one and three-quarter miles east of Prawle on 30 July 1890, but gave her crew plenty of time to transfer items to a passing crabber. In the same area, the Swedish barque *Thekla*, 378 tons gross, was wrecked on 8 May 1891, and might well have been joined by the steamer *Pinedene* on 17 January 1901 which had lost her propellor in a collision, but for strenuous efforts made by local tugs.

Start Point, which lies three and a quarter miles east-north-east of Prawle, is easily identified from seaward by the five hillocks, each about 200ft high, that give it a rugged cockscomb appearance. Since it represents a turning point in coastal navigation, it is not surprising that a great many vessels have come to grief there, either on the rocks or in the immediate vicinity. In 1781, on 26 January, the same day that the brandy-laden *Wierkelyk* was lost at Plymouth, an unidentified ship was wrecked on the Start and all hands lost. Three years later HMS *Crocodile*, a 6th rate, twenty-four gun ship, was also wrecked here, with 200 dead, whilst returning from the West Indies. Even more lives were lost in the disastrous collision between the emigrant ship *Favourite* and the *Hesper* on 29 April 1854. The former was carrying emigrants from Bremen to Baltimore when, in heavy rain and rough seas, she was struck by the American vessel on her starboard side. Capt Hoegman of the *Favourite* was asleep in his bunk at the time and reached the upper deck, still in his night clothes, just as the *Hesper* was beginning to pull clear. To abandon his passengers and command at such a critical moment was un-

Page 107: (*above*) The *English Trader* is cut free of her badly damaged and flooded bow section after going ashore off Dartmouth Castle on 23 January 1937; (*below*) the bow section, after being salvaged and hauled ashore for scrap at Dartmouth later in the year

Page 108: (*above*) The oil tanker *Broadmayne* with salvage vessel standing by, ashore at Newfoundland Cove, Dartmouth, 2 January 1921; (*below*) stranded near Torquay on 22 December 1964, the Danish motorship *Northwind* takes a battering from rough seas

forgivable, yet without a moment's hesitation he leapt for the receding bows of the *Hesper*, gained a handhold, and scrambled to safety, his example prompting the first officer and four seamen to follow suit. As the gap between the two ships widened, so the sea poured into the hold of the *Favourite* and the 191 despairing emigrants and the ten remaining members of her crew were left to their fate. A combination of extreme darkness and rough seas prevented the *Hesper* from effecting any sort of rescue. She remained in the vicinity all night, but at daybreak not a trace of the sinking vessel was to be found. The six men who had so cowardly abandoned their ship were the only survivors from the original complement of 207.

Collision at sea was, of course, common in those days, and another occurred that same year, on 17 September, involving the Norwegian barque *Oceanus*, commanded by Capt Norbeck, and an unidentified American schooner. Carrying 500 tons of rice from Akyab, the *Oceanus* of Kristiansund was run down and cut clean to the waterline off Start Point, after calling at Queenstown and receiving instructions to discharge at Amsterdam. The colliding vessel, after backing off, refused to render any assistance and stood away down Channel. Fortunately, the Brixham lugger *Hero* was on hand and took off the *Oceanus*'s master and some seamen, the remainder landing from their own boat at Gun Cliff, in Lyme Bay. The only casualty was a seaman who was killed outright when the foremast collapsed and struck him on the head. The *British Queen*, an Isles of Scilly schooner of 105 tons gross, also fell victim to the same area when, on 1 February 1860, she was abandoned in a sinking condition. Located at dusk by the brig *Rising Sun* of Sunderland, the schooner, laden with bones and ash, had 3ft of water in her cabin, her upper deck swept clean, and bulwarks on both sides smashed down. Her captain was still in his bunk, seriously ill, and the master of the brig had no option but to save the men and abandon all hope of salvage. Another incident involving collision off the Start took place on 7 August 1862 and sixteen men drowned; this was when the *Moulin* and *Daphne* ran into one another. But when, a year later on 25 May 1863, the *Lovely Lady*, an Aberystwyth

G

PRAWLE TO
SCABBACOMBE HEAD
—Chapter Three—

Sharkham Point

Scabbacombe Head

Dartmouth

H.M.S JED 1920
TWO BROTHERS 1869
MORNING STAR 1910
COMET 1878
WAVE 1871
BROADMAYNE 1921
LONDON TRADER 1937
ANN 1863
EUREKA 1870
DOROTHEA 1972
ROSA 1887
TEST 1932
VICTOIRE 1838
H.M.S CROWN PRIZE 1692
PRINCESS OF THULE 1916
H.M.S SEAHORSE 1711
ELIZABETH LASS 1858
COURSER 1870
ADMIRAL POCOCK 1763
H.M.S FERNWOOD 1942
H.M.S LORD NELSON 1805
MERRY LASS 1889
JESSIE 1881
PICTON CASTLE 1917
ANNA ELISE 1852
GREATHAM 1918
CHARLES JÖSE 1933
AGNETE 1918
FREEDOM 1809
BONITO 1854
HERALD 1853
M.1 1925
JANE BURROW 1852
Start Bay
H.M.S FORMIDABLE 1915
LORD NELSON 1810
CECILIA 1880
HAWTHORN 1881
HENRIETTA 1939
POSTILION 1732
MEDINA 1917
L.C.18 1943
TWO BROTHERS 1852
Beesands
OLIVE BRANCH 1856
WATERLOO 1852
CLAN STUART 1940
PRIUS SENIOR 1878
SIR GEORGE SEYMOUR 1876
ELIZABETH 1871
U.85 1917
WARSAW 1917
DRYAD 1891
LIZZIE ELLEN 1891
H.M.S UNTIRING 1957
GATINAIS 1942
Hallsands
ALBERTA 1891
LADY ALICE 1875
IRA 1878
LUNESDALE 1891
HAZARD 1877
U.72 1917
SANDSEND 1891
MOULINE 1862
JOHN BOYLE 1876
Start Point
ROTORURA 1917
FLORENCE 1905
MARANA 1891
BRITISH QUEEN 1880
TEESDALE 1917
H.M.S CROCODILE 1784
REFORMATION
SPIRIT OF THE OCEAN 1866
OCEANUS 1854
LIVONIA 1917
UNIDENTIFIED 1781
JAMSON 1868
HEIR APPARENT 1880
MARIE THERESA 1872
NYMPH 1891
H.M.S AMAZON 1866
GOSSAMER 1868
SPARKLING WINE 1900
SPENNYMORE 1915
NORDSTERN 1888
UC.51 1917
PREMIER 1916
ST. PATRICK 1912
EMILIE 1870
SUSIE PATOI 1891
THEKLA 1891
THEODORA & SARAH 1851
FAVOURITE 1854
FAVOURITE 1916
Prawle Point
TORBAY LASS 1917
U.18 1917
LYRA 1904
CARIAD 1916
NIMBLE 1888
FLORINDA 1890
OCEANS PRIDE 1916
NEWHOLM 1917
LATONA 1904
AENEAS 1940
NECHES 1918
BOY DENNIS 1917
ONWARD 1917

Slapton Ley

SKERRIES BANK

©R.Larn 1973

schooner, was struck a fatal blow by the barque *Korswein*, the sea claimed only her cargo, 128 tons of salt.

As the volume of sea traffic along the coast increased during the second half of the nineteenth century, so did the number of shipping incidents, and the records are full of founderings and fires brought about by ships blundering into one another. Ironically, not a single steamship was involved until 1866 when, by sheer coincidence, steamship struck steamship, these being the collier *Osprey* and the sloop HMS *Amazon*. The 1,081 ton warship, built at Pembroke Dock only fourteen months previously and armed with two sixty-four pounder cannons, had the worst of the collision and foundered, but without loss of life. On 28 February 1868 the Truro schooner *Samson*, with fifty tons of lime on board for Hull, was run down and sunk during a rainstorm by the brigantine *Mercury* of Llanelly; the *Lady Alice*, a Salcombe schooner carrying coal, was sent to the bottom by the German steamer *Nuonburg* on 10 October 1875, and the second steamship to founder from the same cause was the 633 ton *John Boyle* of Cardiff, on 4 April the following year, after striking the Whitby steamer *Emma Lawson*. A valuable cargo of olive oil was lost when the Dutch brigantine *Hazard* went down in 1877, and in 1878 another Dutchman, the eighteen-year-old galliot *Prius Senior*, sank after running into the *Argonaut* on 27 February.

Inshore incidents must not be forgotten, since in 1881 the 295 tons gross wooden barque *Hawthorn*, of Arbroath, was wrecked on Start Point during a west-south-west gale, the only vessel of over 200 tons to be stranded until 1888. This was the German steamer *Nordstern* of Bremen, loaded with wine from Malaga, ashore on 13 January. Her crew took to their own boats and were partway to Salcombe when met by the lifeboat *Lesty*, out on her first service. The German seamen refused to board the lifeboat and continued rowing towards the harbour entrance, but were taken aback by the huge breakers over the bar. Eventually, a member of the lifeboat's crew was put into each of the two boats to act as a pilot and the procession then gained the inner harbour without incident.

Of the many disastrous storms that have swept over the West

Country, few, if any, could have equalled the violence of the 'great blizzard' that lasted from 9 to 13 March 1891. Not even the hurricane of 1866, which caused so much damage in the Torbay area, or some of the earlier gales that lashed Plymouth Sound, could match this holocaust. Of the many vessels lost in Devon, four were wrecked in the Start Point area. Of these, the worst in terms of lives lost was the steamer *Marana* of Liverpool, a 2,177 tons gross, iron-hulled ship built by Aitkens of Glasgow in 1880. Her last voyage began on 1 March when she left the Victoria docks, London, with railway sleepers for Colombo, under orders to coal ship at Swansea en route. She reached the western end of Lyme Bay during the afternoon of 9 March and shortly afterwards was overtaken by the easterly hurricane which came roaring up astern. The coastguards on duty at Hallsands saw a steamer close inshore during a temporary lull in the driving snow, but it was no more than a fleeting glimpse; it was insufficient to make a positive identification, but there can be little doubt that it was the *Marana*.

Despite near blizzard conditions, which completely blinded her lookouts and helmsman, the *Marana*'s captain kept her at full speed, with the result she plunged into the Blackstone rock, tearing off her rudder and propellor. Conditions aboard must have been appalling since some part of the ship went overboard with every wave. Knowing that she must break up, her crew took to their two boats; the captain, chief engineer, mess steward, and three mates in the smaller, and the remaining twenty-two men in the larger, port lifeboat. Rowing westward towards Prawle, they became separated, the smaller boat frequently disappearing completely from view in the troughs of the huge waves. Nothing of this boat nor its occupants was ever seen again. The larger boat managed to reach Horseley cove, a mile north-east of the coastguard station, but sea conditions were such that the occupants dare not attempt a landing. Though ignorant of the local geography, they had in fact chosen the only practical landing site for miles in either direction, but it was to avail them little. For no sooner had the boat been turned bows-on to the sea than it capsized. A few of its occupants managed to grasp the lifelines and hang on until the boat righted herself, but they were thrown off when the sea turned the boat upside down for a second time. Only four Swedish stokers managed to survive the ordeal, all of whom scrambled on top of Mal rock and from there gained the shore. One of the men, in an advanced state of exhaustion and quite unable to walk the short distance to Prawle village, was left in the care of two companions, whilst the fourth went for help.

He reached Prawle at 10.30 pm, a pitiful, half-frozen and bewildered creature, unable to make himself understood amongst the several households he roused from their beds. Fortunately, the significance of a stranger, soaking wet from the sea and knocking on doors at night, was nothing new to the inhabitants, and a search party was sent out. They scoured the beaches and clifftops, even burning flares in case anyone was in a boat or still clinging to wreckage, but received no reply and found nothing. It was the best part of three hours before the three Swedes, John Neilson, Andrew Johnson and Gustave Anderson, all from Gothenburg, were discovered huddled behind a boundary wall. Next day, the Prawle coastguards walked the clifftop to Start Point, no mean achievement with deep snow obscuring the path and filling crevices. They sighted the broken hull of the steamer and saw five corpses in the water, as well as hundreds of railway sleepers which were later salvaged and sold. One of the four men died from exposure, and nine days later, after the snow had melted, the frozen body of a fifth member of the *Marana* was found close to the main cliff path. At the height of that storm the Hallsands lookout saw another boat amongst the breakers and described it as a hooker, or mackerel boat. The keel of such a craft came ashore to support the story, followed by five bodies, one of which had an artificial foot. This led to identification of the wreck, which proved to be that of the smack *Alberta* of Padstow, Anthony Wells skipper, which had left Par for Gloucester with china clay. What she was doing so far east of her course will never be known.

The same evening that the *Marana* was lost the three-masted schooner *Lunesdale* went ashore at Hallsands. Owned by James Fisher of Barrow, bound for a Lancashire port with whiting, the

141 tons gross schooner was flung beam-on to the sea and bilged. Her crew of four were already in the rigging when she struck, but by the time the local fishermen and coastguards had linked arms in a human chain and waded out to them, only the master remained alive. Successive seas, described by one of the coastguards as 'absolutely frightening', eventually threw the wreck right up the beach, where the ebbing tide left her high and dry. Drenched, and chilled from their immersion, these fishermen had hardly reached their homes before another vessel was reported ashore nearby. This was the *Lizzie Ellen*, a schooner from Chester which had taken on china clay at Charlestown and was on passage to London when the storm broke. Driven before the gale, she was wrecked at the foot of a cliff to the north of Hallsands. Her mate and two seamen were the sole survivors and, like so many before, owed their lives to the local men who waded out to them with ropes. A terrified, screaming cabin boy, who refused to leave the rigging and jump into the sea, cost her master his life. He remained behind, attempting to persuade the lad to leave, and they drowned together when the wreck went to pieces.

But worse was yet to come, for during the early hours of 10 March another sailing ship was lost, this time with no survivors. In the short time it took the coastguards to gather up their equipment and reach the beach, it was all over and the vessel had been smashed to fragments. Chocolate-coloured lettering on a section of white-painted forecastle showed the victim to have been the 1,035 ton, iron full-rigged ship *Dryad*, owned by J. P. Walmsely of Liverpool, which had left Shields for Valparaiso on 3 March. Built on the Mersey by Roydons in 1874, the *Dryad* normally carried a crew of twenty-two, but her owners confirmed that one man had been left behind on the Tyne. It is possible that yet a further wreck occurred at Hallsands during this gale, as lights were seen offshore at the peak of the storm and a piece of broken timber bearing the words, '*Nymph* of T—' was found on the beach, though this could have come from anywhere.

An inquest on the victims of the *Lizzie Ellen* was held in the London Inn, in a room adjacent to that in which the bodies were laid out. A similar scene was enacted in the Prawle schoolroom, where the fate of the *Marana*'s crew was being officially established, followed by a similar event for the *Dryad*. It took the sea less than three days to demolish completely the remains of the steamer at Start Point, and by the time the coroner took his seat at the inquest only one cylinder head of her engine showed above the water, on the eastern side of the Blackstone rock.

Less than a month later, the 642 ton steam collier *Sandsend* was lost on the Start in dense fog, bringing the total number of wrecks at Start within thirty days to six, possibly seven. Since then the sea has almost completely demolished the village of South Hallsands, which was abandoned after a particularly bad storm and tide during World War I. It is quite remarkable that it was ever possible to work fishing boats from off this rugged beach, even in good weather, yet in the old days, the village had a thriving fishing community and kept a number of Newfoundland dogs, magnificent creatures which had been trained to swim out beyond the breakers and bring the end of a rope ashore in their teeth.

Fishing boats from the south coast ports that trawled in the busy shipping lanes ran the perpetual gauntlet of collision, and a great many Brixham and Dartmouth wives became widows in consequence. *Sparkling Wine* was the rather grandiose name of one such Dartmouth vessel, numbered DH57, run down by the Norwegian barque *Eose* on 4 May 1900. The *Latona* (DH192) was lost on 14 January 1902; *Lyra* (BM161) with all hands, after being run down by the British steamer *Heathbank* on 27 September 1904; and the *Florence* on 30 November 1905, sunk by the *Tuskar*. So many have been lost, in fact, that it would be repetitive and impracticable to mention them all, but their names are listed in the index of ships at the end of this book.

Of the many warships lost around the Devon coast, by far the largest was the 15,000 ton battleship *Formidable*, which was torpedoed and sunk with a very heavy loss of life on New Year's Day 1915. Launched at Portsmouth on 17 November 1898, the *Formidable* was built as a Majestic class warship, which embodied many of the improved Canopus class features, making her one of the most powerful ships of her day. She carried four 12in guns in twin turrets as a main armament, plus six 6in guns in single turrets on each side, twenty smaller calibre weapons, and two submerged torpedo tubes. Her peacetime complement was 780 officers and men, which in wartime would almost certainly have been increased to 850. Part of the Channel Fleet, the *Formidable*, in company with other capital ships, was steaming in line ahead towards the west in the face of a gale. At 3 am, when off Start Point and last in the line, *Formidable* was hit on the port side by one, possibily two torpedoes, fired by the German submarine *U.24*; she settled down with a list to starboard and sank within forty-five minutes (Picture, p 90).

Sea conditions were so bad that only four of her boats could be launched. Of these, one capsized, throwing its occupants into the sea. A second got clear with seventy men aboard who were picked up by a light cruiser, whilst the third, a pinnace with sixty survivors, made for Lyme Regis. Before this boat reached the shore, nine men had died from exposure and wounds, all of whom were buried in Lyme cemetery. One young seaman, presumed dead, was covered by sacking, which attracted a dog to sleep on top of the 'corpse'; the animal's warmth revived him and it is understood that he is still alive and visits the area every year.

The last of the four boats to leave the *Formidable* was a launch carrying sixty-nine seamen and one officer, Torpedo Gunner Hurrigan. They drifted out to sea and the boat might well have foundered, since it had a hole in one side stopped only by a pair of underpants. Fortunately, it was seen by the Brixham trawler *Provident*, skipper William Pillar, who carried out a daring rescue in very difficult conditions. He took his boat alongside the big navy launch four times in all, saving everyone aboard, and landed them safely at Brixham. A tablet commemorating the rescue of eighteen officers and 183 men from the *Formidable* was placed on the obelisk on Brixham quay, where it served also as a memorial to her captain and at least 648 dead. The tablet has since been removed and is believed now to be inside the town hall.

Other war losses in the vicinity of Start Point were the Newcastle steamer *Spennymoor* on 4 June 1915; the trawling ketch *Favourite* (BM240), sunk by submarine gunfire in September

Page 117: The cutter *Frisk* saving men from the wreck of HMS *Venerable* on Paignton Ledges, Goodrington, on 24 November 1804

Page 118: The scene at Broadsands, Torbay, the morning after the great gale of 11 January 1866—*From a*

Page 119: (*above*) The Belgian collier *Charles José* ashore on Slapton Sands, Start Bay, on 17 December 1933; (*below*) only survivors among eight vessels thrown against the outer wall of Brixham harbour during the Torbay gale of 1866 were the barques *Wild Rose* and *Leone*

Page 120: (left) Vessels wrecked against the outer wall of Brixham harbour during the gale of 1866, seen from

1916; also the *Premier* (BM129); *Cariad* (BM225); *Ocean's Pride* (BM48); *Boy Dennis* (BM237), the *Onward*, and many fishing boats of the Brixham fleet. In addition, the steamers *Rotorua*, *Teesdale* and *Newholm* were all sent to the bottom during 1917. The *Rotorua*, sunk on 22 March, was a triple-screw liner of 11,140 tons owned by the New Zealand Shipping Co, whilst the Swan Hunter-built *Newholm*, of 3,399 tons, was mined one mile south of the Start, but sank closer to Salcombe. Another more distinguished war loss was that of the *Medina* of 12,350 tons gross, which once had the distinction of serving as the royal yacht. Her owners, the Peninsular & Oriental Steam Navigation Co, were to have taken delivery from the builders, Caird & Co, in June 1912, but before fitting-out was completed she was chosen to take King George V and Queen Mary to India for the Delhi celebrations. In addition to alterations necessary to accommodate the royal family and its entourage, she was fitted with a third mast in order to give her a more 'yacht-like' appearance. This was stepped just forward of her twin funnels, the additional mast being the mainmast from the steamer *Nankin*, still building. On 11 November 1911 the *Medina* left Portsmouth, commanded by Capt Chatfield RN, and was back again in February of the following year on completion of her charter agreement. On return to her builders, she was stripped down for commercial service and started regular runs between London and Colombo, Melbourne and Sydney on 28 June 1912. During the evening of 28 April 1917, having left Plymouth for London earlier the same day on the last leg of a passage home from India, she was torpedoed in her starboard engine room and sank within forty-five minutes. Six of her 'black gang' lost their lives in the explosion, namely the 4th engineer and five native firemen. The incident took place three miles south of the Start, but before she sank the *Medina* drifted into Lyme Bay where she went down in 160ft of water. Her wreck has since been found by divers and a tentative identification made from the two cargo cranes on her forecastle was later confirmed when crockery was recovered bearing the crest of the P & O line.

The war was not completely one-sided in this area, however,

since a number of German submarines were also destroyed hereabouts. The *UC-51* was submerged off the Start, waiting for targets, when on 17 November 1917 some sort of accident caused her cargo of mines to explode. The Admiralty-requisitioned trawler *Lois* was on patrol in the area at the time and her crew were startled to hear a massive underwater explosion, after which the submarine appeared on the surface close at hand, then rolled over and sank. A number of intact horned contact mines floated to the surface, accompanied by a great deal of oil, rubbish and human entrails; positive identification came from a German seaboot marked with the name 'Ewald Metzger'. It was a British minefield in much the same area off Start that brought about the end of the *U-18* the same day as the *UC-51* was lost, and previously the *U-85* on 12 March, and the *U-72* on 12 May. Apart from a few fishing boats sent to the bottom by scuttling charges, the Norwegian steamer *Livonia*, torpedoed on 3 December 1917 with the loss of twenty-three crew, and the *Agnete* on 29 April 1918, were the last of the war losses. A 5,426 ton steamer named *Neches* sank in position 50° 12′ N, 03° 40′ W on 15 May 1918, but this was the result of a collision.

It was mid-November 1925 when the nation learned of another accident involving a British submarine, the fourth since the war had ended. Previously, the *K-5* had gone down off Ushant on 20 January 1921 with the loss of fifty-seven men. The *H-42* had been rammed and sunk by HMS *Versatile* off Europa Point, Gibraltar, with twenty-six drowned on 23 February 1922, and the *L-24* had sunk off Portland with forty-three dead on 10 January 1924. It was the massive *M-1* that was now missing, feared lost, somewhere off Start Point, and half the Royal Navy was out searching for her. The *M-1* started her career at Vickers shipyard, Barrow, during 1917 as the *K-18*, but was selected for conversion to a submarine monitor, intended for coastal bombardment. To this end she was fitted with a single 12in gun taken from one of the King Edward VII class battleships. Four such conversions were made, numbered *M-1* to *M-4*, but they were not the success anticipated. Due to difficulties in sealing the turret when submerged and operating such a massive weapon when half awash, only two of the quartet remained in service for any length of time. These were the *M-2* and *M-3*, which were converted to a seaplane carrier and minelayer respectively after their big guns had been removed.

The *M-1* and eight other conventional boats were placed in reserve as part of the 5th submarine flotilla attached to HMS *Dolphin*. On 12 November 1925, having been brought up to operational standard, the *M-1* put to sea accompanied by the *H-22*, *H-29*, *H-30*, *H-34*, the parent vessel *Maidstone*, and the tender *Alecto*. At some time during the exercises the *M-1* failed to surface and a full-scale search was initiated. A German salvage company called Gutmache offered the use of their deep diving, armoured dress, and diver Otto Kraft went down to 250ft on many occasions, even to 230ft at night when tidal conditions were favourable, but found nothing. The first clue as to the fate of the *M-1* came from the merchant ship *Vidar*, of 2,159 tons gross, after she had docked at Stockholm. Her master, Capt Anell, reported that at approximately 7.45 pm on 12 November, when in position 49° 59′ N, 03° 55′ W, his ship had struck a submerged, or partially submerged object. Examination of the *Vidar* in dry dock showed her stem to be badly bent over to port, with several rivets gone and plating damaged. There were also traces of grey paint with no possible connection with the steamer's own colour scheme. A large Japanese steamer, the *Aden Maru*, passed close to the *Vidar* and on the same track at the instant of the supposed collision, and may have been involved, but she neither stopped nor reported any unusual occurrence. After three weeks of fruitless searching the hunt was officially abandoned on 2 December and the *M-1*, with her entombed sixty-nine crew, has yet to be located. During 1967, a Devon-based salvage vessel claimed to have found the wreck and put a diver down, but this was untrue. The submarine has since been classified as an official grave, and as such it would be an offence to attempt its salvage.

During World War II the twin-screw steamer *Aeneas* sank offshore from the Start after having been bombed on 2 July 1940. Built during 1910 at the Belfast yard of Workham Clark, the

Aeneas had already survived the previous war as a troopship, as well as a stranding on Rathlin island. The *Clan Stuart* also went to the bottom, not as a result of enemy action but through collision with the *Orlock Head* (ex-British Standard Ship, *C-5*) on 11 March, which also went down. Since then the only incident of particular interest was the sinking of HM Submarine *Untiring* on 25 July 1957. During 1945 she was loaned to the Greek Navy and re-named *Zifias*, but on return was considered obsolete and selected for scuttling as an asdic training target in deep water.

During research into wrecks in this area in particular, a great many names and dates were uncovered but seldom was a location given other than 'lost in Start Bay', or 'near Dartmouth'. The stretch of coast between the Start and Dartmouth measures about ten miles, and along with the great Skerries bank lying offshore must have been the scene of many a shipwreck. Known incidents range from the *Postilion* at Beesands in 1732, to the salvage craft *LC18*, stranded and lost on the Skerries on 4 December 1943, the majority being much nearer to Dartmouth. Leyland in his travels visited Dartmouth and described it as 'lying on a very rokky hille on the haven side about half a mile from the very mouth of it, and extendith in length aboute a quarter of a mile. There be good marchaunt men in the towne, and to this haven long good shippes'. There had, in fact, been little or no town here until the end of the twelfth century, when a considerable business grew out of shipbuilding and repairs. The first street in Dartmouth was the 'street of the smiths', which still survives, but in its original form it ran parallel to Millpool. This was a creek or inlet, said to have been a quarter of a mile long, separating Hardness and Clifton. Ships once tied up alongside the wall of St Saviour's church, but this was at a time when Dartmouth was a centre for privateering, and when every shipload of cloth sent down from Totnes was matched by two shiploads of fish from Newfoundland and another three full of European wines. It was a haven for the king's ships for generations, and for a time was the most important seaport in the West Country. A typical early reference to wreck is a mandate issued from Chancery in 1347, addressed to Henry Tirel, Sheriff of Devonshire and his two sergeants at arms,

'. . . directing you to restore certain wines of Spanish merchants which had come into the hands of John Gordon of Dartmouth. In default of restoration, Gordon and others are to be arrested and taken to the tower. The peace of the kingdom is at stake, and there is violation of the king's treaty with Spain to consider'.[2]

Which particular wreck brought the renowned diver Jacob Johnson to the area in 1629 is not known, but it appears that he was 'forbidden to use his endeavour at Dartmouth by the mayor and town clerk'. In August of the same year, Johnson petitioned the Lords of the Admiralty and obtained a warrant to employ his art and industry by diving in the harbours and creeks of the Isle of Wight, the Lizard in Cornwall, Ireland, and elsewhere, for the recovery of bullion, cannon, anchors and cables. By September he was back in Dartmouth again and raised five pieces of ordnance, but was not allowed to proceed 'unless he would compound with the town'. This is the first reference to diving in the area, but it was not long before local men became interested in its possibilities. During the summer of 1716, a Nathaniel Symens of Totnes was able 'to remain submerged in the River Dart before 100 persons for three-quarters of an hour, but complained that though a great number of gentlemen were present, he received but one crown from them all'.

Twenty lives were lost on 9 February 1692 when the twenty-six gun, 6th rate *Crown Prize* was lost outside the harbour entrance, and another queen's ship, the fourteen-gun, 6th rate *Seahorse*, on 26 December 1711 'near Dartmouth'. Wrecks during the following century were mostly small and of less than 500 tons, such as the thirty-one year old schooner *Courser*, Fecamp to Torbay in ballast, stranded one mile west of the Dart estuary in Redlap cove on 13 February 1870 with the loss of five of her six-man crew. An Irish schooner of seventy-nine tons, the *Comet*, stranded within the harbour on 9 November 1878 and became a total loss along with her cargo of oats, and in 1888 there were fears that two local excursion steamers might go the same way. The *Berry Castle*, with 200 passengers aboard, went aground on a bank near Dittisham in fog at 10 pm on 8 August, and the *Dartmouth Castle*, in going to her assistance, also went ashore, but were both refloated the following day without serious damage.

Two rusting boilers and plating in the vicinity of Newfoundland cove are all that remain of the largest of the local wrecks to-date. The oil-tanker *Broadmayne* of London, outward bound for Newport News, stranded in thick fog on New Year's Day 1921, close to the seamark on the Kingswear side. Weather conditions were so appalling, with a full gale blowing from the south-west accompanied by heavy rain, that the launching of the Brixham lifeboat *Betsey Newbon* had to be delayed until 2 am next day, when conditions had improved. Coxswain Sanders and Signalman Noraway went on foot to Brounston farm, from where they set out to search the cliffs and eventually located the wreck. They then climbed down the cliff face in darkness to a point from where they could communicate with the crew, but despite advice to remain on board until the lifeboat could reach them, sixteen of the crew left the ship and climbed to safety. The fog continued so thick that even after the *Betsey Newbon* arrived off Dartmouth, her crew searched the rocks for six hours, but still failed to see the wreck. Finally, at 5.30 am, a rocket fired from the deck of the *Broadmayne* attracted their attention and the lifeboat moved in to rescue twenty-eight men still aboard, some of the crew having already got ashore. The Brixham section of the rocket brigade made a gallant effort to assist, dragging their cumbersome wagon to John Brocks Mews, where three horses were requisitioned. The team then began the long haul up and over Hill Head road and were close to exhaustion when they finally reached the scene of the wreck, and discovered their rope ladders were too short to reach the rocks below. The wreck eventually broke in two, the forepart being refloated and towed into Mill Cove where it was broken up, the stern section being abandoned to the sea (Picture, p 108).

Whereas the *Broadmayne* was broken in two by the forces of nature, the next steamship to be stranded at Dartmouth, the *English Trader*, was deliberately cut in order to save the greater part of the vessel. The lessons of ship surgery had already been learnt in the West Country when two other steamers, the *Highland Fling* and the *Suevic*, had been saved by this method, so that the removal of the *English Trader*'s bow section presented no problem. Built by the Furness Shipbuilding Co in 1934 as the *Arctees*, she was one of the first three 'Arcform' vessels to be built to the order of Sir Joseph Islewood. It was while entering Dartmouth harbour on 23 January 1937 that she stranded close to the castle, and from there she refused to move despite every effort of HM destroyer *Witch* and four tugs. By 3 February her forward tanks had been pierced by rocks beneath her bows and it was decided to cut her in two, the operation being completed nineteen days later and the undamaged after section towed into Dartmouth stern-first. Temporary shoring of the forward bulkhead of the after section allowed it to be towed to Southampton, where tenders were invited for a complete repair, which entailed an almost complete rebuild from the boiler room forward. The Middle Docks & Engineering Co of South Shields secured the contract, and exactly one hundred days later the *English Trader* was finished and ready for sea. This was quite a remarkable achievement considering that over 6,000 tons of cement in the bilges of No 2 hold had to be patiently chipped out before work could even start. The abandoned bow section was later cut up and towed ashore for scrapping (Picture, p 107).

In conclusion, there are the wrecks which occurred to the east of Dartmouth, between the harbour and Scabbacombe Point, which include the wooden brig *Eureka*, the auxiliary cutter *Test* and, more recently, several small fishing vessels. Carrying coal from Newcastle to Devonport, the *Eureka*, of 241 tons, was less than a year old when she struck the cliffs near Pudcombe cove on 6 February 1870, drowning three of her nine-man crew. The *Test* (BM93), was a 3 ton vessel built at Exmouth in 1928. She foundered following a collision with the excursion steamer *Duke of Devonshire* on 15 August 1932. Since then, a number of small, mostly local, fishing boats have been lost, including the crabber *Dorothea*, which went ashore in Newfoundland cove on 17 February 1972 with the loss of all three of her crew, and the 25 ton Brixham trawler *Catherine Allen*, two miles offshore on 28 October 1973.

The *Catherine Allen* capsized when a heavy trawl was being

swung across her deck, and she went down in 120ft of water with a thirteen-year-old schoolboy, Kevin Crocker, asleep in the stern cabin. Despite gallant rescue attempts by the Fishery Protection ship *Kedleston*, divers from RNAS Culdrose, the motor cruiser *John Teast* and the navy salvage vessel *Pintail*, the boy unfortunately drowned.

Page 129: (*above*) The Finnish barque *Berar* ashore and broken completely in two at Charton Bay, exposing her cargo of timber; (*below*) the excursion paddle-steamer *Duchess of Devonshire* aground and holed on Sidmouth beach, 27 August 1934

Page 130: Wrecked near Clovelly, the steamer *Abril* lies with her decks almost awash on 16 February 1906

CHAPTER FOUR

TORBAY

The twenty-five miles of coastline between Scabbacombe and
Hopes Nose, the geographical limits of this chapter, are taken up
almost entirely by the wide sweep of Torbay. Although Lord
Howe is said to have exclaimed in 1795 that 'Torbay will be the
grave of the Navy', having witnessed from the quarterdeck of
HMS *Queen Charlotte* no less than twenty-seven ships in his fleet
lose their anchors and cables in a gale, his prophecy was fortunately incorrect. In fact, less than ten warships have been
wrecked locally, not all of which were British.

Since Torbay is completely sheltered from all westerly winds,
it has been a popular anchorage and haven since earliest times.
Vast numbers of ships, alone or in fleets, have sought the shelter
of this bay; innumerable navy fleet reviews have taken place here,
and it has been visited by practically every reigning monarch and
admiral for generations. There was even a time when Torbay
was regarded by a majority as being a safer haven than Plymouth.
During the middle ages, pirates and their legal counterparts, the
privateers, were not slow to realise the potential of Torbay. Here
they could lay in wait for ships passing up and down Channel, or
entering and leaving Dartmouth, and plunder or sink them as
circumstances dictated. An early instance of this occurred on
29 March 1579, when a company of Scottish merchants complained to the Crown that, 'a month before, a ship of theirs, laden
with sundry merchandise was despoiled at Torquay by one John
Grainger of Plymouth, and one Captain Morrice, along with sixty
other English pirates'.[1] There were, of course, times when even
these gentlemen were outnumbered and dare not remain in the
vicinity—occasions such as the arrival of the Prince of Orange
and his fleet on 5 November 1688, described by one author as

H   131

'Torbay's greatest moment of glory'. This fleet consisted of 400 sail of transport, besides a further fifty men o' war;[2] more than enough to put any marauders to flight.

The Domestic State Papers contain many early references to wreck, some prior to 1300, but the earliest with a positive location relates to 30 November 1657, when a vessel was reported as being stranded in Torbay and 'Captain Pley and constables were recruited to prevent the country people making havoc with her.'[3] During the early part of 1745, Devon and Cornwall were asked to provide recruits for the West Indies expedition, and the transport *Tiger* left Plymouth with hundreds of raw troops aboard on 27 February. No sooner had the *Tiger* reached the open sea than she was overtaken by a hurricane and wrecked under Berry Head. Troops and crew alike leapt overboard in an attempt to get ashore, but the majority drowned like rats and by morning 170 bodies lay strewn along the beach. Those who escaped attempted to reach Plymouth, where posters were already offering the public a reward of one pound for every soldier caught, plus sixpence a day for his subsistence while in custody. At the same time as the *Tiger* was wrecked, Admiral Medlen's fleet, consisting of a large convoy and escort vessels, all lying at anchor in Torbay, were driven to sea before the wind, every single vessel having had to cut its cable. The East Indiaman *Royal George* ran foul of the *Cape Coast*, which foundered without loss of life. Another transport, the *Expeditious*, also went ashore under Berry Head and there was much confusion as to whether survivors were from her or the *Tiger*.

Of the warships mentioned earlier as having fallen foul of the Torbay area, the first was the eight-gun sloop o' war HMS *Savage* of 144 tons, ashore in February 1762, near Roundham Head. The small inlet in which the wreck took place is known to this day as Savage Cove, but anything of the vessel that may remain will be well buried beneath the sand. The second warship to be lost was the *Cerbere*, a French gun brig armed with ten eighteen-pounder cannons. She had been captured by HMS *Viper* when off Mauritius on 29 July 1800. Under the command of Lt Patey, the *Cerbere* left Plymouth on 19 February 1804, but in

working up Channel towards Dover she missed stays near Berry
Head and went ashore during a northerly gale. Having no pro-
truding keel and drawing less than 6ft of water, the wreck lay very
shallow, and all her guns and stores were readily accessible for
salvage. Later that year, on 30 November, the brig *Nelly* of
Teignmouth, carrying clay from Poole to Liverpool, also struck
on Berry Head, bilged and became a total loss.

In the meantime, several wrecks had taken place within Torbay
itself and the inhabitants of 'Torkay', as a 1771 edition of the
Exeter Flying Post shows, were not slow to appreciate the value
of a perishable cargo:

> The brig *St Peter*, William Causey, from London, laden with
> groceries from this [Exeter] city, having overshot her port and got
> opposite Torkay on Friday night last, 1 September, in a heavy gale
> to the eastward, drove ashore about a mile to the westward of Tor
> Abbey, and was dashed to pieces. The cargo was supposed to be worth
> £4,000, the greater part of which was lost, the crew being happily
> saved. Immediately on going to pieces, the country people came down
> in great numbers to plunder the wreck, and even robbed the captain
> of his watch; on which George Cary Esq of Tor Abbey, accompanied
> by his brother and several armed men, seized the ringleaders, of whom
> they immediately sent on board a man o' war, and by their endeavours
> saved all they could of the cargo, and secured it in their cellars.[4]

Whether or not the owners ever saw any of this cargo, once
locked away in Cary's cellar, is left to the imagination!

During the last week of December 1778 the inhabitants of
Torquay flocked to the clifftops to watch a fleet of merchantmen,
some 300 in all, sailing down Channel accompanied by warships.
When off Berry Head HMS *Russell*, of seventy-four guns, collided
with the British East Indiaman *London*, which foundered within
the hour. Unfortunately for the Brixham fishermen, the wreck of
the Indiaman lay in their best trawling ground and for many
years after was responsible for the loss of a great deal of gear.
The year 1748 brought a letter to the *Gentleman's Magazine*
from a correspondent in Torbay giving news of another wreck,
saying, 'This morning, 12 January, in thick snow and a hard gale
of wind at south-east, the sloop *Two Brothers*, Capt West, from
Plymouth to Portsmouth with eleven passengers, ran ashore
about a mile to the westward of Berry Head and instantly went to

pieces, only the captain being saved'.[5] The next incident was on 21 November 1787, when a large Guernsey smuggling lugger was lost in Torbay and her crew of five drowned; the sloop *Active* was stranded and wrecked on 20 December 1794 near Brixham, and on 22 December 1795 George Cary performed yet another public service in connection with shipwreck. This was when the brig *Biscay* parted her cables and drove on to Tor Abbey sands, where she went to pieces. Her cargo, a valuable quantity of groceries, was, needless to say, lost almost entirely to the local wreckers. The ship's mate, four seamen and a boy, the only survivors, were taken in by Cary and given food and clothes, then sent out to help scour the coastline for the body of Capt Burgess, who was reported to be wearing a money belt, containing a large sum in gold. The corpse was found, but there was no sign of the belt.

A particularly severe gale on 12 April 1801 started off another century of shipwreck incidents by adding four more names to the list, namely the *James*, *Reward*, *Leander* and the West Indiaman *Alexander*; but these were minor losses compared to that of the *Venerable* in 1804, the third warship to be lost in the area. Considering the weather conditions and circumstances, it is remarkable that only three men lost their lives out of a crew of 555. It is also probably the only occasion on which a naval ship has been lost because a seaman fell overboard. It was on 23 November 1804 that the fleet blockading Brest, under the command of Cornwallis, returned to Torbay, awaiting favourable winds. On the 24th, the flagship signalled an immediate departure just before dark, a decision which could not have been made at a more inopportune moment. None of the warships had received any warning of departure, which would have allowed them to shorten their anchor cables, most of the fleet were at supper, and movements by large ships in the confines of Torbay at night was inviting disaster. On board HMS *Venerable*, a 3rd rate, seventy-four gun ship renowned throughout the navy as having remained loyal during the Nore mutiny, the call for 'all hands' brought them grumbling and unwilling to the upper deck, and within less than half an hour the ship was in trouble.

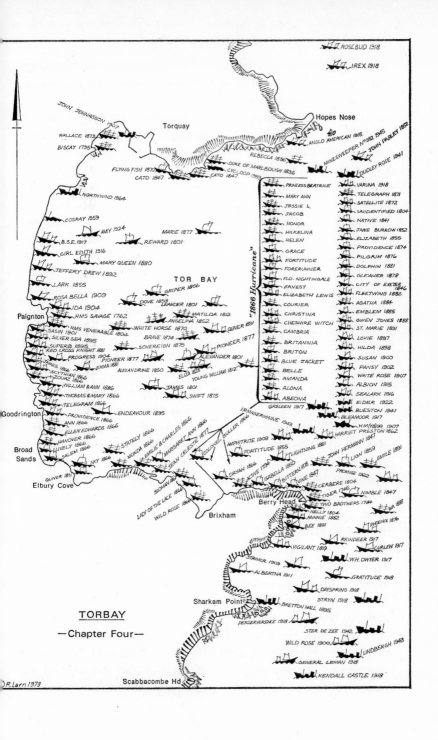

ROSEBUD 1918
IREX 1918

JOHN JOHNASSON 1907
Torquay
Hopes Nose
WALLACE 1873
BISCAY 1795
ANGLO AMERICAN 1915
MINESWEEPER Nº382 1915
JOHN PARLEY 1852
REBECCA 1836
DUDLEY ROSE 1941
FLYING FISH 1870
DUKE OF MARLBOUGH 1836
CATO 1847
CATO 1847
CYCLOOP 1955

NORTHWIND 1964

PRINCESS BEATRICE   VARUNA 1918
MARY ANN   TELEGRAPH 1871
COSRAY 1959
JESSIE L.   SATELLITE 1872
AMY 1924
JACOB   UNIDENTIFIED 1804
MARIE 1877
B.S.E. 1917
REWARD 1801   HONOR   NATIVE 1841
GIRL EDITH 1916   HILKELINA   JANE BURROW 1852
                                HELEN   ELIZABETH 1853
JEFFERY DREW 1892   MARY QUEEN 1880 GRACE   PROVIDENCE 1874
                                FORTITUDE   PILGRIM 1876
LARK 1855   TOR BAY   FORERUNNER   DOLPHIN 1881
                   GRIPER 1856   FLO. NIGHTINGALE GLEANER 1878
ROSA BELLA 1909   DOVE 1853 LEANDER 1852 ERNEST   CITY OF EXETER 1846
IDA 1904   ELIZABETH LEWIS FLEETWING 1882
Paignton HMS SAVAGE 1762 MATILDA 1812 COURIER   AGATHA 1884
SASIN 1901   WHITE HORSE 1870 ANGELINA 1852 QUIVER 1891 CHRISTINA EMBLEM 1885
SILVER SEA 1895   BRAVE 1874   CHESHIRE WITCH GWEN JONES 1888
SUPERB 1895   SOVEREIGN 1875 PIONEER 1877 CAMBRIA   ST. MARIE 1891
RED CROSS KNIGHT 1881   PROGRESS 1904   LOVIE 1897
PIONEER 1877 EMMA 1881   ALEXANDER 1801 BRITANNIA HILDA 1898
JAMES 1866   BRITON   SUSAN 1900
SCYTHIAN 1866 ALEXANDRINE 1850 ELIZA 1828   BLUE JACKET PANSY 1902
ZOUAZ 1866   YOUNG WILLIAM 1812 BELLE   WHITE ROSE 1907
WILLIAM & ANN 1886   AMANDA   ALBION 1915
THOMAS & MARY 1866   JAMES 1801   ALONA   SEALARK 1916
TELEGRAM 1866   SWIFT 1875   ABEONA   EIDER 1922
Goodrington PROVIDENCE 1866 ENDEAVOUR 1895   GRELEEN 1917 BUESTON 1941
ANN 1866   IRMAGERMAINE 1943 BLEAMOOR 1917
ELLEN EDWARDS 1866   H.M.(T&)99 1907
Broad HANOVER 1866 STATELY 1866   AMPHITRITE 1909 HARRIET PRESTON 1862
Sands LIVELY 1866   MONDA 1866 MARGARET ANN 1866   COLONEL BULLER 1866 LIGHTNING 1881
SALEM 1866 SKY 1866 EMILIE & CHARLES 1866 JEAN CELESTE 1877 FORTITUDE 1855 JOHN HERMANN 1866 LION 1859 EMILE 1891
QUIVER 1891   BRYAN 1866 ACTIVE 1794 ISABELLA 1850 PROMISE 1922
Elbury Cove   SLOMAN 1866   BITTERN 1866 VINE 1847 CERBERE 1804
LADY OF THE LAKE 1846 WILD ROSE 1866   TIGER 1746 NIMBLE 1847
Brixham   Berry Head   TWO BROTHERS 1784 IDA 1888
                                                     NELLY 1804
                                                     MINNIE 1882 PHOENIX 1876
                                                     BEE 1891
                                   VIGILANT 1819   REINDEER 1917 CURLEW 1917
                                   RIVER 1909   W.H. DWYER 1917
                                   ALBERTHA 1911   GRATITUDE 1918
                                              DAYSPRING 1918
                                   STRYN 1918
Sharkam Point   BRETTON HALL 1895
PERSEVERENCE 1918
                                   STER DE ZEE 1942
TORBAY
WILD ROSE 1900   LINDBERGH 1943
—Chapter Four—
GENERAL LEMAN 1918
R. Larn 1973
Scabbacombe Hd   KENDALL CASTLE 1918

During the process of 'fishing' the anchor, a seaman slipped from the cathead and fell into the sea. As a boat was being lowered to rescue him, one of the falls was released prematurely, the boat was swamped, and suddenly a dozen men were floundering in the water, a midshipman and two seamen being drowned. A second boat was swung out and managed to save the remainder of the men, including the seaman responsible for the entire misadventure, but by now the *Venerable* had lost her position. She fell away to leeward and in the dark drifted down on to Paignton Ledges, at Roundham Head, and went ashore. Distress signals were fired, but apart from HMS *Impeteux* and *Goliath*, the fleet was out of earshot. Both these ships lowered every boat they had, thinking that the *Venerable* could easily be towed clear, but already the wind had freshened, causing the wreck to be thrown heavily against rock with every wave. Her masts were cut down, and had they fallen towards the shore they would easily have bridged the gap between ship and shore but, as it was, they fell to seaward and by 9 pm, when it was obvious she was doomed, the order was given to abandon ship.

The wind increased steadily from the east until it reached gale force, and soon the *Venerable* was engulfed in surf. Within two hours of first grounding, she lay on her beam ends and was expected to go to pieces at any moment. A number of her crew managed to clamber over the bowsprit and reach the shore, only 25yd away, but the majority were taken off by boat. Most of the ship's company owed their lives to the cutter *Frisk*, Lt Nicholson, which anchored as close as possible to the wreck, then veered out her cable to reduce the distance between the two vessels (Picture, p 117). By daybreak, only the officers and seventeen seamen remained aboard the *Venerable*, all of whom declared they would rather die than abandon their captain and ship. When at last the forecastle went under water, the captain consented to leave, saving not only his own life but those of his devoted crew. Junior officers leading, the men boarded the waiting boats in almost leisurely fashion and by 6 am the wreck was deserted. Within an hour, she had broken in two. Some reports state that a drunken marine was left to his fate on board, having been caught plundering some of the officers' chests and drinking their port,[6] but this is untrue. Admiralty records in the PRO show that this man, the only member of the entire crew to misbehave, was court-martialled on board the *El Salvador del Mundo* in the Hamoaze and sentenced to receive 200 lashes around the fleet.

When the *Venerable* struck, she had a total of 555 men aboard, and since the number rescued by the *Goliath*, *Impeteux* and *Frisk* totalled 547, with three known to have drowned in the boating incident, only five remained unaccounted for, who may well have deserted. During the actual rescue, the *Impeteux* stood so close in to the wreck, that it was feared she, too, would go ashore. In fact her captain ordered her topmasts struck and stationed carpenters at the foot of each mast armed with axes in case it became necessary to cut them down. Those ashore also fully appreciated the situation and lit bonfires on the beach, at the same time holding up large planks of wood on which were burnt instructions as to the best place to beach should the need arise. Sixteen hours after the *Venerable* had been abandoned, nothing of her remained above the surface, but the Torbay beaches were strewn with wreckage from end to end. A guard consisting of the Brixham Sea Fensibles, Volunteers, Royal Marines from the *Impeteux*, and some local cavalry were stationed on the foreshore, 'because wicked fellows are base enough to venture out in the nite to plunder'.[7] To the everlasting shame of the inhabitants of Torbay, not a single boat put out from Brixham or Paignton to assist in the rescue work, the locals being far too busy appropriating what they could for themselves, for which they were roundly condemned. Two days after the wreck, two local farmers were walking the sands out of curiosity, or so they said, when they passed a boundary mark set up by the authorities. They were challenged, then fired on, and one of the farmers, Mr Browse of Paignton, lost his left forearm as a result of the injuries he received. During March of the following year the sloop *Daniel*, Capt Duff, arrived in Torbay from the Scillies, under orders from the Board of Ordnance, to salvage the remaining guns and fittings from the *Venerable*, under the direction of Ralph Tonkin of Penzance. This was the same salvage vessel and crew which, assisted by HM

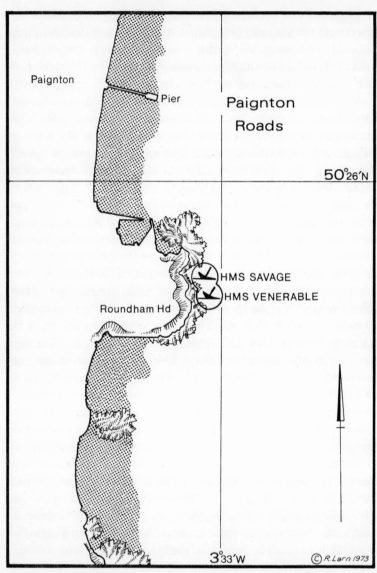

Locations of the wreck sites of HMS *Savage* and *Venerable*

brig *Fearless* and two transports, had successfully raised cannon, stores, and the majority of the works of art from the wreck of HMS *Collossus* on Southward Wells.

There followed a number of smaller incidents, such as the loss of the sloop *Matilda* and the brig *Young William*, both wrecked 'near Torquay' on 29 September 1812; the revenue cutter *Vigilant*, again 'near Torquay' on 5 December 1819, leaving fourteen cannon on the seabed; the *Eliza*, stranded and lost under Waldon Hill during 1828, but only the *Duke of Marlborough*, which followed in 1836, was of any consequence. Formerly a post-office packet vessel stationed at Falmouth, the *Duke of Marlborough* had achieved a measure of notoriety when commanded by Capt John Bull, since she was the ship which fought out a long engagement against the *Primrose*, another British packet, each mistaking the other for an American privateer. Following her purchase out of government service by Messrs Newman and Hunt, she was fitted out for a trading expedition to West Africa but, only a few days after leaving the Downs, sailed into Torbay in September 1836 so that Capt Putt, who had some minor illness, could be taken to hospital. On 11 October, during a severe storm, she parted her main cable; her mate, Gluvias, ordered the second bower anchor to be dropped, but within half an hour its cable also parted and the vessel went ashore beneath a sheer cliff face. From there she swung round, drifted into a small inlet, and came to rest surrounded by rock faces almost the height of her mastheads.

The port shrouds of the mainmast were cut, which allowed the mast to fall against the cliff, and the mate and one seaman began the climb. Just as they reached the topmast futtocks, the wreck gave a lurch which dislodged the mast, crushing the seaman to death and throwing the mate to the deck. For a second time the mate clambered aloft, finally reaching the topmast and then the clifftop, badly cut and bruised. Of the seven men remaining aboard, none would brave that climb and all drowned when the *Duke of Marlborough* finally sank. Next day, when the mate revisited the site, he at first refused to believe that he had been capable of such a feat and swore he could never repeat it. In the

November following the wreck, Mr C. Deane, the celebrated inventor of the standard diving helmet, was engaged to raise the vessel, but recovered only part of her rigging, six cannon, and some fittings. It is worth noting that, from there, Deane moved on to the wreck of the *Venerable* and worked her when weather permitted until November 1848, when he committed suicide by cutting his throat. Many other salvage attempts on the *Duke of Marlborough* are recorded, the most successful being that of a private party of divers on board the smack *Mary Ann* who, in April 1851, recovered many relics and valuables.

Following the *Marlborough* there was a profusion of wreck incidents, commencing on 9 February 1846 with the *City of Exeter*, which took the ground whilst entering Brixham, filled and sank. This was followed on 18 March by the American barque *Nahant*, bound for Galveston with emigrants, which went ashore under Berry Head. Not a single life was lost in this incident, and while another vessel was being chartered her passengers and crew were housed in the old poor house at Baker Hill. The *Nahant*, in fact, floated clear at high water and was later found half awash off Poole Cove, but she was so badly damaged that she was towed into Torquay harbour and broken up in the shallows. On 3 January 1847 the *Cato*, Sprague master, attempted to enter Torquay harbour without a pilot, struck the bottom, and soon afterwards only her masts were showing above water. An Admiralty cutter, the *Nimble*, was another victim of Berry Head when she went ashore without loss of life on 20 February following, and the Brixham trawling sloop *Vine* foundered on 27 October after being run down by the full-rigger *Brunswick*, near the Shoalstone.

Before the year 1847 came to a close Berry Head claimed yet another victim, the *John Hermann*, Capt Leprenz, Hamburg to Sierra Leone, which missed stays on 19 December and went on to the rocks. Within twenty-four hours she had fallen on her beam ends and become a total loss. Her cargo consisted of coloured handkerchiefs, blue beads, and general barter goods for the natives of Africa, a few relics of which still survive in Brixham. Another local wreck, on 5 February 1850, was the *chasse-marée*

Alexandrine, which struck the remains of another wreck, the *Hero*, which had foundered a few years previously. During the same month, the smacks *Isabella* and *Edward Triplett* were lost near Brixham, the *Shamrock* close to Torquay on 11 November 1851, the *Jane Burrow* foundered off Berry Head on 28 April 1852, and was followed by the *Elizabeth* in August.

Elbury Cove, now popular as a holiday beach, saw a sailing ship ashore with its stern section ablaze on 9 December 1861. Fire had been discovered on board the *Sloman* by the captain's daughter when they were some twenty-five miles west of the Start. Two Brixham smacks, the *Sophia* and the *Charles*, helped her into Torbay and managed to beach her in the shallows. As the fire continued to spread, she was towed off at high water and taken into Brixham harbour, where holes were cut in her sides through which the local fire brigade pumped in water. Much to the surprise of the harbour authorities, no assistance was forth-coming from the crew, seven out of eight of whom were drunk and more interested in fighting between themselves than the fire. Although the ship was not completely gutted, she was badly damaged, losing all her sails, mizzenmast, stores and spare gear, and was sold for breaking. Although the name *Sloman* appeared on her bows, lifebelts and boats, it transpired that she was in fact, the *Eliphat Greely* of Maine, her master having assumed a false identity to confuse American privateers.

Of all the gales that have swept through Torbay, there have been none on record to match the fury of the great hurricane of 1866. On Wednesday, 10 January, a total of seventy-four vessels were at anchor within Torbay, the majority of which had made more than one attempt to leave, only to be forced back by what amounted to a month of gales from the south and west. A great calm fell over the western counties that day and most of the ships at anchor made preparations to sail just as soon as there was sufficient wind. By afternoon, a full gale was blowing again, and within a period of three hours had swung, in turn, from south to south-west, then to south-east, finally settling in the north-east. It was the wind, which reached almost 100 mph and was accom-panied by driving snow and hail, that caused most of the damage.

In total darkness, the vessels at anchor heaved and pitched until their cables parted. After which they blundered into each other, were hurled against the breakwater at Brixham, or else went ashore. A number of captains attempted to reach the open sea where they stood an infinitely better chance of weathering the storm, but in so crowded a roadstead this was almost impossible. Those that made the harbour safely were the *Tangerine, Florence* and *Nightingale*, but at least seven others got no further than the breakwater. Two barques, the *Wild Rose* of Whitby, 208 tons, and the Antwerp-registered *Leone*, drove from their moorings and collided with several other vessels, causing them also to go adrift (Picture, p 119). No less than eight ships ground themselves to pieces against the outer wall of the breakwater, where they were later joined by the *Colonel Buller*.

At anchor a mile offshore was the *Cambria* of Exeter, 107 tons —until she, too, parted her cables, and within ten minutes became a total wreck. In that short space of time she was involved in six collisions before striking the pier. Fortunately, her mast overhung the stonework and her crew were able to scramble to safety; seconds later, no recognisable part remained. In his deposition to Mr Hallett, the Receiver of Wreck for Brixham, William Fordyce, master of the 340 ton *Monda*, carrying a general cargo from London to Berbice, stated that he had brought his ship to anchor two miles from Brixham, letting out eighty fathoms of 1½in chain cable on both anchors. At 5.30 pm both cables parted, whereupon he made for the harbour but, in the dark and general confusion, ran ashore on the rocks at Fishcombe Point. The mate attempted to jump ashore but slipped, fell between the hull and rock, and was crushed to death. Four other men in the rigging of the mainmast were all drowned when it fell over the side, and the captain and two seamen only escaped by climbing the cliffs. Long before they reached safety, the *Monda*, valued at £2,000 and her cargo at £13,000, was a total loss, only a part of her keel and a few ribs remaining on the beach.

It was the same story throughout the length of Torbay; beaches strewn with broken ships, corpses, and items of cargo everywhere. In Oxen cove, where four vessels lay stranded, the

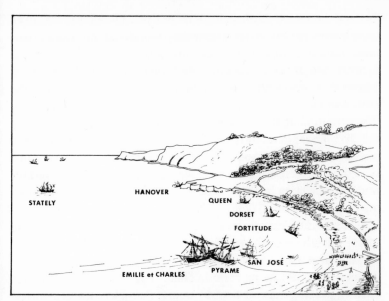

The scene at Broadsands, Torbay, on the day following the great storm
of 1866, showing locations of wrecked vessels

only thing of value remaining was the mast of the trawler *Salem*.
Likewise, Churston cove and Elbury were a mass of tangled
wood and scattered cargo, all that was left of two vessels sunk in
deep water. At Broadsands, where six or seven ships had been
stranded, four were intact and were later saved, but lay amongst
the wreckage of those less fortunate (Picture, p 118). Next day,
the storm having abated somewhat, it was possible to take stock
and to establish with some degree of accuracy how many vessels
and lives had been lost. Of the original seventy-four ships at
anchor, ten were still at their moorings, though much battered
and leaking. A further ten were safe inside Brixham harbour,
eight were ashore with every chance of being saved, forty-one
were total wrecks and five had simply disappeared. The exact
total will never be known since other vessels may have entered
Torbay during the evening, seeking shelter; equally, some may
have reached the open sea only to be overwhelmed. It must
therefore be assumed that, at the minimum, forty-six ships were

lost in the one gale, with seventy-three lives. Many of the corpses washed ashore were fearfully mutilated, some beyond all recognition, being found amongst the rocks without heads or limbs. A local newspaper reporter interviewed a survivor from the snow *Cheshire Witch*, which had apparently foundered, asking him what had happened to his vessel; his reply was simply, 'Sir, I cannot find a stick belonging to her.' Since Torbay at this time had no lifeboat of its own, the nearest which could be summoned was at Teignmouth. Sea conditions prevented it getting round Hopes Nose, so it was taken by road, on its carriage, to Torquay, where it was launched and succeeded in saving eleven men from the ships *Jessie* and *Cheshire Witch*.

Many acts of bravery were performed that night, not least of which were those of the wives of Brixham fishermen, who carried bundles of wood, straw, and other combustible material, even their bedding, to the pier head. There they lit and maintained a beacon, guiding many a boat to safety. Police-constable Amstey waded out into the surf near Brixham and, with the aid of a line, saved the crew of the *Thomas and Mary*, while a fisherman named Mills rescued fourteen people from wrecks near the breakwater. Another local man named Matthews went over the edge of a steep cliff on the end of a rope at the height of the gale and literally plucked several men from another wreck; the same feat being repeated at Broadsands. For well over a week following that awful night, gangs of men were recovering items of cargo and corpses. To quote the *Torquay Times*, '. . . sacks of flour, potatoes, boxes of currants, casks of butter, oil of vitriol, and valuable copper ore, were all placed under the charge of the Receiver of Wreck'. Well, perhaps not all, since the local population made off with a considerable amount. At least one prosecution resulted, which brought William Decent, a Brixham shipowner, before the magistrates charged with possessing wreck not belonging to him. A local lad named Bennetts, in grappling for packages on the sea bed, had brought up the end of a wire rope to which was attached a jib sail from the schooner *Abeona* of Brixham. Mr Decent, having already bought the remains of two wrecks at the back of the pier, on hearing of the sail's recovery, claimed it for himself although the item was clearly marked otherwise. In court, he admitted it had been obtained under false pretences and, after the court had been informed that he had been warned about taking wreck not belonging to him on a previous occasion, he was found guilty and fined £5 with £1 19s costs.

The following, as near as is known, is a list of all the vessels stranded or wrecked during the hurricane. It is possible that a few, although declared a total loss at the time, were subsequently refloated and saved:

Abeona—Brixham schooner, total wreck
Alona—Hull brigantine, total loss
Amanda—Hull brigantine, total loss
Ann—Stranded, but later saved
Belle—French trawler, total wreck
Blue Jacket—Salcombe schooner, total wreck
Briton—Brixham trawler, total wreck
Britannia—Total loss
Cambria—Total loss
Cheshire Witch—Total loss
Christina—Elsfloth schooner, stranded, saved
Colonel Buller—Brixham smack, total loss
Courier—Prussian brigantine, total loss
Deborah—Brig, dismasted, saved
Drian—French brig, total loss
Elizabeth Lewis—French schooner, total wreck
Ellen Edwards—Welsh schooner, total wreck
Emilie & Charles—Brigantine, total loss
Ernest—Brixham trawler, total loss
Florence Nightingale—Total loss
Forerunner—Brixham trawler, total loss
Fortitude—Exeter schooner, foundered, saved
Grace—Brixham trawler, total loss
Helen—Brixham trawler, total wreck
Hilkelina—Hanover galliot, total wreck
Honor—South Shields brigantine, foundered, saved
Jacobe—Dutch brig, total wreck
James—Schooner, total wreck
Jessie—Exeter vessel, total wreck
Lady of the Lake—Brixham smack, total wreck
Lively—Brixham trawler, total wreck
Margaret Ann or *Mary Ann*—London brig, total loss
Monda—Hull brigantine, total loss
Princess Beatrice—Stranded, saved
Providence—Brixham trawler, total loss
Pyrame—French vessel, stranded, saved
Salem—Brixham trawler, total loss
Scythian—Exeter vessel, total loss

Sky—Brixham trawler, total loss
Stately—Newcastle barque, stranded, saved
Telegram—Brixham trawler, total loss
Thomas & Mary—Schooner, stranded, saved
Useful—Blyth brig, stranded, saved
Wild Rose—Whitby barque, total loss
Zouaz—Brig, total loss

The next incident occurred on 23 March 1866 when, during a gale almost the equal of the one in January, the Welsh schooner *Mary Louisa* of Llanelly went ashore on the beach near Paignton pier. Her crew lowered their only boat but would never have made the shore without the assistance of Samuel Wills, a local seaman, who waded out into the surf and took their line. Driven higher and higher with every wave, the wreck eventually finished up at the back of Torbay House, 600ft from where she first struck.

One of the most dramatic shipping incidents to take place at Torquay concerned the *Wallace*, which caught fire and came so close inshore that she threatened the whole waterfront. The *Wallace* of Boston, after discharging petroleum at Antwerp, was on passage back to Key West when she was forced to seek shelter from the weather in Torbay, on 2 January 1873. Between 3 and 4 am on 6 January, fire was discovered in her forehold, which her crew tried to extinguish but without success. Signals for assistance were not seen ashore, so attempts were made to sail her to Paignton sands where she could be scuttled. While she was standing across Torbay, the wind changed and she was blown north until she grounded 100yd west of Sulyarde Terrace, settling right across the main sewer outfall of the town, only 50yd from what was to become the entrance to Princess pier.

Until then the fire had been confined to the forepart of the *Wallace*, but it now quickly engulfed the entire vessel, putting the safety of the town itself at stake. The site of the blazing wreck is now occupied by the Torbay Hotel, which was at one time virtually the waterfront but which land reclamation has now placed some distance from the sea. Every fire appliance in the area was called out and soon the entire harbour was full of smoke and flying sparks. As it was possible that the *Wallace* would have

Page 147: Her stern section broken off and under water, the steamer *Huddersfield* lies wrecked on the rocks under Gawlish Cliff, near Clovelly, on 27 January 1908

Page 148: (*above*) Knapp Head, one mile from the North Devon and Cornwall border, claimed the coaster *Eilianus* on 16 June 1936; (*below*) the Dutch steamer *Flora* high and dry ashore at Hartland Quay on 14 April 1915

to be scuttled, the Torquay Military Volunteers brought a carriage gun from Corbyn Head and were prepared to fire shells into her waterline. A fire engine was put aboard the barge *Tavistock* and towed to windward of the burning hulk so that water could be played on the fire from both sides, but it made little difference and the *Wallace* burnt for two days and nights before becoming a total loss.

Since there was once a time when Brixham could boast of a fishing fleet in excess of 300 vessels, it is not surprising that a great many of these came to grief, usually being run down and sunk offshore. The 27 ton *Brave*, lost in Torbay on 14 June 1874 was a typical case; *Providence*, 34 tons, was run down off Berry Head on 29 July, the same year; the Dartmouth sloop *Swift* foundered at her moorings in Brixham Roads on 28 March 1875, being in very poor condition, whilst the *Sovereign* was wrecked in Torbay on 14 September 1875. These were followed by the fifty-six year old sloop *Phoenix* on 21 April 1876; the *Pilgrim*, run down by an unidentified ship on 28 July 1876; and the *Dolphin* on 6 August 1881 following a collision with the barque *J. B. Sprott*.

Although, technically, the *Shamrock* in 1851 was the first steamship to be involved in an incident in Torbay, the first steamer wreck was that of the *Bretton Hall*, which went ashore on Mudstone beach, near Sharkham Point, on 6 December 1885. Registered and owned in Liverpool, she was on passage to Newport from Antwerp, intending to take aboard some 2,000 tons of coal. Steaming through dense fog at eleven knots, her captain had every confidence in his dead reckoning, which placed the ship well south of both Prawle and Start Points but was, in fact, thirteen miles in error. After going ashore, distress rockets were fired, which were sighted by Harry Parker, a local miller, who obtained several lengths of rope. These he managed to pass across to the wreck from the clifftop, and in this manner thirty-six Lascars and Portuguese seamen, out of a crew of fifty, got ashore. The Brixham lifeboat was launched but found its services were not required, although it later assisted in the recovery of some valuable cargo. It is interesting to note that the *Torquay Times* reported, '. . . the Mansands lifeboat also put out,

I

to assist at the wreck', but to which boat this referred is uncertain, probably a coastguard boat.

Following the abandonment of the *Bretton Hall*, a party of some fifty local fishermen went on board and remained there all night, probably in hope of some salvage award. After one night on the beach, the ship began to take in water rapidly and was abandoned for a second time with her stern now completely submerged. Her cargo, amongst other items, included 450 tons of best Belgian malleable iron, in ingots and used in sword making, which was of little interest to the waiting crowd. But as she began to break up, fifty tons of general cargo were released into the surf and literally thousands of people scavenged along the beach, picking up packs of playing-cards and boxes of eau-de-cologne, much to the frustration of the Torbay Customs officers.

As the nineteenth century entered its last decade Torbay was faced with the full fury of the 1891 blizzard, which appears to have either been accurately forecast or anticipated, since only two vessels were reported as being in difficulties, namely the *Emilie* and *Quiver*. At 3 pm on 10 March the former, a sixteen-year-old Cherbourg brig, drove ashore directly beneath Berry Head House, less than 150yd from the coastguard lookout. Her crew of eleven were all taken off with the aid of a breeches-buoy, the last to leave being Capt Viget, who insisted on going below again to collect his umbrella! The *Quiver*, a Brixham cutter of forty-eight tons, was at her moorings and empty when the gale struck her, causing her cable to part so that she drifted ashore in Oxen cove. So the toll continued into the turn of the century, with a profusion of trawling ketches, sloops and cutters being lost, mainly off Berry Head.

No further incident of any note occurred until 1907 when, in June of that year, the naval torpedo-boat HM (*TB*) *99* was lost while on trials, some four and a half miles off Berry Head. Built by Thornycrofts in the late 1880s, this steel-hulled 15 ton warship was armed with two torpedo tubes and a machine-gun. At the time of her loss she was being used to evaluate a new design of propeller which, during a fast run, vibrated so violently that she sprang a leak and sank. Salvage operations were in progress by mid-July, with the gunboat *Spanker* and the tug *Etna* in attendance. Diver Trapnell, aged forty-eight, went down in 'standard dress' to 150ft and within a few minutes reported over his telephone that he had located the propellor and shaft, and that it had broken away from the main hull. He asked for a rope to be sent down so that these items could be raised, then, without warning, his voice became weak and strangled and he told his attendant that his air line and breast rope were both badly tangled in the wreck. A second diver went down and it took over two hours to free Trapnell, after which the second man returned to the surface bleeding from the nose and in a state of complete exhaustion. By now, Trapnell had spent almost three hours at 150ft, which was outside any of the normal decompression tables, so that bringing him to the surface was a matter of guess work, and 'stops' which amounted to five hours. Once back aboard and undressed, Trapnell was unable to stand up and was put to bed in the *Etna*. Next day he was transferred to Torquay general hospital, where he became delirious and died from a combination of decompression sickness, shock, and physical exhaustion. Later in 1907, both sections of the wreck of the torpedo-boat were salvaged and taken to Devonport, where the bow portion was scrapped in No 4 Dock, the stern section being rebuilt into a new boat on the south yard camber.

By comparison with other areas of Devon, there have been few steamship incidents in Torbay, but one of some note was the sinking of the *John Johansson* alongside the south pier at Torquay. Carrying 800 tons of coal, this West Hartlepool vessel arrived in Torbay during a severe south-east gale and had not long berthed when a particularly large wave caused her to strike the seabed. Several plates were sprung and her engine-room flooded. Hand pumps failed to get her afloat again on the next high water, so Capt Anderson and his famous *Lady of the Isles* were called in the following day, 11 October 1907. The salvage men discharged her cargo, cemented over the leaks as a temporary measure, pumped her out, and towed the steamer away to Plymouth.

The war years saw a great deal of U-boat activity off Torbay and during 1917–18 alone at least five steamers were torpedoed and sunk in the area. The *W. H. Dwyer* of Sunderland, torpedoed and sunk on 26 August 1917, was presumably a tanker, since *Lloyds' Register* states that her machinery was aft, and she was too large to be a coaster. One month later the *Greleen*, built by Harland & Wolff for the Haenton Shipping Co in 1894, was sent to the bottom with nineteen lives lost on 22 September, to be followed by the *Bleamoor* on 27 November, the *Styrn* on 10 June 1918, and the *Kendall Castle* on 15 September 1918, all less than four miles from shore and in the same area.

Between the two world wars there were very few incidents. A pair of destroyers went ashore on Roundham Head and Preston beach respectively on 12/13 December 1920, and the crew of the Torbay and Brixham lifeboat no doubt imagined themselves in for a busy night until they learnt that the warships were, in fact, the German ships *T189* and *S24*, carrying only six steaming crew between them. They were under tow by the London tug *Warrior*, from Cherbourg to Teignmouth for scrapping, when both parted their tow ropes and stranded in Torbay. The *T189* broke her back and had to be abandoned on the rocks, but her partner was patched up and towed away, despite 30ft of her bow being badly buckled. Three steamers were ashore for various reasons between 1922 and 1929, namely the *Eider*, beached near Berry Head after springing a leak on 2 March 1922; the *River Lagan* on 8 January 1924 on Goodrington beach; and the Spanish *Sebastian* on Broadsands on 6 December 1929, but all were refloated and saved.

During World War II the majority of losses brought about by enemy action were well offshore from Torbay, so have no part in this chapter. In more recent years, the large Dutch steel barge *Cosray 10*, one of three under tow of the tug *Cycloop*, broke adrift and was wrecked beneath the cliffs at Daddyhole Plain on 5 December 1959. A Danish motor coaster, the *Northwind*, had a lucky escape on 22 December 1964, when a north-easterly gale forced her ashore on Hollacombe beach, between Paignton and Torquay (Picture, p 108). She lay beam-on to a 90ft high cliff, from where a breeches-buoy was rigged and Capt Kirkeby and his five crew speedily rescued. When the weather abated she was successfully refloated, having suffered virtually no damage, as was the *Trinity Navigator*, a tanker of 42,844 gross tons, which went ashore on the north side of Berry Head at 3.30 am on 2 March 1971, the last shipping incident near Torbay to date.

CHAPTER FIVE

HOPES NOSE TO DORSET

It is not necessary to be a connoisseur of shipwreck to appreciate the marked change in wreck incidents from here on along the south coast, as the coastline swings north-east towards Lyme Bay and the Dorset border. Although this chapter in fact embraces the longest single stretch of Devon's coast, the wreck incidents will be found to diminish not only in number but also in tonnage, the most obvious decline being in 'deep-water' sailing ships and steamers. Vessels passing up or down Channel normally set course between St Catherine's Point on the Isle of Wight, and Prawle Point, or the Start, which keeps them well clear of Lyme Bay. Only those unfortunate enough to become embayed before a south-easterly gale or, in more recent times, coasters entering or leaving Exmouth and Teignmouth, were in real danger. Consequently this area is far from notorious for its shipping losses.

The majority of incidents occurred at Teignmouth, which in bygone days enjoyed not only a brisk interchange of trade with Newton Abbot but also supported a shipbuilding industry. It was even considered of sufficient importance for de Tourville's ships to select it as a secondary target for attack in 1690, after being thwarted by unfavourable winds from attacking Plymouth. The French swept in and sacked East Teignmouth, leaving it almost completely destroyed, but it was soon rebuilt. There are few early references to wreck here, but in 1825, in its first annual report, the Royal National Institution for the Preservation of Life from Shipwreck made two references to a lifeboat having been installed, which points to an existing need for one in the area. However, since no record of any such lifeboat has been uncovered it must be assumed that it did not materialise until 1852, when

the Shipwrecked Fishermen and Mariners Benevolent Society
provided a 28ft boat, rowing ten oars.

The wreck of the *John*, of Lympstone, appears to have been
the subject of the earliest account recorded in any detail, and
the following is an extract from the records of the High Court of
Admiralty for the year 1573:

> . . . it is pronounced, decreed and declared, that the aforesaid
> Gilbert Peppett, Robert Vinton, and John Hillman, loaded a certain
> ship called the *John*, in parts beyond the seas, called Newfoundland,
> with 70,000 salt fish called Newfoundland fish, and that the ship
> with the fish arrived safely off the port or river of Exmouth, and that
> the aforesaid John Parsons was hired as a pilot to conduct the ship
> and fish into the port or river of Exmouth aforesaid. That he, Parsons,
> and others, his associates in that behalf, hired his services to the
> aforesaid Peppett, and that the said John Parsons taking upon him-
> self the duty of conducting the ship and the rest of the premises into
> the port, by his craft, fault, ignorance, rashness and negligence, caused
> the aforesaid ship, with the aforesaid fish, to strike upon the sands
> and rocks of the sea, and that in consequence the *John* was wrecked,
> and that by reason thereof, 18,000 of the fish were sunk in the sea,
> utterly perished, and were lost . . . valued at the sum of £200 . . . that
> by reason of the breaking up and loss of the ship in like manner, the
> sustained loss was to the amount of £66 13s 4d in addition to the
> cargo.[1]

There then follows a considerable gap in time, until the late
1700s, when we hear of a privateer named *Bellona*, belonging to
an ironmonger named Leake, of Exeter, which foundered in
sight of Teignmouth after leaving port on 5 September 1779.
Sixty-one years later, in 1840, a Teignmouth trawler brought
ashore a piece of the wreck in late September, having found the
remains of the *Bellona* near the Clerk rock. Another West Country
privateer, the sixteen-gun *Thornborough*, Capt Crowte, fell victim
'to the high rocks off the land at Orcombe' on 2 November 1806.
During a hard gale from the south-west, the schooner-rigged
vessel was sighted off Exmouth bar in distress, having lost her
foretopmast and jib boom. After striking the rocks, she bilged
and sank, her 1st lieutenant, Mr Salter of Topsham, and two
seamen getting ashore. At 9 pm the same day, the deck parted
from the rest of the wreck and a further nine men were saved, but
her captain and two men were drowned.

On 16 November 1812 the Cardiff collier *Brothers* was wrecked

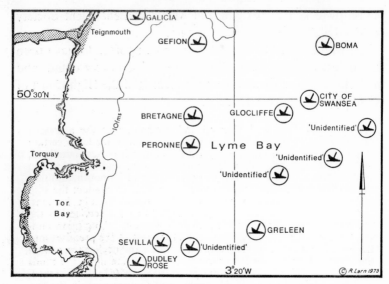

Locations of wrecks offshore from Teignmouth

on Orcombe Point, followed by the *Moon*, carrying pipeclay for Topsham, at the same spot, during February 1817. Both losses were directly attributable to bad weather, but the next wreck, if we are to be influenced by public criticism, was brought about by the reluctance of Exeter pilots to put to sea when it was rough. The 73 ton Exeter schooner *Friends*, on passage from Hartlepool with £100 worth of coal aboard, anchored off Exmouth on 3 January 1854 while her master burnt flares for a pilot to come out, but received no response. A strong north-east wind was blowing at the time, which soon increased to force ten on the Beaufort scale. Unwilling to enter the Exe at night without assistance, the master attempted to reach the shelter of Torbay, but struck a rock and had to beach his ship between Dawlish and Langstone rock. The crew of five were saved, but the schooner, valued at £400, quickly went to pieces. In their defence, a spokesman for the local pilots stated to the Board of Trade, that 'they never went to sea at all on such occasions'.[2]

Further south, in Babbacombe Bay, was where the American full-rigged ship *Caroline* of Charlestown was stranded on 12

Page 157: Wreck of the steamship *Cingetorix* on the rocks near Hartland Quay on 2 March 1911

Page 158 The Royal Fleet Auxiliary tanker *Green Ranger* wrecked at Longpeak, Hartland Point, on 17 November 1962

Page 159: Stranded in thick fog on 27 May 1904, only yards from the old coastguard station at Hartland Quay, the Italian steamer *Rosalia* became a total wreck

Page 160: The shattered hull of the Lorient trawler *Goliath* on the rocks beneath Sandor Cliffs, Hartland Point, on 16 March 1969

March 1860, the largest vessel to go ashore in the locality. Having discharged her cargo from America at Hamburg, she loaded railway iron and sailed for Cardiff. In dense fog, Capt Haynes mistook Straight Point for Lands End and turned inshore. When close to Gull rock, the *Caroline* was sighted by a local fisherman named Harris who put out in his own boat to warn them of the danger, but before a tug could be called the *Caroline* went ashore and was badly holed forward. Valued at $30,000, both wreck and cargo were sold to a syndicate of ten local men for the ridiculous sum of £250. To the original owners' intense chagrin, they landed and sold the entire cargo of iron at a handsome profit, then proceeded to refloat the ship, refitted her, and returned her to service!

Only five years later, on 29 April 1865, the remains of the *Friends* was joined by those of the Brixham fishing trawler *Ranger*, which leaked so badly that she had to be put ashore, where she went to pieces. During the year 1867 there was a particularly unfortunate incident on the Pole Sand, at the entrance to the Exe. This concerned the Exmouth brigantine *Julia*, of 148 tons, owned by a Mr Norrer, which was carrying 240 tons of Newcastle coal consigned to P. Varwell at Exeter. She was driven on to the bar by a furious south-easterly gale on 5 January, striking at the back of the Pole, nearly opposite the lifeboat station. There was considerable delay in launching the lifeboat and even then, because of the tremendous surf running, it was necessary to prolong things even further by dragging her seaward with ropes. The lifeboat *Victoria* was no sooner afloat than she drifted away up river, and the exertions of her crew were quite useless against the wind and tide. Within fifteen minutes of going ashore nothing of the *Julia* or her seven-man crew was to be seen, and the hundreds of spectators ashore had only been able to watch in horror as she quickly disappeared. A small boat, described as belonging to the 'preventative officers', was launched and manned by Exmouth fishermen, who reached the brigantine where the lifeboat had failed. Only one man remained alive for them to rescue, Adam Stewart of Aberdeen, who had shipped aboard at Shields at the last minute to replace crew who had run away. Of the remainder of the crew, the body of Capt Canham was the only one recovered, being found by HM cutter *Nimble* between Exeter and Lympstone. This time it was the lifeboatmen who bore the brunt of public criticism, it being maintained that they were 'fine weather men', and that on this occasion, long after the crew had mustered, 'the coxswain was not to be found'.[3] But things were not entirely one-sided, since at the Board of Trade enquiry held at the Royal Hotel, Dawlish, it was found that the 'vessel *Julia* was not in a fit and proper condition to go to sea'.

There followed a great many incidents on both the Pole Sand and Teignmouth Bar, during which the lifeboat saved a great many lives and vessels, the majority of them fishing boats or small coasting ketches. Typical of these was the 76 ton wooden smack *Melbury*, which became a total loss on Exmouth Bar on 19 November 1867. An unnamed lighter sank in Exmouth Bight during the November of 1869, the French sloop *Marie Elizabeth* was yet another victim of the Pole Sand on 25 February 1874, and on 14 October 1877 a southerly gale sank the *Annie, Hope* and *Richard*, all luggers. Another wreck of somewhat larger proportions was the London brigantine *Warrior*, carrying coal, which stranded on the beach on 7 January 1882. Built in America in 1853, the *Warrior* was one of a fleet of twenty-eight ships owned by Hall Brothers of Newcastle.

Collisions at sea in other areas of Devon were frequent occurrences but rare off Teignmouth, one of the few concerning the three-masted schooner *Scud* which was cut in two by the steamer *Blanchard* in 1885. A Guernsey-registered vessel, the *Scud* had been in the hands of a shipbuilder for some time in order that she could be lengthened. On completion, she loaded china clay at Melbury docks and sailed for Leith. On 12 January the lights of another vessel were seen ahead and identified as those of a steamship. As the two vessels came abeam of each other the *Blanchard* inexplicably turned directly towards the *Scud* and ran her down. She sank in less than two minutes, fortunately without loss of life, the prompt action of her mate being directly responsible for saving the captain, who was trapped with both legs broken by the fallen mainmast. One more stranding occurred prior to World War I, that of the Russian schooner *Tehwija* of

HOPES NOSE TO DORSET

— Chapter Five —

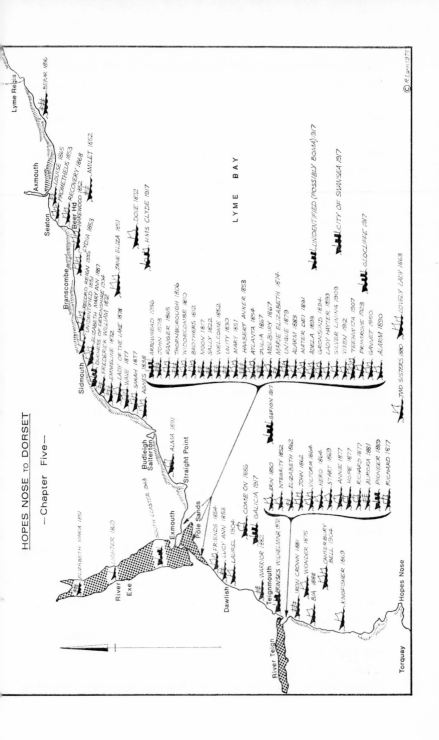

© R.Larn 1973

Lyme Regis
BERAR 1856
Axmouth
LOUISE 1865
PROMETHEUS 1853
Seaton
RECOVERY 1868
Beer Hd
HAREWOOD 1852
LYDIA 1853
AMILET 1852
Branscombe
SECOND REIGN 1935
UNIDENTIFIED 1851
ELIZABETH MARY ANN 1887
DUCHESS OF DEVONSHIRE 1934
FREDERICK WILLIAM 1822
EMMELINE 1672
JANE ELIZA 1851
Sidmouth
LADY OF THE LAKE 1878
DOVE 1872
HMS CLYDE 1917
WADE 1877
SARAH 1877
AGNES 1838

LYME BAY

ARROWHEAD 1856
JOHN 1573
RANGER 1865
THORNBOROUGH 1856
WIDDECOMBE 1810
BROTHERS 1812
MOON 1817
SALLY 1822
WELCOME 1852
UNITY 1830
MARY 1851
HALBERT ANKER 1853
ATLANTA 1854
JULIA 1867
MEL-BURY 1867
MARIE ELIZABETH 1874
UNIQUE 1879
ALARM 1883
MATER DEI 1891
ADELA 1893
GROWSUND 1894
LADY HAYTER 1893
SILVER LINING 1909
VIXEN 1912
TEIGNWTA 1907
PRIMROSE 1923
GAWET 1950
ALARM 1890

UNIDENTIFIED (POSSIBLY BOAM) 1917
CITY OF SWANSEA 1917
GLOCLIFFE 1917

TWO SISTERS 1800
LOVELY LADY 1863

Budleigh Salterton
ALMA 1851
Straight Point

SOUTH COASTER 1943
River Exe
LIGHTER 1810
ELIZABETH MARIA 1854

Exmouth
Pole Sands
COME ON 1866
GALICIA 1917
FRIENDS 1854
LUCY ANN 1853
LAUREL 1854

Dawlish
GAFFION 1917
ERIN 1850
INTEGRITY 1852
ELIZABETH 1862
JOHN 1862
VICTORIA 1864
HERO 1864
START 1863
ANNIE 1877
HOPE 1877
RICHARD 1877
AURORA 1881
PIONEER 1889
RICHARD 1877

WARRIOR 1882
PRINSES WILHELMINA 1971
IRON CROWN 1881
WONDER 1875
BIA 1888
CANTERBURY BELL 1904
KINGFISHER 1869

Teignmouth
River Teign
Torquay
Hopes Nose

Riga on 10 October 1907. From Lappvik to Exmouth with a cargo of timber, she went ashore on the outer Pole Sand. The Exmouth lifeboat made several attempts to reach the wreck but was beaten back by huge seas. An urgent call was sent to the Teignmouth lifeboat for assistance and after an exhausting row the *Alfred Staniforth* reached the schooner and saved her eight-man crew. Shortly afterwards the Russian vessel went to pieces.

Wartime incidents were confined almost solely to 1917, in which year four large steamers were sent to the bottom by enemy action at the western end of Lyme Bay. The first and by far the largest was the Pacific Steam Navigation Co's liner *Galicia*, of Liverpool. This twin screw, 5,922 tons gross vessel, built by Swan Hunter of Newcastle in 1901, struck a mine and sank in eight and a half fathoms on 12 May. The Teignmouth lifeboat, assisted by a tug, brought ashore fifty passengers and crew, the remaining nine being taken off by a naval patrol boat. During mid-August the *Glocliffe*, of 3,281 tons gross, was torpedoed and sunk off Exmouth, and on 25 September the *City of Swansea* went down with her cargo of Newcastle coal. Exactly one month later the Norwegian *Gefion* met the same fate, sinking in eleven fathoms in a position given as 50° 32′40″ N, 03° 21′42″ W. Since then, the only incidents of note have been the wreck of the *South Coaster* and the stranding of the *Arrowhead*. The coal-burning steamship *South Coaster*, of Cardiff, went ashore on the Pole Sand on 13 December 1943. She was eventually refloated by Admiralty tugs and beached in the shallows close to the railway lines that run along the Warren. She was scrapped where she lay, but her remains can still be seen at low water. Dense fog, the cause of so many tragic losses in the past, put the Guernsey motor vessel *Arrowhead* on the Maer rocks on 2 February 1956, but fortunately the damage was only slight and she was saved.

Before moving east towards Sidmouth and Beer Head, an unusual 'wreck' incident—if that is the correct description—was reported in local newspapers during 1907. On 31 May the Brix-ham fishing ketch *Skylark* was fishing some eight miles south east of Exmouth when her crew spotted what they at first thought to be a hayrick floating on the surface. Drawing closer, they found the

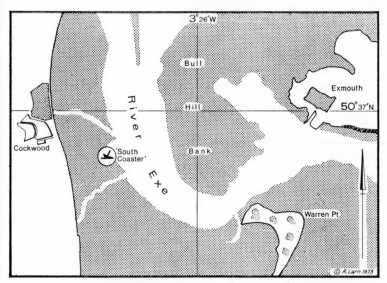

Location of the wreck of the steamship *South Coaster* in the river Exe

object to be a derelict army observation balloon and four hours of frustrating effort were spent in chasing the partially deflated balloon all over the sea before it was finally secured and the 'catch' could be examined. Attached to the balloon was a wicker basket, which contained nothing but an officer's riding crop. Not appreciating the implications, the crew of the *Skylark* resumed their fishing and remained out for a further three days before reporting the incident on their return to port. A massive search was at once launched, the balloon being identified as having come from Aldershot, manned by two officers of the Royal Engineers, but no trace of them was ever found.

From Exmouth to where the border between Devon and Somerset meets the sea, a little to the west of Lyme Regis, lies a quiet and peaceful stretch of coast with an infamous reputation for smuggling but with few wrecks. An expression once common in this part of the world stated that, 'Sidbury financed—Branscombe landed—Sidmouth found wages, and Salcombe carriers'. Branscombe and Beer were, of course, celebrated villages from which smuggling was organised, the most outstanding individual concerned being Jack Rattenbury, a notorious smuggler who was born at Beer in 1778 and published his memoirs in 1837. A memorial tomb in Branscombe churchyard dedicated to John Hurley and describing him as 'an active and diligent officer, inoffensive in his life and conversation', is silent testimony of the sort of things that went on locally. John Hurley was a preventative officer who met his death in 1775 by going over the cliff; everyone connected with the incident maintained that he must have slipped and fallen but, considering the circumstances, it is more likely that he was pushed. On the night in question, the smugglers were out awaiting a cargo carried in a lugger. The night was so dark that it was necessary to light a small beacon on the clifftop between Beer and Seaton to guide the boat to land, and it was this fire that Hurley was attempting to extinguish when he met his death.

The much travelled Leyland visited Seaton during the period 1534–43, and described it as, 'the Town of Seton is now but a meane Thing, inhabited with Fischar men but it hath bene far larger when the Haven was good'. He then went on to Beer and wrote, 'Ther longid to Seton and doth yet a Chapelle of stone, caullid Berewood, nere the Shore, scant half a Mile distant from the very Towne of Seton, and there is an Hamlet of Fischar men. There was begon a fair pere for Soccow of Shippelettes at this Berewood, but there cam such a Tempest a 3 yeres sins as never in mynd of men had before beene sene in that shore, and tare the Pere to Peaces.' Since then, it has been the practice at Sidmouth, Beer and Seaton, along with other small ports, to work ships directly off the beaches, embarking or landing cargo over the side at low water from horse-drawn carts. Such operations always involved an element of risk, since a sudden change of wind direction or a ground swell uncovering rock on an otherwise sandy beach could spell disaster. The case of the *Samuel*, in August 1812, was typical of what could happen. She had partially discharged her cargo of coal at Sidmouth when the wind suddenly went onshore and though every effort was made to save her, she was finally wrecked on Otterton Ledge, near Budleigh Salterton. The number of vessels lost in this manner are

legion; a Guernsey-registered schooner, the *Agnes*, was wrecked
on Sidmouth beach on 19 March 1838; the *Jane Eliza* of Caernarvon, carrying pipeclay, was lost on Chit rocks on 15 January
1851; the *Harewood* on Beer Head on 16 June 1852; the *Amulet*
near Seaton on 28 October 1852; the *Lydia* at Seaton Sluice on
17 March 1853; the *Prometheus*, another Seaton wreck, on 29
November 1853; the Penzance brig *Louise*, also at Seaton on
8 February 1865, and many others.

It was this practice of landing passengers and cargo over the
side which brought about the total loss of a once well known
excursion steamer, the *Duchess of Devonshire*, on 27 August
1934. The ship had been laid up for some time after the Devon
Dock, Pier & Steamship Co of Exeter had found her no longer
economic. In 1933 a local syndicate headed by a Capt Coleberd
bought her and put her back on excursion work between Seaton
and Torquay. She arrived at Sidmouth shortly after noon on 27
August with forty passengers aboard, some of whom wished to
disembark. This necessitated running her bows ashore and rigging
a small gangplank, but while this was being done a heavy sea
lifted her stern and swung her beam-on to the beach, where she
stranded on top of some concrete slabs. At low water the obstructions pierced her hull and she began to fill. Even when the
hole was plugged and the pumps started, she refused to be
refloated and had to be abandoned, eventually to be broken up
for scrap. As late as 1950, some of her bottom plates were uncovered by the sea and had to be removed by the local council
(Picture, p 129). Since that day, the motorised topsail ketch
Record Reign, stranded on 8 February 1935, has been the last
vessel lost in this manner. She had got off course in fog and after
striking a rock offshore was beached at Littleham Shute. She had
an interesting past, having been one of the famous 'Q' ships
during World War I. Offshore, there are few deepwater wrecks,
only the Admiralty requisitioned trawler, HMS *Clyde*, lost in
collision off Sidmouth on 14 October 1917, and the still unidentified wreck eight and a half miles, bearing 179° 40′ from Sidmouth church, falling into this category. The latter could well
be that of the Liverpool steamer *Boma* of 2,694 tons register,

thought to have been torpedoed in position 50° 32'10" N, 03° 14'12" W.

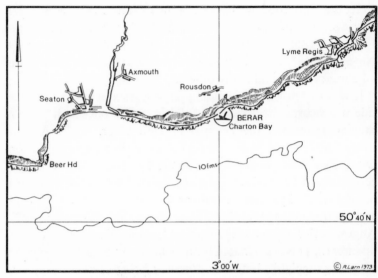

Location of the wreck of the sailing-ship *Berar*

Only one further wreck remains to be mentioned on the few remaining miles of the south Devon coast, and this is the Finnish barque *Berar* which went ashore in fog on 7 October 1896. She carried a massive quantity of sawn timber, en route from Baga to Swilley, and shortly after going ashore broke in two, leaving the wood free to float away so that it covered local beaches for miles. She struck a rock almost mid-way between Culverhole Point and the centre of Charton Bay, and it was here, during 1972, that her remains were relocated by John Moore, a diver employed by the Unit of Coastal Sedimentation (Picture, p 129).

Page 169: (left) The topsail schooner *Madeleine* stranded on the beach at Westward Ho!, 31 August 1908

(right) The three-masted schooner *Fimmo* ashore at Braunton Sands on 1 May 1923

Page 170: (above) Following an offshore collision, the schooner *Nikita*, seen to the left of the picture, capsized and sank in Ilfracombe harbour in September 1894; (below) the Ketch *Marie Emilie* stranded almost at the entrance to Ilfracombe harbour

HARTLAND TO WESTWARD HO!

Situated at the extreme north-west corner of the county, Hartland Point dominates the entire sixty or so miles of north Devon coastline, stretching from Marshland Mouth east to Glenthorne. Although a mere 350ft in height, compared with the Great Hangman and Holdstone Barrows which are both in excess of 1,000ft, the cliffs at Hartland offer some of the most impressive and spectacular coastal scenery in the whole of England and Wales. Rightly called, 'the sailors' grave', it is an area notorious for shipwrecks and steeped in legend. Once the lonely domain of a small community of Augustin monks, who founded Hartland abbey, the headland was also at one time a part of the royal estate and was bequeathed by King Alfred to his son, Edward.

Despite documentary evidence of wreck here as early as 1321,[1] the details are sketchy, as is to be expected, and it is not until the early 1800s that specific details can be found. During 1821, a tremendous October gale put forty fishing vessels ashore near Clovelly with the loss of thirty-five lives and an unspecified number of boats; again, in October 1838, a similar incident claimed a further twenty-one lives and fourteen locally-owned fishing craft. These losses were followed by that of the *Auspicious*, wrecked at Hartland on 21 October 1842, then the *Sir R. R. Vyyan* on 8 March 1845, but it was not until 1851 that a vessel of any size was lost.

This was the Finnish ship *Pollux*, of Bjorneborg, which left Dublin for Alexandria on 9 November in ballast. Shortly after her departure from Ireland she encountered a furious gale, her ballast shifted, and she went over on her beam ends. She could only be righted by cutting away her main and mizzen masts, after which the vessel drifted helplessly into the Bristol Channel and it was the 6th before she was sighted by two pilot skiffs off Devon. The pilots went aboard to offer their assistance, but to their astonishment, instead of welcoming their help, the crew of the *Pollux* promptly abandoned ship, leaving the locals to get the vessel into Clovelly roads as best they could. Next day the crew of the *Pollux* returned aboard, with the exception of Capt Lindstrom who claimed urgent business elsewhere. For reasons best known to themselves, the crew refused to render any assistance to the pilots and the Clovelly smacks which were still struggling to get the ship into Bideford. Twice en route she grounded but got off, and in desperation the Lloyds' agent requested the help of a steamship or tug. Less than half an hour after the *Pollux* had been taken in tow, a member of her crew deliberately cut the towing hawser, so that, adrift and helpless again, she finished up on the beach at Clovelly close to the pier.

Repudiating her as a wreck, the local Receiver of Wreck insisted that everything possible should be done to save the vessel and her contents. He ordered her ballast to be discharged, all spirits and stores unloaded and placed under lock and key, and before nightfall she was once more afloat. She was then towed a short distance offshore, anchored and left empty for the night, but within hours a full north-easterly gale was blowing. She rode safely until 10 am next day, then both cables parted and within ten minutes she was ashore and being smashed to pieces, her few remains later being auctioned off as firewood.

There was great concern when several large pieces of wreckage, thought to have come from a foreign vessel of some 150 tons, were found among the rocks at Hartland on 10 February 1852, but a search revealed nothing and the wreck was never identified. On 24 March 1857 the crew of the St Ives schooner *Sarah* managed to row themselves to Clovelly in their own boat, leaving their vessel to break up on the rocks, one of the few contemporary instances of the entire complement of a wrecked ship being saved. Another schooner, the Brixham owned and built *Fame*, of 85 tons, was wrecked at Hartland on 14 March 1866, and only seventeen days later the first steamer wreck in the area occurred. The wooden paddler *Queen* was well known locally, having been on the Hayle to Bristol packet service for fourteen years. Owned by the Hayle & Bristol Navigation Co, the *Queen* normally made the 150 mile journey on a single tide, and during her many years of service, involving some 4,000 trips, had not been involved in a single incident. There can be no doubt that this splendid record was due entirely to the vigilance of Capt Spray, who commanded her from her launching up until October 1865. He then handed over to his son Granville, who had served aboard as a seaman for five years, and then as mate for a further three.

The *Queen* left Bristol on 29 March with forty passengers and 100 tons of general cargo on board, calling at Ilfracombe only. She left there at 10.30 in the evening, and after following her normal westerly course for an hour and fifty minutes as usual, which took her five miles past Hartland, the mate ordered a new course of south-west-by-west. Shortly afterwards, to his horror, steep cliffs loomed ahead and the vessel struck the Tinge rock a terrific blow. She was got off and headed back towards Ilfracombe, but when the ship's carpenter reported 3ft of water in the hold, the *Queen* was run ashore at Clovelly, a ship's length from the pier head. It was now obvious that she was seriously damaged, so the remaining thirty-seven passengers and sixteen crew were ferried ashore. Work began next morning on the removal of her cargo and continued uninterrupted until the Wednesday, when she broke her back and went to pieces. The inevitable Board of Trade enquiry opened on 1 May in the Penzance guildhall, where Capt Spray was found guilty of neglect in not using the lead and of having failed to keep and maintain a ship's log since he had assumed command of the packet.

Although there had been one or more lifeboats at Appledore since 1825, the Manby mortar life-saving apparatus at Clovelly was for many years considered sufficient to cover the entire Hartland area. Then, in the 1860s, there came such a succession of small wrecks that public attention was drawn to the need for an additional lifeboat at the western end of Barnstaple Bay and a local subscription fund was opened. On 22 August 1868 the polacca schooner *Queen Victoria* of Bideford was blown ashore at Clovelly and wrecked. Another schooner was to follow, the

91 ton *Nancy*, which foundered off Hartland on 18 March 1869 with the loss of all six crew, and on 12 September a Genoese barque named *Odone* was lost at Portledge. On this occasion it was the local coastguards who went to her rescue; they manned the station's galley and went out beyond the line of breakers, from where they were able to guide the thirteen Italian survivors to safety in their own boat. The first Clovelly lifeboat, the *Alexander & Matilda Boetefeur*, arrived at her new station on 18 June 1870 but, for reasons unknown, did not attend the wreck of the schooner *Saltash* which stranded at Hartland on 28 August with the loss of five lives. It was, in fact, October before the lifeboat was put to use, when it went out to rescue the crew of the herring boat *Gem* which had sunk in bad weather, and but for its intervention another fishing vessel, the *Sisters*, would also have been lost. During 1871, the Clovelly lifeboat herself had a lucky escape when she was capsized by a gale during an exercise launch. Fortunately, all the crew wore regulation lifebelts and managed to retain a hold on the lifelines, so that not one of them was lost, as was so often the case in similar accidents.

Although the records of the Royal National Lifeboat Institution show that the Clovelly boat went out to a great many wrecks, for every occasion it was launched there were an equal, if not greater number, when it remained in its house unused. A typical instance concerned the steamer *Silurian*, of 1,252 tons gross, which struck Chapman rock, two and a half miles east of the point, on 2 September 1880. Built at Newcastle in 1876 and owned in Salonica, the *Silurian* was carrying patent fuel from Cardiff, which at one time had been her port of registry. Some three months later, on 23 November, the 50 ton Jersey schooner *Florida* was run down offshore by the French steamer *Charles Godard* and sank, and on 1 July 1882 the *Hoche*, also a French steamship, was wrecked two miles south-west of the headland, near Spekes Mill Mouth. Two other vessels went ashore at Hartland that same year. The French-owned brig *St Joseph*, on passage from St Malo to Swansea in ballast, stranded on 10 September to become a total loss, but the fishing lugger *Start*, stranded on 7 December, was later refloated and saved.

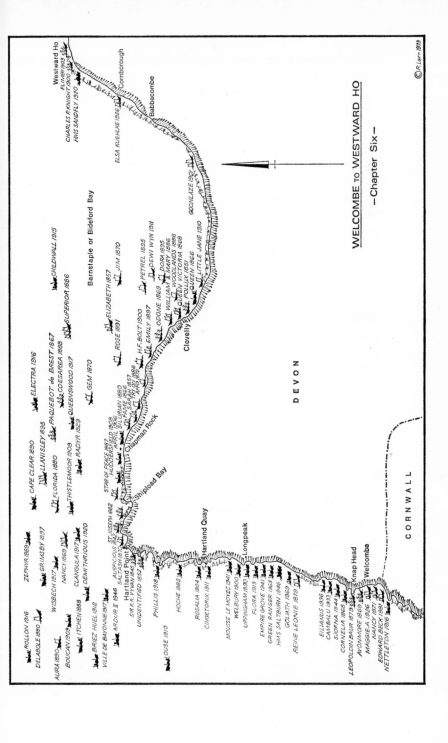

WELCOMBE to WESTWARD HO

—Chapter Six—

© R. Larn 1973

CORNWALL

DEVON

Barnstaple or Bideford Bay

Westward Ho
FLIMBY 1803
CHARLES P.KNIGHT 1900
HMS SANDFLY 1920
Comborough
ELSA KUEHLKE 1926
Babbacombe

CHILDWALL 1915
SUPERIOR 1886
GOONLAZE 1921
LITTLE JANE 1910
QUEEN 1866
POLLUX 1851
QUEEN VICTORIA 1868
WOODLANDS 1886
DORA 1895
MARY 1866
WILLIAM & MARY 1866
DEWI WYN 1911
PETREL 1895
JIM 1870
ELIZABETH 1857
EMILY 1897
ODONE 1869
H.F. BOLT 1900
ROSE 1891
GEM 1870
Clovelly

ELECTRA 1916
PAQUEBOT de BREST 1867
COESAREA 1888
QUEENSWOOD 1917
RADYR 1929
FLORIDA 1880
LLANISLEY 1895
CAPE CLEAR 1890
THISTLEMOOR 1909

STAR OF PEACE 1887
HUDDERSFIELD 1908
APRIL 1936
SILURIAN 1880
SARAH 1857
FAME 1866
PROVIDER 1886
APRIL 1864
Chapman Rock

Shipload Bay

ST. JOSEPH 1682
AUSPICIOUS 1842
SALTASH 1801
SIR R. R. VYNER 1865
Hartland Point
UNIDENTIFIED 1852
Hartland Quay

Longpeak

PHILLIS 1918

HOCHE 1882

OUSE 1910

ROSALIA 1904
CINZETORIX 1911

MOUSSE LE MOYEC 1941
WELBURY 1900
UPPINGHAM 1800
FLORA 1913
EMPIRE GROVE 1941
GREEN RANGER 1963
HMS SALTBURN 1946
GOLIATH 1869
REINE LEONIE 1879
Knap Head
Welcombe

ELLIANUS 1936
CAMBALU 1933
SJOFNA 1944
CORNELIA 1868
LEOPOLDIN BAUR 1879
AVONMORE 1869
MAGGIE A 1926
NANCY 1871
EDWARD BECK 1881
NETTLETON 1916

ROLLON 1916
DELABOLE 1880
ZEPHYR 1869
WISBECH 1917
AURA 1890
BOUICAN 1909
NANCY 1869
ITCHEN 1888
CLANGULA 1917
DEMITHRIOUS 1920
BRIEZ HUEL 1912
VILLE de BAYONNE 1971
ARDUR II 1949
GRIMSBY 1897

There followed an almost frightening number of wreck incidents, starting with smacks and coasting ketches of less than five tons, followed by larger sailing ships, and finally an unprecedented number of steamers. The smaller losses include the *Try On*, *Woodlands* and *William and Mary*, all on 15 October 1886; the *Rose* during December 1891; the *Petrel* and the *Dora* in October 1895; the *Emily*, 1897, and the *H. F. Bolt* in 1900. In contrast to their generally small tonnage, the Plymouth schooner *Star of Peace*, of 142 tons register, was rated locally as a 'proper wreck' when she struck the Hartland rocks on 18 February 1887 while carrying copper ore and zinc ash. Among the steamships were a number which went almost unnoticed locally, such as the *Itchen*, registered at Southampton, 193 tons gross, which foundered off Hartland on 28 August 1888, and the Waterford Steamship Co's *Zephyr*, which sank somewhere between Lundy and the mainland on 29 September 1889. She ran headlong into a severe gale off Lundy while carrying coal from Cardiff to Flushing. The sea tore away her engine-room skylight, flooded the tiny boiler room and extinguished the fires, so that her complement of sixteen crew and one passenger were forced to abandon ship. They got away in a lifeboat and a small dinghy, both of which reached Ilfracombe safely. The following year the Newcastle-owned *Cape Clear*, outward bound from Liverpool to Rosario and St Vincent with a general cargo, also went down in the same area, between 20–23 January, but with a tragic loss of life. Wreckage from this vessel was found ashore on Lundy on 31 January, and four days later two lifebuoys bearing her name, six hatch covers, and broken cabin furniture were found south-west of Hartland. Later still, another of her lifebuoys came ashore at Hartland Quay. She was posted as missing at Lloyds on 5 March, presumed lost with all hands, and the wreck was never found.

Exactly mid-way between Hartland and the border with Cornwall stands the bleak and desolate point known as the Longpeak, which claimed the 1,431 ton steamer *Uppingham* of London on 23 December 1890. Bound from Cardiff to Port Said with coal, she developed engine trouble when off Bude and, after setting auxiliary sail, put about for Lundy where Capt Lilley hoped to find shelter. Her engine then failed completely and she drifted helpless on to the rocks, to be wrecked with the loss of eight of her twenty-eight crew. One of the survivors was second officer Teck who, by coincidence, was on board another steamship, the *Welbury*, of West Hartlepool, which was wrecked almost on top of the *Uppingham*'s rusting remains on 24 April 1900.

Although salvage tugs were available at both Lundy and Ilfracombe on 4 October 1895, there was no way in which they could be contacted from out at sea, with the result that the Norwegian brig *Haabet* had to be abandoned and allowed to drift ashore at Croyde, where she became a total loss. Her distress signals were sighted from the cliffs above Clovelly, and the lifeboat was quickly launched. The brig was found to be leaking badly, with most of her canvas blown away and not one boat left intact, so the lifeboat took off her crew of nine, together with the captain's young daughter. Another set of distress signals sighted by the Hartland lighthouse keepers on 13 August 1897 indicated that the Cardiff collier *Grimbsy* was in trouble a short distance offshore. Again the crew of the Clovelly lifeboat found her full of water, and as she was in imminent danger of foundering, her four passengers and thirteen crew were taken off by the lifeboat.

The stretch of high cliffs between Clovelly and Westward Ho! is a particularly fearsome place in which to be wrecked. Even today, the cliffs are virtually uninhabited, and in 1901, when the *Goonlaze* was lost there with tragic result, the area must have been desolate indeed. It was the body of a seaman, found on 5 February in a field at Peppercombe about four miles east of Clovelly, that first indicated a vessel had gone ashore. A search of the coastline showed a mass of wreckage concentrated below Cockington Head, but no sign of survivors. So completely had the sea demolished the wreck that it was some time before it was identified as the Hayle schooner *Goonlaze*. In time, the corpses of all four of her crew were found, only one of whom had managed to scale the 300ft high cliffs before he, too, succumbed from exposure and injuries. It appears that the schooner came into Bideford Bay to shelter and was unable to get clear when the wind veered to the north-west. Possibly she parted her cables and stranded so close under the cliffs that her distress signals could not be seen.

The year 1904 marked the beginning of a long series of steamship wrecks, almost as if Hartland was some monster with an insatiable appetite for ships and men. The first of these was the Italian-owned *Rosalia* which, on 27 May, crashed on to the rocks at Hartland Quay in dense fog, tearing such holes in her bottom there was no hope of salvage. Unlike the *Goonlaze* incident, her presence could neither be mistaken nor ignored since she stranded immediately in front of the naval-manned coastguard station. Had the *Rosalia* been driven a further 200yd over the rocks, her bow would have destroyed the parapet surrounding the station and lookout post (Picture, p 159). It was fog that also brought about the end of the *Abril* on 16 February 1906. This Spanish steamer, loaded with 1,700 tons of coal from Cardiff, went ashore in the Beckland Bay area, close to Chapman rock. She filled so quickly that her crew of twenty promptly abandoned ship in two lifeboats, the larger of which, with sixteen men aboard, reached Clovelly. The smaller boat, unable to make headway against the tide, was missing for a time, but was later found by a steam tug which had put out to assist the Clovelly lifeboat. Built at Campbeltown in 1897 by Cuncliffe & Dunlop as the *Ardgour*, the 1,334 gross tons *Abril* broke her back and became a total wreck (Picture, p 130). This service by the lifeboat *Elinor Roget* was its last on this station, and by coincidence its replacement, the larger twelve-oared *Elinor Roget II* which arrived in June 1907, performed its first useful function in almost identical circumstances. This was at the scene of the wreck of the 2,055 gross tons *Huddersfield*, of Cardiff, on 27 January 1908. Yet another victim of fog, she stranded under Gawlish cliff, west of the *Abril*. As with so many previous incidents, the first anyone ashore knew of the wreck was the arrival at Clovelly of survivors, in their own boat. By the time the *Elinor Roget* had reached the scene, huge ground seas were sweeping the steamer from end to end. She was already breaking up, and with no boats remaining intact the twelve men still aboard would certainly have drowned but for the lifeboat's timely rescue (Picture, p 147).

It was 2 November 1909 before the next incident occurred, the victim being the *Boucan*, of 1,216 tons gross and owned by Cie de Navigation d'Orbigny, which sank following collision with the *Salglia*. The *Thistlemoor* foundered off Hartland exactly one month later, after being struck by a succession of giant waves which tore off all her ventilators and flooded her forward hold to such an extent that her bows were forced down and her propellor made ineffectual. Despite every assistance from another steamer, the *Arndale*, and the Clovelly lifeboat, the *Thistlemoor* went down in deep water, taking with her twenty-six crew including her master. Fifteen months were to pass before Hartland again echoed to the crash of distress rockets. This was in March 1911, when two more steamships were lost within twenty-four hours. During the evening of 2 March, a Mr Oatway, proprietor of the Hartland Quay hotel and leader of the local LSA team, noticed thick fog sweeping in from seaward. As a precautionary measure, a Mr Slute was sent up to the cliff lookout post to keep watch and had hardly reached his station before the deep bellow of a ship's siren was heard close inshore, followed immediately by distress signals. Fog hampered rescue operations and it was some time before the ship was located, driven deep into the ridges of rock at St Catherine's Point, only half a mile south from the old quay. The 1,375 tons gross *Cingetorix*, of Antwerp, having struck at low water, lay some 700yd offshore and presented so difficult a target for the rocket apparatus that its crew were obliged to climb down the cliffs to the rocks below. Even then, four rockets failed to send a line across the Belgian steamer's deck, and eventually it was a line fired from the wreck itself that established contact and enabled all nineteen crew to be saved. On this occasion the Clovelly lifeboat, unable to weather Hartland Point, had to put back, its services fortunately not being required. The sea quickly pounded the *Cingetorix* down until only her bridge showed, and despite salvage attempts by the now famous Western Marine Salvage Co, of Penzance, she went to pieces, scattering her cargo of 2,100 tons of steel sheet and billets on the seabed (Picture, p 159).

The very next morning, the Cardiff collier *Ouse* sank off Hartland, after developing a serious leak. Capt Wicklin and his crew of thirteen saved themselves, but not one of them had sufficient time to collect any belongings. Though the *Ouse* was forty-two years old when she foundered, she was perfectly sound, having undergone a complete refit in 1905 at a cost of £2,000. In view of this, the Board of Trade enquiry accepted the possibility that some rivets had been sprung when she had hit the Black rock leaving Falmouth on 21 February. Two more steamers were to be added to the tragic list before the outbreak of World War I; the *Briel Huel* on 9 March 1912, and the *Katina* a month later, on 24 May. Of these, the former was by far the largest being of 3,074 tons register. Carrying coal from Barry, destined for Algiers, and with thirty-nine crew and two passengers aboard, she struck the steamer *Tempest*, foundering as a result. The *Flora*, an Amsterdam-registered vessel of 725 tons gross, went ashore at Longpeak on 4 April 1915 and was wrecked (Picture, p 148), whereas the Greek-owned *Katina*, although badly damaged in stranding close at hand, was eventually refloated and saved.

Following the declaration of war with Germany, there was a tremendous increase in the demand for Welsh coal and the number of steamers entering and leaving the Bristol Channel increased a hundredfold in as many weeks. The commanders of U-Boats found easy targets amongst the slow, and as yet, unarmed merchant ships. Between 1914 and 1918, 268 vessels were sunk by enemy action in the Bristol Channel, but many others were lost by collision or wreck. In the immediate vicinity of Hartland Point, twenty losses were recorded, eighteen of which were steamers, enemy action accounting for thirteen. The *Childwall* of Liverpool was in collision with the *Trinculo* on 1 April 1915 and foundered; the 2,413 tons gross *Nettleton* of Hull was wrecked in fog on 11 February 1916, south of Knap Head, only half a mile inside the Devon border. Although the Bude LSA team was summoned and struggled along the clifftop with their apparatus, by the time they arrived the crew of the steamer, assisted by two local youths, had rigged an improvised breeches buoy and got ashore safely. The underwriters later sold the wreck to Thomas Wall & Co, who carried out extensive salvage. These wrecks were followed by that of the *Electra* of Liverpool, 495 tons gross, sunk following collision with the steamship *Margaret* on 4 October 1916, and of the Norwegian *Rollon*, which foundered following a leak on 27 October in a position given as four miles north-by-west of Hartland Point.

Of the war losses connected with this part of the Devon coast, the first were the French-owned *Ville de Bayonne*, and the British *Queenswood*, both torpedoed by *UC-65* on 16 February 1917. From that date onwards, hardly a month went by without some unfortunate crew having to row themselves ashore, more often than not into Clovelly harbour. A Newcastle steamer, the *Wisbech*, was sent to the bottom west of Hartland on 14 August, to be followed by the Cork Steamship Co's *Clangula* on 19 November. She sank in thirteen fathoms, taking with her a general cargo, her master, and fourteen crew, four miles south west of the point. By far the largest vessel sunk was the 7,388 tons gross hospital ship *Rewa*, owned by the British India Steamship Co and on passage from Madras to Avonmouth with 362 crew and patients aboard, when torpedoed on 4 January 1918. Sailing ships formed a small fraction of the total war losses, but included the *Marsouin* on 6 February 1918; after which, all in 1918 and all steamers, came the *Dalegarth* and the *Gregvnog* both on 18 April; the *Rimfakse* on 28 April; the *Girdleness* on 2 May; the *Phyllis* (ex-*Hesleden*) on 17 May; the *Moliere* (ex-*Calanas*) and the wooden schooner *Annie B. Smith* on 12 October. Of these, only the *Phyllis*, a French vessel of 1,455 tons gross, reached the Devon coast, going ashore 500yd south of Hartland Quay.

In the decade following the end of the war there were less than a dozen occasions on which the services of the Clovelly lifeboat were required. One of these was to save the crew of the Greek steamer *Demithrious* (ex-*Ben Ledi*), which was on passage from Par to Runcorn with china clay. She sprang a serious leak when five miles east-north-east of Hartland on 4 September 1920 and foundered after her crew had been taken off. The *Radyr*, which went down with the tragic loss of all twenty-one crew on 7 December 1929, was a loss which remained in the memories of local lifeboat men for years. An SOS radio message from this 2,280 tons gross Cardiff collier was relayed to both the Clovelly and Appledore lifeboats, but the seas were so huge that neither boat could get out to her in time. Built at Belfast by Harland & Wolff in 1918 as a 'standard ship' named *War Tabard*, she later became the *Jura* and then the *Radyr*.

Mystery wrecks are not common, and for that reason an incident which happened at Hartland on 4 January 1921 is worth special mention. A Mr Goaman, looking down at the beach from the overhanging cliffs at Elmscott, noticed a great deal of wreckage, and not long afterwards part of a large vessel, 120ft long and with a 40ft beam, was discovered on the pebbles. The timber and paintwork were fresh and carried no marine growth or barnacles, galvanised ironwork still shone as new, and tar smelt strongly. As the wreckage lay upside down, a huge iron propellor could be seen on the end of a shaft and was said by locals to be much larger than those of some of the steamers wrecked nearby. Yet there was no sign of an engine, only masses of electrical cable hanging down. Eventually the sea demolished the section, and to this day it is not known what type of vessel she was, let alone her identity. It was Knap Head, already well littered with wreckage, that claimed the next casualty, this being the Liverpool coaster *Cambalu*, of 496 tons gross, which went ashore there to become a total loss on 30 January 1933. Her bow section was still intact and showing at low water when she was joined by the 333 ton *Eilianus* (ex-*Wyke Regis*) in fog, on 16 June 1936. She had previously discharged her cargo at Dunkirk, then proceeded to Le Havre to take on board some 800 tons of scrap steel, destined for Britton Ferry. Her crew drifted about in the fog all night, before coming ashore at Marshland Mouth and scrambling up the cliffs (Picture, p 148).

War losses during World War II were small compared to those of 1914–18 and began on 30 September 1940 with HM Tug *Comet*. A French collier, the *Mousse le Moyec*, was wrecked at St

Catherine's Tor on 6 December, victim of a north-westerly gale which unfortunately coincided with an engine breakdown. Another victim of the elements was the 320 ton Liverpool motor vessel *Empire Grove*, lost on the return part of her maiden voyage on 18 October 1941. By late 1944, the bow section of the *Cambalu*, still intact, had been thrown close to that of the *Eilianus*, so that they propped each other up and very nearly became the scene of three bow sections in one place when the Norwegian steamer *Sjofna* stranded almost alongside on 23 November. She was carrying 500 tons of china clay in bags from Fowey to Larne, and both the Padstow and Clovelly lifeboats went to her aid, saving seven lives before the rocket line parted and heavy seas forced them to seek shelter. The Hartland LSA crew then took over the rescue and saved two more men, but the whip of the breeches buoy had to be cut to save the second man from drowning when it became entangled. Another line was fired but fell short, and the second went straight into the wheelhouse where it broke the captain's right leg and set fire to the ship's cat! Eventually the injured captain, nine remaining crew, and three animals, plus the unfortunate cat, were landed safely, the *Sjofna* going to pieces shortly after.

At the end of the war, on 10 August 1946, a small steam tug, the *Ardur II*, foundered off Hartland following a series of events so bizarre that one can hardly believe in their authenticity. The flush-decked steam tug *Ardur II* was launched in 1912 by Heffled & Co of South Shields. Her subsequent career is of no consequence, at least not until 6 May 1946 when she was sold by Cowington & Sons Ltd of Chelsea to the Standard Lighterage Co of Liverpool for the sum of £1,050, their intention being to use her on the Mersey. Her new owners contracted with Tonmouth Lister & Co of South Shields to deliver the vessel for £495, plus demurrage of £12 a day. She was insured for £2,000 after inspection on 17 May but a number of points would appear to have been overlooked. Her steam windlass was inoperative, her pumps defective, there were faults and blockages in the bilge lines and she carried no lifeboat, nor did she have Ministry of Transport permission to sail without one. In addition, her only liferaft was inadequate and there was not a single flare or distress signal on board.

Nevertheless, a certificate of seaworthiness was eventually issued, and she sailed with a recently demobbed, temporary lieutenant (RNR) as master, plus a crew of four. There followed a chapter of disasters that surely can have no equal. She left Chelsea on 13 June, but when approaching Tilbury landing stage, where a compass adjuster was to be embarked, her engines refused to go astern and she collided with a moored vessel, sustaining damage to her bow plates. Further down river a leaking rivet made its presence felt by partially flooding the engine room, but whether it was the bow leak or water coming in round the stern gland is difficult to say, since both let in several gallons a minute. The tug was then anchored for repairs, after which, lacking a windlass with which to heave in her cable, her crew slaved for the best part of a day with blocks and tackle to get the anchor up and stowed. Off Beachy Head, the bracket holding the standard compass in place collapsed, allowing the instrument to fall and be smashed, after which there was further flooding and the tug headed for Newhaven. At noon on 14 June her pumps choked and the depth of water in the boiler room had the crew frantically bailing with buckets, as well as passing lumps of coal by hand into the furnace in order to maintain steam pressure. She reached Newhaven at 8 pm with her engine making fearful knocking noises and on the instructions of the harbour master she was moored to a buoy. Her exhausted crew turned in but were rudely awakened next morning with the news they were sinking. Fortunately, they all got off just before she heeled over and went down.

By 28 June she was afloat again and had been repaired, cleaned out, painted, and leaks made good—or so it was thought. The *Ardur* left Newhaven on 28 July, but within five hours was again leaking so badly that she had to put into Yarmouth, on the Isle of Wight. On leaving there, the low-pressure cylinder knocked so badly that she was forced to berth alongside at Portland, where her engineer, with outside assistance and tools, worked on her for forty-eight hours without rest. Brixham was another port of call, where more leaks were plugged, after which the low-pressure cylinder took her into Falmouth. Here she took aboard eight tons of coal, the leaks were again plugged and she sailed on 9 August, having already taken two months to get from the Thames. The final act came on 10 August, when she leaked so badly that her fires were extinguished, her pumps choked, and she sank one mile north of Hartland Point. With no flares or radio, the crew's

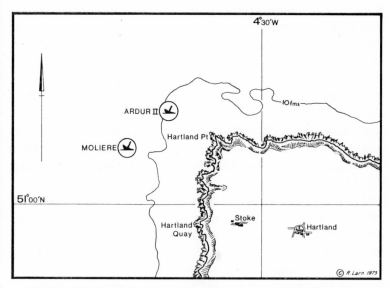

Location of the wrecks of the tug *Ardur II* and the steamship *Molière*

only means of attracting attention was the steam whistle, and the captain continued to send out S-O-S in morse code until the steam pressure failed. Although the tug was too far from shore for her whistle to be heard, an alert Hartland coastguard recognised the puffs of steam for what they were and called out the Clovelly and Appledore lifeboats, plus the Hartland LSA crew. Two of the tug's crew were rescued from off the liferaft, the remainder from the sea, but despite prolonged artificial respiration the engineer died. A Ministry of Transport enquiry was opened at the Temperance Institution Hall, Southampton, on

15 September 1947 and resulted in the new owners being fined £400 for negligence.

Four months after the *Ardur II* incident, an obsolete warship, the 710 ton minesweeper HMS *Saltburn*, fell victim to the Longpeak on 7 December after breaking tow on her way to a scrapyard. Built in 1918 by Murdoch & Murray, the *Saltburn* was bought for scrap by a Mr Gifford of Bude, who broke her up where she lay, salvage being complete by 1948. Only two other vessels have been lost at Hartland since 1946, the *Green Ranger*, another obsolete naval vessel on her way to the breakers, and the French trawler *Goliath*, driven ashore in a gale during 1969 and the last wreck in the area to date.

The *Green Ranger*, a Fleet Auxiliary tanker, was in tow of the tug *Caswell*, from Devonport to Cardiff, when, during the afternoon of 17 November 1962 in a force eight gale from the northeast, she broke adrift and went on the rocks half a mile south of Longpeak. Distress signals from the tug were relayed to secretaries of both the Appledore and Clovelly lifeboats and both boats were launched, but only the more powerful Appledore could weather the seas around the point, where she began to search for the wreck close inshore. Sleet and driving rain reduced visibility to a few yards, so that the lifeboat crew went past the wreck without sighting it and continued to search right down to Knap Head. Here they met up with the destroyer HMS *Agincourt*, which had been sent by the navy from Milford Haven to assist, and followed the warship back north as her searchlight probed every crevice of the coast. An hour later they found the *Green Ranger* and the lifeboat went alongside, but failed to attract the attention of the seven-man steaming crew aboard, who were below decks at the time. It was an extremely hazardous position for the lifeboat, in danger of being either smashed against the wreck or on the rocks with every wave, yet Coxswain Cann held his boat in this position for fifteen minutes, with a grappling hook aboard the tanker and his searchlight shining on her superstructure. Prudently, he then slipped the line and stood out to sea, to hear three hours later, over the lifeboat's radio, that all the tanker's crew were safe ashore. Mr Cann rightly received the silver medal of the RNLI,

Page 187: (above) Stranded on the Morte Stone on 16 September 1936, the Barnstaple ketch *Dido C* was refloated undamaged; (below) the ketch *Arabella* on Brittons Rock, Ilfracombe, 2 October 1895

Page 188: The brig
A.C.L. under repair at
Ilfracombe after strand-
ing on Woolacombe
Sands, Morte Bay

while the Hartland LSA crew were awarded the Ministry of Transport's shield for the most distinguished rescue of 1962–3, having clambered down the cliff face in appalling conditions in order to get within 120yd of the wreck. The *Green Ranger* broke in two amidships soon afterwards and was lost, parts of the wreck still showing at low water (Picture, p 158).

The last wreck in this chapter had much in common with earlier incidents, since the first knowledge of the disaster was the appearance of two French seamen in the doorway of Elmscott farm at 7 am on 16 March 1969. And much the same scene was being enacted at South Hole Farm, one mile away, where two more survivors were calling a Mr Gifford from his bed. It transpired they were four of the five survivors out of a crew of seven from the Lorient trawler *Goliath*, which lay on her starboard side a short distance from the foot of the 500ft high cliffs at Sandor, less than half a mile from where the *Green Ranger* had been wrecked. Her helmsman was steering the ordered course of 165° when she struck, but in the dark the crew had no idea as to where they were. The four men who had appeared at the two farms had, in fact, scaled the almost sheer cliffs in bare feet, scrambling over razor sharp granite outcrops and thick brambles to reach the top. After the trawler had gone ashore, her crew of six left in the ship's dinghy, an inflatable liferaft type, but were thrown out, two of the men drowning in their attempt to reach the rocks. Only twenty-four hours after going ashore, the trawler's stern broke off and she very soon went completely to pieces, but even the steep cliffs did not deter a number of people from going down to the site to recover a souvenir or to take photographs (Picture, p 160). Her captain, who stayed aboard when the rest of the crew left, was later rescued by Mr Gifford and his two sons, but by this time the *Goliath* was high and dry.

L

WESTWARD HO! TO SOMERSET

'The John and Lilley came ashore
To feed the hungry and cloathe the poor'

The north Devon ports of Barnstaple, Bideford and Appledore, all of which centre on the rivers Taw and Torridge, have historic connections with the sea and ships stretching back to the beginnings of recorded history. Since time immemorial, the high cliffs that run almost unbroken from Hartland to the Somerset border have offered shelter from the prevailing wind. Vessels leaving the Severn Sea, later referred to as the North Channel and today as the Bristol Channel, found Barnstaple or Bideford Bay a safe and welcome anchorage, and in consequence brought about the growth of these ports. Barnstaple in particular, whose chief trade was once wool from Spain coupled with a local textile industry, enjoyed a prominent position until incessant wars brought about its collapse in the eighteenth century. In the same way, many private fortunes were made at Bideford from Virginian tobacco and Newfoundland fish, leading later to the development of a booming emigrant trade with North America. Eventually, silting of the rivers and creeks restricted the size of vessels using the ports and Appledore came into its own with coasting traffic, handling vast quantities of culm and limestone.

Leyland, in his chronicles, dismissed Appledore as being, '. . . a smaul thing at ebbe of water. The Haven entry is barrid with Sande and the enterie into it is daungerous',[1] a condition which remains to this day. His opinion of Bideford and Barnstaple was not much better, yet it was not many years after his visit, according to tradition, that a Bideford ship fought and beat a galleon of the Spanish Armada, bringing it back to the port as a prize. When England was threatened by Spain in 1588, Bideford was ordered to provide six ships for the defence of the realm, three of which, the *Victory*, *Bullett*, and *Bulldog*, were retained locally for protection of the north Devon coast. On 22 June the *Victory* of 250 tons, carrying a crew of sixty-five and armed with twenty-five guns, put out to intercept an enemy ship at loose in the Channel. They met up some twenty miles west of Bideford and fought a gun battle for the best part of twelve hours, then parted company and drifted eastward. Next day they met again and fought to a standstill, the *Victory* firing a final, double-shotted broadside that caused the Spaniards to strike their colours and surrender.[2] The Spanish ship's name is quoted as being the *San Juan*, Capt Don Pedro Valvez, and the town still boasts an iron sea chest and several iron cannon said to have come from the prize, but the authenticity of the incident is in question. Certainly, standard reference books relating to the Armada mention ships in the fleet of this or a similar name, but there is no mention to be found of a *San Juan* being captured, lost in the Bristol Channel, or unaccounted for in the final reckoning. It is, however, possible that she was one of the many merchant vessels which accompanied the fleet from Spain and, being relatively insignificant, went unrecorded.

As is so often the case, there are few early references to shipwreck in this area, though there is evidence of its extent and, inevitably, the volume of shipping in and out of such a treacherous estuary must have led to losses. A customs collector at Bideford in 1852, at a time when the port required twenty-six such officials to conduct its business, listed seventy-five ships which had been wrecked locally over a period of forty years, and in 1858 an Appledore man stated that,[3] 'sixty-two wrecks had taken place locally in the previous fifty-nine years'. The earliest recorded wreck in the vicinity dates back to the time of Gytha, wife of Earl Godwin and mother of King Harald. She attributed her husband's delivery from a shipwreck near Hartland to the agency of St Nectan, and as a mark of appreciation founded a collegiate church at Stoke. Another example was a vessel from Flushing, which was driven ashore and wrecked at Appledore early in 1627. Of English origin, ship and crew had been captured by the Spanish some six months before and had remained in the service of the French, the seamen then making their escape and sailing back to England. Sir John Drake's men took possession of the goods cast ashore from the wreck, but a gentleman by the name of Kift, the Admiralty judge, ordered them to be restored to the owners, whereupon Drake complained to the king and wished that Kift should be dismissed.[4]

The earliest authenticated wreck on the 'bar' at Bideford was that of the *Johannah & Mary* of Bristol, which stranded and was smashed to pieces with the loss of all hands on 28 November 1735. Similarly the *Salisbury*, carrying rum and sugar from Jamaica, was lost in March 1749 in Barum Bay at the back of Northam Burrows, an area described in documents of the time as being 'on Mr Benson's manor'. More detailed information about wrecks is to be found in Customs deposition books, and that for the loss of the *Sally* of Bristol on 15 September 1769 states;

> ... at two of the clock next morning, it came cloudy and thick and squally weather for some time. Soon afterwards, there was so little wind, the master could have no command of the ship, and he imagined further to the eastward than he really was, on which he sounded six or seven fathoms of water, and let go his best bower. She still driving till at last she struck aft, and came abroard side to, upon which this deponent and the rest of the crew took to their boat to save their lives, and got on shore at a place called Burroughs, in the parish of Northam.

There followed, on 12 December 1770, the wreck of the snow *Juba*, another Bristol-owned vessel. She quickly went to pieces and her crew drowned, leaving, to quote the Customs record book, 'a cask of palm oil, with a few elephant's teeth, were taken up and put under the care of the Riding Officer'. One year later, in October, there were two wrecks on the same day, the brigantine *Diana*, from Boston with timber, lost on Pickwell sands, and the Barnstaple-owned *Cato*, also carrying wood, on Saunton sands. It was also about this time that a large Dutch East Indiaman went ashore at Westward Ho! and was wrecked. At irregular intervals, the timbers of a ship uncover on the beach there so that the complete outline of the vessel can be traced, in much the same manner as the *Amsterdam* at Bexhill, near Hastings, but the wreck as yet remains unidentified. Until it was demolished in 1952, an interesting structure connected with wreck was the stone tower known as Chanter's Folly. It was erected in 1800 by a Bideford merchant named Chanter to afford a vantage point from which to watch for the return of the various ships in which he had a financial interest. On the very first occasion he used it, he saw his son's ship wrecked on the bar. In his anguish, he ordered that the tower was never to be used again, and it subsequently fell into ruin.

Despite an obvious need for a lifeboat at Appledore, by the early 1800s the only assistance available from the shore in the event of shipwreck was the Manby rocket apparatus. 'Scarcely a year has elapsed without a shipwreck having taken place within the bay', wrote the Barnstaple Collector of Customs, in 1815, and already local businessmen were talking of subscribing towards a professional life-saving boat and crew, but the project received little support. Then, on 2 October 1821, the Fowey-registered schooner *Bee* fell victim to the estuary, the remains of another vessel, still unidentified, were found ashore on Saunton sands, and Appledore got its first lifeboat. This was the one ton, four-oared *Volunteer*, which arrived towards the end of February 1825 and was installed in a barn near the old King's Watch House. She performed no useful service until 11 September 1829, when she made two trips to the south tail of the bar in appalling conditions during a north-west gale to save all twelve crew and passengers from the Bristol packet sloop *Daniel*. The fact that the Royal National Institute for the Preservation of Life from Shipwreck rewarded three of the lifeboatmen with silver medals, and the others with money, speaks for itself. But even the *Volunteer* was unable to save the lives of the three local men aboard the sloop *Betsey*, which capsized on the bar on 3 March 1831. A contemporary newspaper account states, 'A melancholy accident occurred in Barnstaple Bay on Thursday, when the sloop *Betsey*, Charles Lake master, on her return from Wales with coal, in endeavouring to cross the bar, capsized, and the master, his brother, and a man named Shaddick, all unfortunately perished. The hull of the vessel was driven in at Appledore the succeeding tide.'

As a direct result of this tragedy, the local businessmen formed themselves into the North Devon Humane Society, which set about the provision of another lifeboat and a larger boathouse nearer the sea. As a result, a second lifeboat, the *Assistance*, arrived on 27 December 1831 and was not idle for long, being called out on 6 March 1833 to save the lives of nine men who had been working on the hull of the schooner *Delabole*, blown ashore and wrecked at Saunton sands on 20 February that same year. This wreck had been sold to two Braunton men who had engaged labourers to discharge her coal cargo and it was they who were in danger when a northerly gale sprang up. Some seven months later the *Assistance* was called out again, this time to investigate a report that a brig had foundered off Northam on 24 November. She proved to be the *Mary Ann* of Exeter, whose crew had drowned long before the lifeboat arrived, so that it was obliged to return empty-handed. Some hours later, when movements in the brig's rigging suggested that someone had managed to get back on board, the lifeboat went out for a second time, manned by a fresh crew. The movements seen from the shore proved, however, to be a piece of flapping canvas, and it was while this was being examined at close quarters that a huge wave caught the coxswain unawares and the *Assistance* capsized. All but three of her crew swam clear, but these three, rather foolishly perhaps, had lashed themselves to their thwarts and two of them were drowned. The third man managed to keep his head above water in the upturned boat and was, providentially, still alive when the boat washed ashore. Less than a month later both boats were out again, this time to the Liverpool ship *Elizabeth*, from Calcutta, which stranded near Westward Ho! on 17 December.

For the next two years things were very quiet, then in 1836 three incidents took place, one of which very nearly brought about a second lifeboat disaster. The sloop *Lovely Peggy* of Cardigan got on the bar on 16 January, her crew being saved by the *Volunteer*, after which the same lifeboat rescued eight men from the Irish brig *Erato* on the 30th. It was the Plymouth schooner *Henrietta* that rolled right over on top of the lifeboat, after it had gone to her assistance on 29 November. Miraculously,

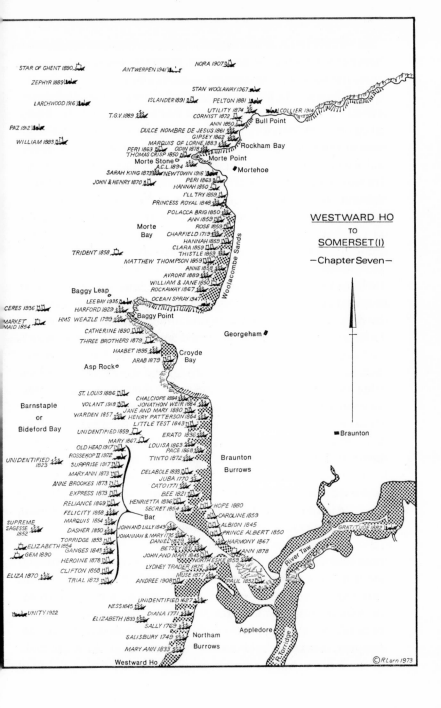

STAR OF GHENT 1890

ZEPHYR 1889

LARCHWOOD 1916

PAZ 1912

WILLIAM 1883

ANTWERPEN 1941

NORA 1907

STAN WOOLAWAY 1967

ISLANDER 1891

PELTON 1881

T.G.V. 1889

UTILITY 1874

COLLIER 1914

CORNIST 1872

Bull Point

ANN 1850

DULCE NOMBRE DE JESUS 1861

GIPSEY 1862

MARQUIS OF LORNE 1883

Rockham Bay

PERI 1863

ODIN 1878

THOMAS CRISP 1850

Morte Point

Morte Stone

A.C.L. 1894

Mortehoe

SARAH KING 1873

NEWTOWN 1916

PERI 1863

JOHN & HENRY 1870

HANNAH 1850

I'LL TRY 1859

PRINCESS ROYAL 1848

POLACCA BRIG 1850

Morte
Bay

ANN 1859

ROSE 1859

CHARFIELD 1719

HANNAH 1859

CLARA 1859

TRIDENT 1858

THISTLE 1859

MATTHEW THOMPSON 1859

Woolacombe Sands

ANNE 1858

AVRORE 1889

WILLIAM & JANE 1850

ROCKAWAY 1867

Baggy Leap

LEE BAY 1935

OCEAN SPRAY 1947

CERES 1936

HARFORD 1829

HMS WEAZLE 1799

Baggy Point

MARKET
MAID 1854

CATHERINE 1890

Georgeham

THREE BROTHERS 1879

HAABET 1895

Croyde
Bay

ARAB 1879

Asp Rock

WESTWARD HO
TO
SOMERSET (I)
—Chapter Seven—

Barnstaple
or
Bideford Bay

ST. LOUIS 1886

CHALCIOPE 1884

VOLANT 1918

JONATHON WEIR 1884

WARDEN 1857

JANE AND MARY 1880

HENRY PATTERSON 1864

LITTLE TEST 1843

UNIDENTIFIED 1859

ERATO 1836

MARY 1867

LOUISA 1863

OLD HEAD 1917

PACE 1868

ROSSEKOP II 1972

Braunton

UNIDENTIFIED
1823

SURPRISE 1917

TINTO 1872

Burrows

MARY ANN 1873

DELABOLE 1833

ANNE BROOKES 1873

JUBA 1770

EXPRESS 1873

CATO 1771

RELIANCE 1869

BEE 1821

FELICITY 1858

HENRIETTA 1836

HOPE 1880

SECRET 1854

MARQUIS 1854

CAROLINE 1859

SUPREME
SAGESSE
1852

DASHER 1850

JOHN AND LILLY 1843

ALBION 1845

JOHANNAH & MARY 1735

PRINCE ALBERT 1850

TORRIDGE 1853

DANIEL 1823

HARMONY 1867

ELIZABETH 1854

GANGES 1843

BETSEY 1851

ANN 1878

GEM 1890

HEROINE 1878

JOHN AND MARY 1845

NORTH ESK 1859

ELIZA 1870

CLIFTON 1858

LYDNEY TRADER 1878

River Taw

TRIAL 1873

MUSE 1877

ANDREE 1908

PAUL 1852

UNIDENTIFIED 1627

UNITY 1922

NESS 1845

DIANA 1771

ELIZABETH 1833

SALLY 1769

Appledore

SALISBURY 1749

Northam

MARY ANN 1833

Burrows

Westward Ho

Braunton

GRATITUDE 1882

R. Torridge

© R Larn 1973

both vessels righted themselves, the lifeboat suffering only a few broken oars, and all eleven men aboard the schooner were rescued.

A long series of furious gales, which came to a climax between 14–16 January 1843, brought about another series of wreck incidents, one of which, the *John & Lilley*, prompted a local man to compose the couplet at the beginning of this chapter. A barque with the regal name of *Albert Edward, Prince of Wales*, carrying soap, candles, and other general cargo, had already been stranded on Northam Burrows and well looted on the night that the West African trading vessel *John & Lilley*, of Liverpool, was wrecked near Saunton, at the northern end of Braunton Burrows. For eleven days her crew had battled against the elements, being blown from the north coast of Cornwall across the Bristol Channel to south Wales, then back to Devon, where finally they lost their rudder and went ashore. Capt Towns and his crew of twenty-five, the majority of whom were by now very drunk, were saved, but the same cannot be said of her valuable cargo. Bound for Africa, the *John & Lilley* carried cotton goods, domestic pots and pans, muskets, gunpowder, foodstuffs, and other luxuries which the locals were not slow to appreciate. Not only did she 'feed the hungry and cloathe the poor', but she also put a great deal of money into the pockets of the local gentry. Several of them, charged with stealing from the wreck, were put on bail for £200 pending trial, and items of cargo were even found hidden in the vault beneath the pulpit of the Baptist church at Appledore.

It was on 14 February 1845 that the Bideford-owned *John & Mary* was wrecked, and two days before Christmas of the same year the barque *Ness*, carrying rum for her home port of Bristol, and the Dartmouth schooner *Albion* were lost on the coast. The latter went to pieces on North Tail before either lifeboat could reach her, and six seamen drowned as a result. This particular incident, all too familiar at the time, made it perfectly obvious that the existing position of the lifeboats, as well as the boats themselves, were inadequate to meet the ever growing number of incidents. Arrangements were, therefore, made for the old six-oared *Assistance* to be moved to a new site on the north bank of the estuary, but the new boathouse was not completed until the summer of 1848 and the *Assistance*, strangely enough, was never used from this site, being replaced by the *Dolphin* in 1857. Earlier that year, yet a third lifeboat, the *Petrel*, was added to the growing fleet and stationed on the south bank, near Appledore. On 29 February 1848 she went out on her first service, to help the schooner *Bideford*, but became swamped and was forced to return empty-handed. Although it must have been obvious that there was something drastically wrong with the new boat, she was put back in her boathouse without any sort of trial or investigation to evaluate her seaworthiness and remained there for two years before being called out again. This time it was to assist the crew of the brigantine *Dasher* of St Ives, which stranded on the bar on 23 March 1850 during a north-westerly gale. Predictably, the *Petrel* filled with water before she had gone half way to the wreck, and had it not been for the timely intervention of the *Volunteer* all five of the brigantine's crew might have been lost; as it was, John Ninnes, the cabin boy, was drowned.

By 1856, with the original *Volunteer* replaced by a newer boat named *Mermaid*, the area was well prepared for the spate of wrecks that were to follow, despite the fact that the useless *Petrel* continued to be retained until 1861. On 8 October 1857 the American ship *Warden* was stranded and broken up in the vicinity of Baggy Point, seven of her crew losing their lives; the *Felicity* of Milford was wrecked on the bar on 18 December 1858, to be followed by the Fowey-owned schooner *Caroline* on 11 March 1859 and another schooner, the *Clifton*, the next day. A night rescue by Appledore men in the two lifeboats saved six lives from among the crew of the brig *North Eske* on 2 November 1859, but they were unable to reach the *Meridian* of Fowey on 15 November 1864 and she was lost with all hands. While no two wreck incidents are ever exactly alike, most of those that followed during the 1860s and '70s were almost pure repetitions of those already described. These include the brig *Altivo* on 23 February 1866; the *Wool Packet* on 21 September 1866; the smack *Mary* on 5 January 1867; the *Harmony* on 29 March 1867; the barque *Pace* on 28 December 1868 and, the day following, another barque, the *Leopard*, both of which resulted in epic lifeboat rescues. In ballast for Newport, the Bideford-owned *Mary* was running up Channel at night when another vessel was sighted dead ahead. Capt Glover called out to her 'Port your helm!' and did the same himself, but the other vessel went to starboard and the two ships collided. Locked together by a fouled anchor, they drifted for over a mile, during which time Glover attempted to ascertain the name of the other vessel but her crew refused to tell him. After being ordered back aboard the sinking smack, the Bideford men were abandoned to their fate but, fortunately for them, they were taken in tow by the schooner *Polacco* and managed to reach Saunton sands, where the *Mary* went to pieces.

So the incidents continued; the schooner *Reliance*, lost with all her crew on 12 September 1869; the brigantine *Nigretta* on 15 November 1871; the barque *Tinto* on 8 December 1872; the *Express*, *Anne Brooks* and *Mary Ann*, all on 4 April 1873, and the brigantine *Spec* on 24 December of the same year. Of these, the Cardiff-owned *Tinto* was perhaps the most tragic incident as, long before the crew of the lifeboats were aware of her stranding on the west side of Down End, she had broken up with the loss of eight lives. In addition to her crew of sixteen, she carried eleven survivors from another vessel which had foundered in the Atlantic, four of whom were amongst the dead.

Typical of the many wrecks which do not appear in the lifeboat records was that of the 84 ton, wooden brigantine *Muse*. Carrying pitch from Gloucester to St Nazaire, with a crew of five, she got into the bay on 20 February 1877 and was unable to beat clear. At 4.30 am, with the wind blowing a full gale from the north-west, she went ashore and within three hours nothing remained but a few planks. There was only one survivor, Charles Le Croix, who managed to get ashore on a piece of wreckage. During 1880, a similar incident concerned the Barnstaple schooner *Hope*, Vaggers master, which went onto Braunton sands on 24 November and deserves special mention as she was an incredible 102 years old when wrecked. Surprisingly, there had been no steamer incidents until 1881, when there were two within ten months. The first was the British collier *Ranee*, stranded on Saunton sands on 7 October during hazy weather. Less than nine months old at the time, the 617 ton ship was refloated and saved, whereas the second was completely destroyed by fire. This was the 14 ton, wooden-hulled paddle steamer *Gratitude*, which was lying alongside Westacott's shipbuilding yard, close to Barnstaple bridge. It was a Sergeant Eddy of the local police who first spotted the fire and roused her crew during the early hours of 2 July 1882. Every effort was made to extinguish the flames, but she was completely gutted and sank after burning to the waterline.

A great many of the sailing vessels which met with disaster on this stretch of coast had, in fact, reached the open Atlantic outward bound, only to encounter some accident or unfavourable wind which forced them back. Typical of these was the brigantine *Jonathon Weir* of Monckton NB which left Newport for Cuba with coal and ran into a series of gales off the Scillies on 23 January 1884. Several huge seas broke over her deck, causing the backstays of both fore and main masts to part, so that all sail had to be taken in. Drifting helplessly before the wind, she was blown into the bay, then onto Saunton sands near Down End, and finally wrecked. Fortunately her crew of eight, plus one passenger and a stowaway, remained aboard until low water, when they were able to scramble to safety. Another brigantine, the *Chalciope* of Fleetwood, inward bound from Corunna with pitwood, was forced by bad weather to heave-to near the Bishop Rock on 7 December of the same year. Following a moderation of the gale, she was squared away on a course of north-east and at 4 pm, with Hartland Point just visible on the starboard bow, Capt Whiteside ordered an alteration to east-north-east, then went below for a well-earned rest. On returning to the upper deck an hour and a half later he found the helmsman steering a completely different course to the one ordered and the coast dead ahead, less than half a mile distant. Unable to save the vessel in the short time available, the captain ran her ashore and her crew took to the rigging to await the arrival of the lifeboat which rescued three seamen, the remaining five walking ashore at low tide.

Yet one more loss took place in 1884, that of the ketch *Strathisla* of Barnstaple, which left Kinsale for Newport in ballast on 23 September. While attempting to enter the Taw in fog without a pilot, she struck on the north ridge. The impact brought down the main gaff, which smashed the steering wheel, and this damage, additional to a bad leak and a choked bilge pump, were sufficient excuse for the crew to abandon ship. She drifted away on the rising tide in a derelict condition, striking first the rocks east of the lighthouse, then Millstone Point, where several locals boarded her and took charge. A prolonged legal battle ensued when they claimed salvage, since the master of the *Strathisla* refused to admit that she had been abandoned.

A marked decline in the number of wreck incidents is apparent for the period 1885 to 1900, with only four vessels lost in the vicinity. Of these, the schooner *St Louis*, stranded on 12 December 1886 with five of her crew drowned, was the only wreck close to Appledore. A Norwegian brig showing distress signals was sighted off Clovelly on 4 October 1895 and the lifeboat put out and rescued her crew of ten, but the ship herself, the *Haabet*, drifted right across to Croyde Bay before being stranded on the beach. Since then, this particular part of Bideford Bay has seen less than a dozen ships lost, amongst which were the brigantine *Charles P. Knight*, at Westward Ho! on 4 October 1900; the *Flimby*, also at Westward Ho! on 11 September 1903, and the eighteen-year-old French ketch *Andree*, near the bar on 21 April 1908. Carrying coal, the *Andree* struck some submerged wreckage two miles south of the bell buoy, so that she had to be put ashore, in what proved to be a vain attempt to save her. Two schooners, the *Surprise* and the *Volant* were other victims of the bar during World War I, and the obsolete coastal destroyer HMS *Sandfly* got on Pebble Ridge, at Westward Ho! on 7 October 1920, whilst being towed to a breaker's yard at Milford Haven. Two years later the *Unity*, a steam trawler, foundered about 500yd offshore and the wreck had to be dispersed by explosives as it had become a navigational hazard.

There then followed the disgraceful business of the *Elsa Kuehlke*, which revived some traditional wrecking instincts locally. It was Sunday, 24 October 1926, when this German schooner appeared off Westward Ho! with a bad leak and carrying a cargo of clay from Fremmington. Her captain decided to beach her, but she was badly holed in the attempt and became a total loss. Hundreds of scavengers invaded the wreck, taking anything of value, and a West Country newspaper reported, '. . . they behaved in the most disgraceful manner, pillaging all they could lay their hands on, even personal photographs'. Eventually someone set fire to her remains, which put an end to any further theft, but pieces of her still remain beneath the cliffs on the Cornborough side of the beach. The last wreck here to date was the 114 ton motor fishing vessel *Rossekop II*, which went to pieces on Airy Point at 9.45 pm on 4 November 1972.

At the north-east corner of Barnstaple Bay two prominent headlands, Baggy Point and Morte Point, along with the infamous Morte, or Death Stone, form the pincers of a giant trap. In the days of sail it was feared by shipmasters even more than Hartland Point, and vessels at anchor in the bay maintained a constant watch in case the wind changed, for this stretch of coast is particularly vulnerable to gales which thunder in from the west or north. Without question, dozens of sixteenth- and seventeenth-century wrecks took place here, but only details of the snow *Charfield*, stranded on Woolacombe sands in June 1719, have been passed down to the present day. The only eighteenth-century wreck recorded in great detail was, in fact, the most tragic on the entire north Devon coast. The vessel was the naval sloop o' war HMS *Weazle*, which sank near Baggy Point on 12 February 1799 during a furious north-north-west gale. It is best described by John James of Bideford, who, five days after the event, wrote this in a letter to a friend:

I heard on Wednesday last, a funeral sermon for 106 persons unfortunately lost in the *Weazle* on Sunday night. She was in the bay that afternoon, and as people went to church, the seafaring men felt some anxiety, if the wind should shift a point and blow, which it did. They made every effort to get out to sea, and in vain kept firing signals of distress. It is supposed she got round Baggy Point and struck upon Morte rocks; that fine ship perished and as yet only one body has been taken up, but many are watching from opposite the beach, both yesterday and today, and are fishing up fragments of the wreck. We have since heard the wreck is visible at low water, this side of Baggy Point. A sloop that was in distress in the bay on Monday or Tuesday has also gone down, her fate is uncertain. It is expected many bodies will float and be driven on shore the coming spring.[5]

There was one woman among the 106 dead, a memorial to whom still exists at Northam church, although a great many were laid to rest at Braunton, and a gravestone to William Kidman, one of the victims, survives at Georgham. Quite recently, the *Weazle*'s remaining iron cannon and other items on the seabed were located by a local diving club, whose members, after commendable efforts, landed one of the guns.

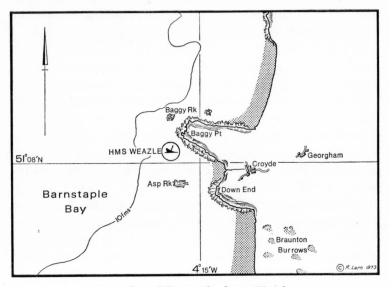

Location of the wreck of HMS *Weazle*

A notable feature of shipwrecks in this corner of Devon was the unusually heavy loss of life. Few ships went ashore here with any survivors, and by far the greater number were lost with all hands. A contributory factor was the complete absence of local boats in Morte Bay, and although a Manby twenty-four pound mortar apparatus was installed in 1823, it proved too unwieldy and heavy to transport over rough ground. A newer, lightweight rocket apparatus was introduced in the 1850s and this was to prove most useful.

The Swansea brigantine *Harford*, loaded with copper ore for south Wales, was one of the unlucky vessels to strike Baggy Point and was lost with all six of her crew on 26 August 1829, but some were not so unfortunate and the *Princess Royal* of London, wrecked off Baggy Point on the last day of March 1848, lost no one. She is worth mention, since her cargo of sugar from Mauritius attracted a great many wreckers to Barricane Cove, where she was stripped bare before the authorities could intervene. It was the Morte Stone that claimed the next victim, the Bristol schooner *Thomas Crisp*, on 18 January 1850, after she had left Bristol for Barbados with a general cargo. Fog and gale-force winds in the Channel caused her master, Francis Farr, to put about for Penarth Roads, but with the lookouts unable to see an inch beyond their own jib-boom, she went ashore on the Devon coast. The jollyboat was prepared for launching, but before it could be put over the side a huge wave washed boat and crew overboard. All but her captain, who drowned, managed to scramble back aboard the boat. Bailing furiously with seaboots and sou'westers, they managed to remain afloat until rescued by the packet paddle-steamer *Brilliant*, which landed them at Hayle.

The 1850s saw a total of fifteen wrecks here, the most tragic period being 24–26 October 1859, known better perhaps as the *Royal Charter* gale and the worst on record in the British Isles. During its first day, 195 wrecks occurred around the country, but it was the third day, the 26th, that saw seven vessels lost in Morte Bay. The first to go down was a forty-year-old schooner, *Ann*, lost with all seven of her crew; she was followed shortly afterwards by the *Rose*, another schooner, with only one survivor; the *Hannah*, again with only one saved, and the pilot cutter *I'll Try*, from which only two were saved. The brigantine *Thistle* went ashore and her entire crew managed to save themselves but not one person survived from the schooners *Clara* and *Matthew Thompson*.

Rockham Bay, to the north of Morte Point, has been the grave for many a fine ship, and it was here that the brig *Dulce Nombre de Jesus* met her end on New Year's Day 1861, with five crew members drowned. The brigantine *Gipsey* followed, on the Slipper Rock in 1862; the *Peri*, a two-masted schooner in 1863;

the barque *Janvrin* in 1864; the barque *Rockway* in 1867; the *Dart* in 1869; and the *Mary Matthews* on 17 March 1870. Storm and fog brought about the majority of these losses, but fire and collision continued to take its annual toll, with incidents such as the *Sarah King*. Late in the evening of 25 January 1873, the deck officer of the Hayle packet steamer *Bride* sighted a green light on his starboard bow, which appeared to follow him round when he made a change of course. Four minutes later the packet sliced into the side of the brigantine *Sarah King* of London, when close to Morte Point. So quickly did the sailing vessel fill and sink that the fourteen crew and three passengers aboard had no alternative but to leap overboard, but all were rescued and landed at Ilfracombe. Had bad weather not delayed the 248 ton brig *Odin*, so that she missed the tide at Llanelly and was unable to enter port, she would not have ended her days on the north face of the Morte Stone during October 1878. Rather than risk his ship, with its cargo of cut timber, at anchor off the port, her master stood to the south, away from the Welsh coast, but seemingly in ignorance of the confines of the Bristol Channel, put his ship onto the rocks in the darkness. Valued at £1,050, the vessel became a total loss and both ship and cargo provided many a Devon household with wood that day.

It was the 1880s before the first steamship was lost hereabouts, this being the *Pelton* on 26 March 1881. Then, as if to confirm the old superstition that such events always happen in threes, the steamer *Uzzia* went ashore in 1882, and the *Lynx* the following year. The *Pelton*, a Newcastle-registered ship of 816 tons gross, laden with coal for Havre, foundered near Bull Point with the loss of sixteen of her seventeen crew, a particularly tragic outcome and fortunately not repeated in either of the other steamship incidents. Thomas Hogg, a seaman, was the sole survivor from the *Pelton*, and stated in his deposition that all had gone well until they were off the Scillies. A severe gale then caused the ship to assume a list to port, and when she began to take water into the hold, seven of the crew elected to leave the ship in a lifeboat, Hogg among them. They got clear in the starboard boat and saw the steamer founder shortly afterwards. For five hours they

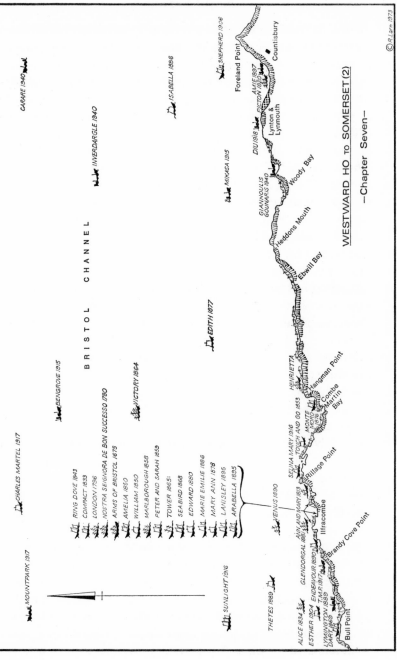

WESTWARD HO TO SOMERSET (2)

—Chapter Seven—

© R.Larn 1973

M

BRISTOL CHANNEL

CARARE 1940

MOUNTPARK 1917

CHARLES MARTEL 1917

BENGROVE 1915

INVERDARGLE 1940

ISABELLA 1886

EDITH 1877

VICTORY 1864

RING DOVE 1843
COMPACT 1833
LONDON 1796
NOSTRA SEIGNORA DE BON SUCCESSO 1780
ARMS OF BRISTOL 1675
AMELIA 1850
WILLIAM 1850
MARLBOROUGH 1858
PETER AND SARAH 1859
TOWER 1651
SEABIRD 1868
EDWARD 1860
MARIE EMILIE 1886
MARY ANN 1878
LANISLEY 1895
ARABELLA 1895

SUNLIGHT 1916

VENUS 1890

THETES 1889

ALICE 1834
ESTHER 1904
GLENDORGAL 1891
ENDEAVOUR 1890
T.M.P.1917
LYMINGTON 1889
DART 1669

Bull Point

Brandy Cove Point

Ilfracombe

Rillage Point

ANN AND MARY 1813

SELINA MARY 1916
TOUCH AND GO 1853

MONTE MORO 1878

Combe Martin
Bay

Hangman Point

HENRIETTA

Ebwill Bay

Heddons Mouth

GIANNOULIS
GOUNARIS 1940

MIKASA 1915

Woody Bay

DIU 1918

Lynton &
Lynmouth

AMIE 1897
PICTON 1882

Foreland Point

SHEPHERD 1906

Countisbury

rowed around, bailing all the time, and in this short period of time five of the men died from exposure, one with his arms around Hogg's neck. The schooner *Ureah* then sighted them and went to their assistance but, in getting close alongside, caused the lifeboat to capsize. The two remaining survivors were thrown into the sea and drowned, only Hogg escaping from beneath the upturned boat.

Although the lifeboat *Grace Woodbury*, previously named the *Jack-a-Jack*, had been installed at Woolacombe in 1871 as a secondary boat for the Ilfracombe station, whose principal boat could not always get round Bull Point to Morte Bay in bad weather, she was only launched to perform a service twice in twenty-nine years! One of these occasions was to the steamer *Lynx*, on 6 March 1883. Carrying coal for Portreath, in Cornwall, the *Lynx* sprang a leak and had to be run ashore at Woolacombe to prevent her foundering. Although the lifeboat was launched, the steamer had been driven so far up the beach that the *Grace Woodbury* was unable to get alongside without going aground herself. At low water the leak was repaired but attempts made to winch her off by means of kedge anchors all failed. Worsening weather conditions opened up other leaks and it began to look as if the *Lynx* was finished, until the lifeboatmen set to work, refloated her, and got her safely into Appledore.

Of the many ships stranded at Baggy Point, the largest and certainly the most welcome so far as the locals were concerned, since it took place in the depths of a particularly hard winter, was the iron, full-rigged ship *Penthesilea* on 19 January 1890. She went ashore during a west-south-west hurricane, leaving what one inhabitant described as 'a prodigious amount of coal on the beach, free for the asking', which naturally provided fuel for many a local hearth. Two years later hopes ran high that a cargo of pitprops was also in the offing, since the *Maria* of Gloucester, on passage from Cork to Llanelly, went ashore at midnight on 22 April 1892. Her crew reached Ilfracombe in their own boat, but on returning to the Morte area overland next day in the hope of salvaging personal effects, found that the vessel had refloated herself and drifted out to sea, never to be heard of again. From then on, the majority of wrecks, as one would expect, were steamships, starting with the *Paz* of Montevideo, which collided with another Uruguay-registered steamer, the *Olavarria*, seven miles west of Bull Point on 25 May 1912. The *Paz*, built by Priestman of Sunderland as the *Sir Richard Grenville*, foundered as a result, but without loss of life.

Although the remains of wreck are not usually visible for long on the coast of Devon and Cornwall, the boiler and some iron frames of the Bristol-owned steamer *Collier* can still be seen, despite the fact she stranded and broke up on 28 January 1914. One of the smallest steamers to be lost on the Devon coast, the 114 ton net *Collier*, had a remarkable career which began at the shipyard of J. Reid, Port Glasgow, in 1849, and ended with her being the oldest steamship on *Lloyds' Register* by a long way when she was lost. She served as a cross-Channel packet from Dover for many years and once, despite her small tonnage, went as far afield as Australia before settling down to routine Bristol Channel work. She was on her way to Hayle in ballast and was steaming in dense fog with both captain and mate on deck when they saw the red light of Bull Point, which indicated they were in the dangerous sector. Before they could take avoiding action, the ship went ashore on Rockham beach at dead low water and, as the tide turned, she washed higher up on the beach until she became wedged between two rocks. Capt Dyer of the Morthoe rocket brigade assembled his team and apparatus on the clifftop, but the *Collier* was too far away for them to be of any assistance. In any case their efforts were wasted, since the steamer's crew had already got away in the ship's punt. Under tow from the steamer *Devonia*, the Ilfracombe lifeboat then appeared on the scene and took aboard Capt Wright, Mate Jefferies, Engineer Thompson, two firemen, three able seamen, a dog, a cat, and a pet goldfinch in a cage. During World War I the only casualty due to enemy action close enough inshore to class as a Devon wreck was the Liverpool steamer *Bengrove*, torpedoed and sunk on 7 March 1915, but strandings and collisions still took their toll. A London steamer, the *Newtown*, went ashore on Barricane beach on 7 January 1916; the *Larchwood* sank three miles off

Bull Point on 14 January; the sailing vessel *Sunlight* on 16 November, in a position given as seven miles north-west of Bull Point, and the French dandy *Charles Martel* and the British steamer *Mountpark*, both during 1917.

Without question, the most spectacular wreck photograph taken on this part of the coast was of the wooden ketch *Dido C* of Barnstaple, as she lay perched high and dry on the Morte Stone on 16 September 1936 (Picture, p 187). After stranding in hazy weather, her three-man crew were taken off by the Ilfracombe lifeboat *Rosabella*, since it was feared she would break her back, but at high water, still intact, she was refloated and towed clear. Built at Lysekil, Sweden, in 1921, the *Dido C* continued to work out of the north Devon ports until World War II, when she was sold to a Scottish firm of shipowners. She sank at Ardrossan, on the west coast, following a collision in 1947, but was salvaged and taken to Ireland, where she lay at Kircubbin for about ten years, slowly falling apart from decay. In 1964, tired of her presence, the villagers set her on fire and pushed her out into Kircubbin Bay, part of Strangford Lough, but she drifted ashore to sink on the eastern bank, where her charred timbers still show.

Another interesting wreck took place in 1936, that of the motorised sailing ketch *Ceres*, the oldest vessel registered at Lloyds. She had been built at Salcombe in 1811, four years before the battle of Waterloo, and had served as a munitions carrier throughout the Napoleonic wars. In 1936, with a cargo of slag and a crew of two, she was on passage from Swansea to her home port of Bude, where she was owned by Messrs Petherick & Sons. She sprang a leak on 25 November when off Baggy Point and finally sank 500yd from the point, leaving her topmasts showing above the surface until, soon afterwards, she went to pieces. The last foundering here was that of the 278 ton sand dredger *Stan Woolaway*, which sank a mile offshore on 13 March 1967. She was returning to Barnstaple, full laden, when she developed a list and sank shortly afterwards. Three years later, from amongst the wreckage on the bottom, members of the Ilfracombe and North Devon sub-aqua club recovered the ship's bell, which was returned to its original owners. In appreciation, they, in turn, granted sole ownership and salvage rights of the wreck to the club.

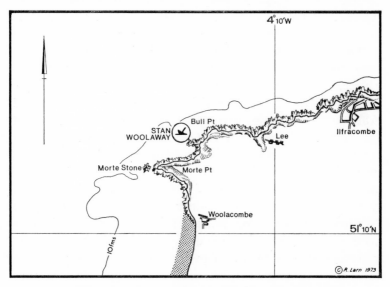

Location of the wreck of the sand-dredger *Stan Woolaway*

From Bull Point, east to Glenthorne, which marks the border with Somerset, lie twenty-three miles of the highest and most formidable cliffs in the whole of Devon. Its general inaccessibility, sparse population, and open countryside, made this stretch of coast popular with the smuggling fraternity and history records a great many seventeenth- and eighteenth-century 'goings on' connected with this activity. West of Watermouth can be found Samson's Bay, named after a notorious smuggler, while place names such as Shipload Bay and Brandy Point all have obvious connections. Chambercombe Farm, inland from Ilfracombe, has, however, a more sinister connection with gentlemen of 'the other trade', the wreckers, if legend is to be believed. It is said that here, very many years ago, a small, sealed room was discovered, in which was found the skeleton of a young woman lying on a bed, and everything covered in thick cobwebs.[6] It was said to be the body of a Spanish girl who had

survived the wreck of some ship lured ashore by the infamous
wreckers of Hele Bay, and that she had been immured after being
stripped of valuable jewellery; but it is not in character for
wreckers of this coast to go to so much trouble when another
corpse on the beach was neither here nor there.

Punctuated with dozens of small headlands and inlets, the
coast here abounds with hazards and represents a formidable
obstacle to shipping, with no haven other than at Ilfracombe.
The Doomsday Book records that in 1086 a small port called
Alfreincombe occupied part of the present-day Ilfracombe, and
tradition has it that Alfred the Great fitted out the harbour as a
royal dockyard and kept a fleet there to oppose the Danes, then
encamped in south Wales. The earliest recorded wreck at Ilfracombe appears to have occurred in 1635, as in the parish church
there is a tomb marked 31 October of that year and bearing the
inscription 'Bryant Tooker and two Frenchmen, parte of a shipps
companie called ye *John*, were drowned at our harbour mouth.'

At some time during the following century, a rich Spanish ship
came ashore during a gale in a cove once outside of the harbour
but now enclosed by the breakwater. Gold and silver coins have
been found there from time to time ever since and a contemporary
report suggests that this wreck was, '. . . a big ship, ashore in
1782, said to have been one of Rodney's prizes, but by others
that she was a Bristol slaver'.[7] Yet another source states, '. . . a
vessel, returning from the West Indies with black prisoners, was
driven ashore at Ilfracombe early in the 19th century, and that for
years coins, both gold and silver, along with jewels, were found
at low water, in the shingle. The vessel was ballasted with yellow
shingle and this can still be seen.'[8] Perhaps these reports all refer
to the transport *London*, carrying British troops and French
prisoners-of-war, lost in Rapparee Cove on 9 October 1796.
Thirty people were drowned in this wreck, sixteen of whom were
local men who had attempted to swim out to her from ashore.
Since the dates of wreck incidents are often grossly distorted, it
should not be overlooked that the incident bears a resemblance
to the loss of the *Arms of Bristol* on 26 March 1675. This particular wreck is well documented and described as: '. . . a very fine

ship of 350 tons, armed with twenty-six guns, from Bristol to Barbadoes, in the West Indies, cast away near Ilfracombe, but forty got to land, some in ship's boats and some driven in on wreck, sixteen persons being drowned. Very little of her cargo has been saved, and very little likelihood of saving much more.'[9]

Of course, there must have been many earlier losses, details of which are regrettably lost, but a reminder exists in the form of the ancient chapel of St Nicholas, on top of Lantern Hill and built around 1320. By the early 1400s, it was an accepted place of pilgrimage, where prayers in thanksgiving for deliverance from shipwreck were offered. Later, the chapel displayed a light for the benefit of shipping, and during its long history has been in turn a place of worship, a lighthouse, a dwelling house, a laundry and a cafe. Unfortunately, no further authenticated incidents of wreck are known till 1780 when, on 2 October, the *Nostra Seignora de Bon Successo* of Lisbon stranded at the harbour mouth and went to pieces. It has been suggested[10] that another vessel, with an almost identical name was lost on the Morte Stone the same year, but if this is so, the coincidence is remarkable, unless she was stranded but got off, only to be lost at Ilfracombe.

Although it is maintained at Ilfracombe that the town's first lifeboat, provided by private subscription, was stationed there in 1828, there is no record of its service, so that it must be assumed that local boatmen rescued the crews of the schooner *Compact* in 1833, the brig *Alice*, near Bull Point in 1834, and the schooner *Ringdove* in January 1843. It was a particularly fierce gale, eventually reaching hurricane force, which wrecked the 54 ton smack *William* of Fowey on 5 January 1850 and, later the same day, the Padstow schooner *Amelia*. Carrying a cargo of iron and coal valued at £130, the *Amelia's* master, Thomas Avery, attempted to enter the harbour at night in fog, but struck a rock and sank. He was severely reprimanded at the Board of Trade enquiry for not having gone up channel and anchored in Penarth Roads to await daybreak. Although a great many similar incidents followed, and are listed in the ship index, the majority were of little or no present-day significance.

It was 1889 when the steamer *Lymington* was lost near Ilfracombe with no survivors, the one and only steamship to be stranded near the port. A public enquiry into the loss opened at Ilfracombe town hall on 8 February, the first witness being William Robins, caretaker of the auxiliary lifeboat at Morthoe. He stated that just before 2 am on Saturday, 2 February, he heard that distress signals had been fired in the vicinity of Bull Point. He informed the coastguards, who set off with their rocket apparatus while he rode to Ilfracombe to tell the lifeboat secretary. On arrival, he found the lifeboat crew already assembled, dressed, and preparing to launch, having been summoned at least an hour previously by maroons fired from Lantern Hill, the news having reached there from Lee, the scene of the wreck. William Barbeay, coxswain of the lifeboat, was the next witness and said that he had been summoned at 9.15 pm the previous day, when a large white light, or flare, had been seen off Lee Bay. He had gone along the coast as far as the Capstone, but had seen nothing other than the normal steaming lights of a vessel some distance offshore.

A messenger arrived at the lifeboat station shortly after Mr Robins' appearance to say that the lifeboat would be useless, and that it was the rocket apparatus that was required. The entire crew had then set off on foot, pushing the heavy rocket cart to the Castle coffee shop, where horses were waiting. Unfortunately, it was 3 am before they reached the village of Lee, and another hour passed before they were on the clifftop overlooking the wreck site, by which time the *Lymington* had gone to pieces and all her crew had drowned. The stern of the wreck was later found near the bathing cove, half a mile from Lee, and the bow section was seen drifting around offshore. At the time of the enquiry, only two bodies had been recovered, those of Edward Miller, her twenty-one year old 2nd engineer, and John Millthorpe, the chief engineer. Millthorpe must have been fated to lose his life in this manner, as less than four weeks previously he had been chief engineer in another steamer that had also been wrecked with a heavy loss of life.

Few wreck incidents have taken place east of Ilfracombe, where

Page 213: The Italian steamer *Carmine Filomena* of Genoa, wrecked on Lundy, 1 July 1937

Page 214: HMS *Montagu*, a 14,000 ton battleship wrecked on Lundy during fog on 29 May 1906. The catwalk allowed salvage crews to board the vessel in all weather conditions

Page 215: (*above*) Salvage men crossing from the island of Lundy to the wreck of the *Montagu* on Shutters Reef, 1906; (*below*) one of the main condensers being removed from the wreck of the *Montagu* by members of the Western Marine Salvage Co

Page 216: Ashore at the 'quarries', Lundy, on 25 March 1929, the Greek steamer *Maria Kyriakides* remained stranded for a year before being re-floated and towed into Ilfracombe

Lynmouth is the last remaining haven in Devon. Although of no size, Lynmouth housed a lifeboat from 1869 to 1944, performing on average one service every three years, which indicates the frequency of incidents. An iron schooner, the *Monte Moro* of South Shields, struck a rock some two miles offshore and had to be beached in Combemartin Bay on 4 August 1876, but the obstruction was more likely to have been floating wreckage than rock. A similar incident caused the Swansea smack *Edith* to founder in a position two miles north-east of Hangman Point in 1877, while the Barnstaple polacca *Henrietta* became a total loss after stranding near Higher Hangman on 2 October 1880.

Although the sailing ship *Forrest Hall* was subsequently saved and hence cannot be classified as any sort of wreck, no record such as this would be complete without reference to what was probably one of the most spectacular and arduous services to date in the history of the Royal National Lifeboat Institution. It began on 12 January 1899, when the lifeboat secretary at Lynmouth, Tom Bevan, received a telegram from the Anchor Hotel, at Porlock Weir, stating that a large sailing ship was in distress in the bay and flying signals requesting assistance. Normally, the Lynmouth lifeboat would have been launched and gone east along the coast, but with a full north-westerly gale blowing, seas were breaking clean over the esplanade and the approach roads were flooded to a depth of 3ft, so that it was out of the question to risk the boat and its crew. No one had even contemplated taking the heavy boat and carriage by road to Porlock before but, with no alternative, it was unanimously agreed they would attempt to get the ten-oared *Louisa* over Countisbury Hill. Unless one has traversed this route, the significance of this decision cannot be fully appreciated, since it represented a journey of twelve miles from sea level up to 1,400ft and back to sea level again, at night in the pouring rain and a full gale, and with only oil lamps for illumination. Even today, with every possible mechanical aid, it would be considered a remarkable achievement.

It was an operation that required the utmost co-operation from everyone in the village and before the lifeboat and carriage, weighing some eight tons, could set off at 7 pm, a gang of men and horses went ahead, measuring the width of the road, demolishing obstructions, and tearing down any banks that might impede the boat's progress. Twenty horses were harnessed together and, assisted by every able-bodied man, woman, and child, they set off up the fearful slope. Their first mishap occurred, fortunately, after they had reached the top of Countisbury, when a wheel fell off the carriage. By the time this had been refitted and everything was ready to proceed, everyone was soaked to the skin and enthusiasm for the task had begun to wane. More than half of the helpers declined to go any further and turned back for Lynmouth, leaving about twenty men to complete the journey. Not long afterwards, they met up with the advance gang who had completely removed a long length of stone wall on the Lynmouth side of Glenthorn White Gate, only to find that the carriage could not get down Ashton Lane. Without hesitation, they removed the boat from its carriage and took it through the narrow section of road on skids, moving it forward 6ft at a time. Meanwhile the bulky carriage was taken through a side gate, across several fields, and back on to the main road further ahead, where it awaited the lifeboat's arrival. From this point on, every- thing was downhill, but it was necessary to employ almost all the men on the drag ropes, or in checking the wheels with giant wedges, as they slipped and skidded down a gradient of one in four. In Porlock itself, finding a cottage was in the way, they knocked down a corner of the building, much to the indignation, at first, of the old lady who lived there. She had never seen a lifeboat before but when told of the ship in distress, she readily helped to remove granite blocks from her own home. With the sea so close, the men hoped that all the obstacles had been over- come, only to find that the seawall at Porlock Weir had been washed away and the road made impassable. So back they all went with the *Louisa*, along the higher road, where a fallen tree was found blocking their path, and had to be cut up before they could proceed.

Eventually, at six o'clock in the morning, they reached the beach, exhausted and utterly soaked. With the *Forrest Hall* still in the bay and her anchors dragging closer and closer to the shore by the minute, they had no alternative but to launch the boat immediately and go to her assistance. They reached the ship, but found there was nothing they could do until daybreak, when it was hoped that the tug which had been towing the *Forrest Hall* when she broke adrift would re-appear. At 7 am the tug, the *Jane Jolliffe* of Liverpool, came into the bay, reconnected her tow, and took the ship to Barry none the worse for her experience. The Lynmouth men, though in an advanced state of exhaustion and in worse condition than the ship's crew, insisted on making the trip and arrived in Barry on the 13th, having eaten nothing and been without sleep for well over twenty-four hours. After a well-earned meal and a rest, they returned to Porlock, from where the lifeboat was towed back to Lynmouth. Ten years later, the *Forrest Hall* was wrecked and lost near Auckland, New Zealand, on 27 February 1909.

CHAPTER EIGHT

LUNDY ISLAND

In the year 1786 the merchants of Bristol, claiming that Lundy took such a 'great toll of shipping', offered to build, equip and maintain a lighthouse on the island entirely at their own expense. In retrospect, this reference to a great many wrecks was undoubtedly an exaggeration, since even during the second half of the nineteenth century, the peak years for shipping losses around the United Kingdom, an average of less than one vessel a year was lost on Lundy and the toll during the 1700s is most unlikely to have been greater.

Situated twelve miles north-west of Hartland Point and the north Devon coast, this lonely, three-mile-long granite platform of volcanic origin lies at the entrance to the Bristol Channel, directly in the path of what was once a major shipping route to the coal ports of south Wales and, of course, Bristol itself. Considering the vast numbers of ships that have passed this way during the last two centuries alone, it is remarkable that so few losses have occurred on the island. Chanter estimated a million annual passings and, if this should seem an exaggeration, he goes on to say that 300 ships were within sight of Lundy at one time, and that 170 others of good size were at anchor in Lundy Roads.[1]

Described appropriately as 'a pocket kingdom, over which the owner has complete jurisdiction',[2] Lundy has a recorded history going back to the year 1199 and the reign of King John, since when its ownership has changed hands many times. With no natural resources other than stone, the island had precious little to offer prospective settlers and in the old days must have been a fearful place indeed. Storm-bound in winter for days, even weeks at a time, and with only one landing place, Lundy is a natural stronghold and as such became a centre for pirates and smugglers

220

alike, as well as being a constant thorn in the side of the authorities. Its coastline of almost continuous cliff, rising sheer from the sea to a height of 300, even 400ft in places, made it well nigh impregnable and as admirably suited as a stronghold to seventeenth-century Algerian pirates as it had been to the infamous Mariscos five hundred years earlier.

Like the Isles of Scilly, its Cornish counterpart, Lundy has never had its own newspaper, so that apart from the logbooks of the Trinity House lighthouse-keepers—started in 1819 but unfortunately no longer in existence—no complete record of wreck was maintained on the island. For a short time during the late 1800s, there was a Receiver of Wreck on Lundy, but apart from one incomplete volume covering the period 1868–85, even these depositions and letter books have been lost. With no lifeboat and a population seldom greater than three dozen, information concerning losses on Lundy have, in general, been passed on by word of mouth. In all probability shipwrecks during the 1700s never reached the ears of those on the mainland at all, and in support of this it is worth noting that issues of *Lloyds' List* between 1742 and 1756 make not one mention of a ship being lost on Lundy.

The earliest reference to wreck here is that of the *Marie*, a collier, which was lost on Lundy on 19 September 1757, after which it was February 1793 before news was received that the *Nancy & Betty*, St Ives to Swansea, had sunk close inshore. A Chepstow vessel, the *Wye*, is said to have been wrecked and lost with all hands in December 1796, and the Bristol ship *Jenny* on 20 February of the following year. Homeward bound from West Africa with ivory and some gold dust, she was lost on the west side of the island at a spot known to this day as Jenny's Cove. Much has been made of this incident and one source[3] insists that the *Jenny* was a British frigate, lost on 28 December 1809 with $1,000,000 of gold specie, but the Royal Navy has certainly never owned a frigate by this name.

Although north Devon newspapers have printed full accounts of many wreck incidents on Lundy, for the majority only the bare details are known. The only practicable course here, then, is to catalogue them in chronological order, giving such detail as is available.

1811   *Estrella de Mar*, schooner, 104 tons, of St Ubes in Portugal, for Bristol. Built 1798. Wrecked on Lundy, crew saved.

1816   *Rover*, 17 November, British sloop, 40 tons, Newport to London with coal. Wrecked on Lundy.

1819   *Unidentified* foreign ship sank near Lundy, six bodies recovered.

1819   *Unity*, 1 May, British sloop, Charlestown to Barry, foundered north of Lundy, crew saved.

1820   *Unidentified* schooner sank on 20–21 January, north of Lundy. Three bodies and an oar marked *Lamb* washed up. No record of such a vessel lost, or missing at Lloyds.

1822   *Fame*, 7 February, Bristol cutter, for Cork, wrecked on Lundy, crew saved.

1823   *Morrison*, British brigantine, Cork to Newport, foundered off Lundy, three lives lost.

1825   *Unidentified* vessel wrecked on Lundy.

1827   *I.O*, 24 April, Bristol schooner, 51 tons, built in 1821, owned by B. Hawkes, Jersey to Cardiff, master J. Le Gallis. Run down near Lundy 21 April, put ashore at South Hole on 24th and wrecked.

1829   *Francis Anne*, 21 March, Bristol barquentine, 372 tons, built, 1825, owned by P. Morris, Bristol to St Ives, master E. Grandy. Struck a rock and sank three cables south-by-west from the east end of Rat Island.

1833   *Unity*, 12 January, British smack, 39 tons, built 1829, foundered off Lundy.

1835   *Rapid*, 21 August, British, Llanelly to London with coal, wrecked on Lundy.

1836   *Abbotsford*, April, barque, Bristol to Boston, went ashore on Lundy, refloated, taken to Ilfracombe and returned to service.

1838   *Unidentified* ship, belonging to Shields, stranded on Landing Beach during a gale.

1841   *Sarah*, abandoned off Lundy, thought to have sunk.

1842   *Mary Ann*, 2 February, British barquentine, Whitehaven to Cardiff with iron ore, foundered 10 miles north-west of Lundy, crew saved.

1842   *Mariner*, 19 March, Dartmouth smack, foundered in Lundy Roads.

1848   *Ann*, 2 February, St Ives brigantine, built 1794, 104 tons gross, owned by Mollard & Co, St Ives to Cardiff, master Richards. Stranded on west side of Lundy, lost with entire crew.

1848   *Sylphiden*, 12 February, barque, Cardiff to Havanna with coal. Stranded on Lundy in fog, crew all saved.

1849   *Archelaus*, 7 November, French sailing vessel, master Boutelle, Cardiff to New York with railway iron. Foundered in Lundy Roads, crew all saved. Cargo was salvaged in 1850.

1850   *Unidentified*, 2 January, barque, foundered in Lundy Roads, four lives lost.

1850   *Thomas Crisp*, 18 January, British brig, 195 tons gross, built 1838, carrying stores. Wrecked on Lundy in a gale, one member of crew of nine drowned.

1850   *Unidentified*, 18 February, sailing trawler, found wrecked on West Point, Lundy.

1850   *Glenlyon*, 29 May, London-registered barque, built at Sunderland in 1845, 348 tons gross, owned by T. Cropton, Cardiff to San Francisco, master L. Flick. Wrecked on island.

1851   *Unidentified*, 8 January, French lugger, wrecked on Lundy, and all four crew drowned.

1851   *Unidentified*, 8 January, schooner, wrecked on Lundy, four of five crew drowned.

1851   *Panaja Eleusa*, 22 October, foundered 20 miles south-west of Lundy.

1851   *Janet*, 17 December, foundered off Lundy.

1852   *Wizard*, 13 January, Guernsey-registered fruit schooner, 58 tons gross, owned by Le Page & Co, master Guille, Bristol to St Michaels, in ballast. Wrecked during south-east gale in Lundy Cove. Six crew, all saved. Wreck sold for £40 on the beach.

1852   *Eliza*, 14 January, Ilfracombe brig, 108 tons gross, Newport to Hayle with railway iron. Leaked and foundered when 14 miles south-west of Lundy, five crew, all saved.

1852   *Orange Branch*, 23 July, Exmouth-registered schooner, 54 tons register, Newport to Plymouth with coal, foundered after striking floating wreckage 14 miles south-west of Lundy. Four crew, all saved.

1853   *Ariel*, 30 April, known only to be carrying coal, exploded and sank near Lundy, and was a total loss. One corpse recovered.

1855   *Joseph F. Votsam*, 14 May, sailing vessel, Cardiff to New York, with iron and passengers. Stranded on the Hen and Chickens rocks at night, sixty-two people aboard, all saved.

1855   *Avon*, 15 May, British barque, 408 tons gross, built at Sunderland in 1850, owned by H. Moon of Sunderland, master W. Moor. Wrecked on Lundy during a gale.

1856   *Wesleyana*, 18 January, Goole schooner, built at Knottingley in 1846; 75 tons gross; owned by Green & Co. Master Green. Wrecked off Lundy near northern end.

1856   *Choice*, 20 April, Bideford three-masted schooner, built at Prince Edward Is in 1854; 181 tons, owned by T. Williams. Leaked and foundered 6 miles south-east of Lundy. Crew saved and landed at Ilfracombe.

1856   *Loire*, French steamer, Cardiff to Rouen, carrying coal, wrecked on Lundy.

1857   *Frederick*, 4 November, Dublin-registered smack, 50 tons; carrying coal. Found abandoned in Lundy Roads, taken to Clovelly in a sinking condition, became a total loss.

1858   *Charles*, 13 March, Dartmouth-registered schooner, in ballast; Plymouth to Llanelly. Stranded at night at north end of Lundy in fog. Valued at £600, she became a total loss. Five of her seven crew were drowned.

1858   *Trident*, 15 April, smack, built in 1816; 41 tons; carrying coal. Wrecked on Lundy during a severe gale, one member of three crew drowned.

1859   *Plymouth*, 29 August, Plymouth-registered schooner; Newport to London with railway iron. Cargo shifted and foundered when 12 miles south-by-west of Lundy.

1859   *Unidentified*, 24–25 October, a barque, brigantine, and a schooner wrecked on Lundy in a gale.

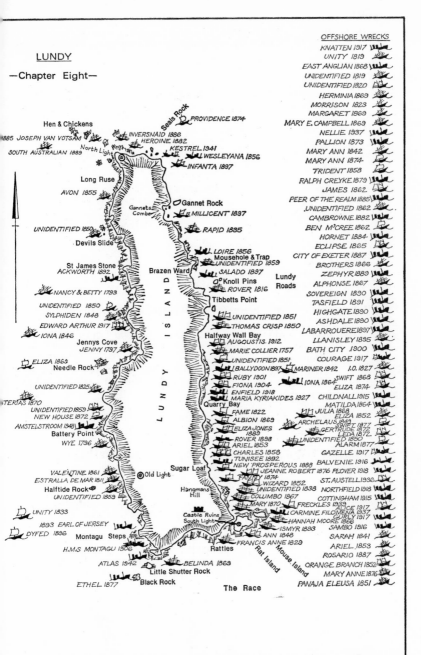

LUNDY

—Chapter Eight—

N

1859 *Peace*, 2 November, Dartmouth-registered smack, 44 tons; Newport to Plymouth with coal. Abandoned and foundered, 1½ miles south-by-east of Lundy. Crew saved.

1861 *Lewis Charles*, 9 February, schooner, 91 tons; carrying coal and six crew. Run down by the *Bottreaux Castle*, and sunk. One man drowned.

1861 *Valentine*, 23 May, Cork-registered brig, 53 tons; Waterford to Llanelly in ballast, master Williams. Wrecked on west side of Lundy near the Old Light. Crew saved and landed at Appledore.

1862 *James*, 19 March, St Ives schooner, 85 tons; with coal from Swansea, leaked and foundered when 15 miles east-north-east of Lundy. Five members of her crew reached the island in their own boat, which capsized in the surf, drowning four of them.

1862 *Cheasapeake*, 28 June, new schooner, 55 tons; carrying coal. Sank following a collision 8 miles west-south-west of Lundy. One member of crew of four drowned.

1862 *Ben M'Cree*, 3 November, wooden pilot cutter, sank off Lundy.

1864 *Iona*, 2 January, Dundee steamer; built at South Shields in 1856; 246 tons; from the Clyde to Kingstown; master Chapman. General cargo and a crew of forty. Suspected of being a blockade runner to American Confederate ports. Masts of wreck showed at low water and a diving bell was used on her salvage[4]. Foundered 1 mile east of Lundy.

1864 *Matilda*, 4 April, steamship; 544 tons gross; carrying coal and steel. Foundered north-east of Lundy.

1865 *Eclipse*, 5 April, sailing vessel, stranded on Lundy.

1866 *Hannah More*, 18 March, Liverpool-registered ship; built at St Johns in 1856, 1,129 tons gross. Master Haughton, Callas to Queenstown with guano. Stranded and lost on Rat Island, Lundy. Twenty of her twenty-six crew were drowned.

1866 *Brothers*, 28 November, Guernsey-registered sailing vessel, 379 tons gross. Built in 1841; Swansea to Dieppe, with 632 tons of coal. Leaked and foundered when some 20 miles north of Lundy. Crew saved and landed at Padstow.

1867 *Colombo*, 27 October, Genoese-registered barque. Stranded and lost on Lundy Beach.

1867 *Alphonse*, 7 October, St Malo barque, abandoned off Lundy following collision. Drifted ashore on island. Refloated by Ilfracombe boatmen and saved.

1868   *East Anglian*, 14 January, Liverpool-registered steamer, owned by London and Liverpool SS Co; 395 tons gross. Porthcawl to Plymouth with coal, master Demsey. Leaked and foundered 7 miles south-west of Lundy. Crew of twenty, all saved.

1868   *Caroline*, 19 February, Barnstaple-registered smack. 44 tons register, carrying granite from Lundy quarry to London. Stranded on beach and became wreck.

1868   *Swift*, 8 October, Teignmouth-registered schooner; 81 tons register; Cardiff to Plymouth with coal; master Carlisle. Leaked when off Lands End, turned back, but sank when at anchor in Lundy Roads, $1\frac{1}{2}$ miles from shore.

1868   *Julia*, 1 November, Penzance-registered schooner; 78 tons gross; built Prince Edward Is in 1839; Swansea to Penzance with coal; master Steel. Foundered in Lundy Roads, 1 mile from shore.

1869   *Hermina*, 30 January, Dutch brig; foundered 1 mile east-by-north of Lundy. Only two from crew of eight saved.

1869   *Albion*, 20 March, Bristol-owned pilot-cutter; 38 tons register. Stranded in Lundy Roads. Four crew, all saved.

1869   *Belinda*, 6 April, Weymouth-registered brigantine; 156 tons register; London to Swansea with 220 tons of copper bar, valued at £3,000; master Randell. Ran ashore on the cliff, east of the south-western point of the island. Part cargo salvaged shortly after.

1869   *Margaret*, 22 April, Liverpool-registered brig; 142 tons register; Cardiff to Montevideo with coal. Put back to Cardiff following a collision; sailed again after repairs had been carried out, but leaked and sank off Lundy. All nine crew saved.

1869   *Eliza*, 30 December, Bideford-owned smack; 32 tons. Foundered off Lundy with the loss of all crew.

1870   *Asterias*, 21 May, barque, 800 tons gross; Cardiff to Hong Kong with coal. Caught fire and exploded before sinking, 2 miles west of Lundy. Two lives lost.

1870   *Mary*, 16 December, Isles of Scilly-owned brigantine; 219 tons; Swansea to Bordeaux with coal. Stranded between Rat Island and Lundy, and became total wreck. Enquiry into loss held at Liverpool.

1871   *Brenda*, 14 February, Liverpool-registered barque; 958 tons register. Built Nova Scotia in 1864; Newport to New Orleans with railway iron. Struck between the Knoll Pin and Brazen Ward. Vessel later refloated after all cargo removed.

1872 *Leda*, 28 February, French schooner; built 1847; 94 tons register. Cardiff to Nantes with coal; master Tascon. Foundered following collision 10 miles south-west of Lundy. One member of crew of five drowned.

1872 *Gertrude*, 7 May, brigantine. Foundered in Lundy Roads, following a collision.

1872 *New House*, 5 September, St Ives-registered sailing vessel. Wrecked on Lundy.

1873 *Eliza*, 27 March, St Ives-registered sailing vessel. Foundered off Lundy, after being run down by the steamer *Sir Bevis*. Four of her crew drowned, two floated nearly to St Ives on a hatchcover and were saved.

1873 *Mary Ann*, 27 April, Newport-registered 16 ton pilot-cutter. Foundered 3 miles south-south-west of Lundy.

1873 *Pallion*, 5 November, London-registered steamship; built 1871; 1,146 tons gross; Cardiff to Suez with coal. Foundered 7 miles south-west of Lundy. Crew saved.

1874 *Providence*, 7 June, Bristol-owned smack: built at Bristol in 1823; 23 tons net. Cruising in channel, foundered half a mile north of Lundy.

1874 *Fanny*, 5 October, Bideford-owned smack; 30 tons register. Stranded on Landing Beach, Lundy.

1876 *Jeanne Robert*, 15 January, French schooner, carrying coal from Newport. Stranded in Lundy Roads, three crew drowned.

1876 *Mary Anne*, 13 August, Aberystwyth brigantine; built in 1857; 122 tons. Middlesbrough to Swansea with 195 tons of pig iron. Foundered 10 miles east-north-east of Lundy.

1877 *Ethel*, 3 February, Newcastle-registered steamship; built in 1871; 811 tons gross. Bilbao to Newport with iron ore; master Reeves. Stranded on Black Rock, part of the outer Shutters, on the south-east side of Lundy in fog, and sank. Nineteen of her crew drowned, only the mate survived.

1877 *Alarm*, 12 August, Newport-owned smack; 13 tons; built in 1862; cruising in the channel. Foundered after collision with the steamer *Pelan*, when 7 miles east of Lundy.

1877 *Swift*, 17 October, Cardiff-owned dandy; 65 tons gross; Swansea to Hull with 86 tons of copperas and 10 tons of arsenic. Leaked and foundered when 10 miles north-east of Lundy.

1879 *Ralph Creyke*, 20 February, Goole-registered steamship; built at Sunderland in 1878; 750 tons gross. Cardiff to Dieppe, with

750 tons of coal; master Wright; owned by Goole SS Co Ltd. Leaked and foundered 10 miles south-west of Lundy. Nine of her crew of fifteen were lost, including the master.

1882 *Pasla Kevello*, 31 August, Genoese barque; 547 tons, built 1871; Cardiff to West Africa, with coal. Stranded in fog, on the east side of Lundy. Was refloated, repaired, and renamed before returning to service.

1882 *Cambronne*, 26 November, French steamship, of 811 tons gross; built in 1877; Cardiff to France with coal. Foundered after collision with the SS *Marion*, off Lundy.

1882 *Heroine*, 13 December, Newport-registered brigantine; built Prince Edward Is in 1876; Newport to Rosario, with coal and railway iron; master J. Kirby. Stranded on the north-east corner of Lundy in fog, leaked, and sank. Crew of ten, all saved.

1882 *Burnswark*, 13 December, Bristol-registered barque; 253 tons; Bristol to Old Calaba, in West Africa, with a general cargo; master W. Luke. Stranded in dense fog on the western side of Lundy. Crew of thirteen rescued by pilot cutter No 22.

1884 *Hornet*, 27 January, British steamship; built in 1874; Newport to Marseilles with a general cargo. Foundered off Lundy after developing a severe leak.

1885 *Peer of the Realm*, 11 February, Newcastle-registered steamship; 1,813 tons gross; built at Sunderland in 1870; owned by Foster & Irving, of Bristol. Cardiff to Bombay with coal; master Edwin Knowles. Stranded on the east side of Knoll Pin Point, east Lundy, in fog, All crew saved.

1886 *Bosweden*, Penzance-registered iron schooner of 214 tons. Neath to Penzance with coal; master R. Boyns. Sighted off Lundy on 15 October, then disappeared and was never seen again.

1886 *Inversnaid*, 16 October, Glasgow-registered ship; built at Greenock in 1884; Cardiff to Singapore with coal; master Dodds. Foundered off the Hen and Chickens Rocks during a severe gale, lost with all thirty crew.

1887 *Rosario*, 4 March, Spanish brigantine; 223 tons gross; Cardiff to Majorca; master Fernandez. Foundered after collision with the ss *Glenmauis* when 5 miles west of Lundy. Crew saved.

1887 *City of Exeter*, 11 March, Exeter-owned steamship; 1,054 tons gross; built at Stockton in 1870. Cardiff to St Nazaire with coal; master R. Popham. Foundered during a force 10 gale, 4 miles south-west of Lundy. Sixteen of her seventeen crew drowned.

1888   *Elsie*, 3 January, Whitby-registered steamship; 2,374 tons gross; built at Sunderland in 1881. Cardiff to St Vincent with coal. Stranded on the Knoll Pin, Lundy, in fog. Refloated and saved without loss of life.

1888   *New Prosperous*, 14 February, Bristol-owned pilot cutter of 24 tons; built in 1836. Stranded at Landing Place, Lundy.

1888   *Electric*, 8 May, Gloucester-registered wooden steam paddle tug of 12 tons net; owned by W. Williams of Newport; built in 1874. From Newport for towing work; master Thomas. Stranded at Pilots Quay, Lundy.

1888   *Radnor*, 9 May, Cardiff-registered steamship; 812 tons net; built by Palmers of Newcastle in 1879. Stranded on the eastern side of Lundy.

1889   *South Australian*, 14 February, British-owned steamship. Foundered west-north-west of Lundy.

1889   *Eliza Jones*, 16 December, Caernarvon schooner; 63 tons gross; built in 1857. Hayle to Bristol in ballast. Stranded and lost on Lundy, with three crew drowned.

1890   *Sovereign*, 19 February, Southampton-registered steamship; 110 tons gross; built at Southampton in 1870. Foundered after collision with the *Highgate* off Lundy.

1890   *Highgate*, 19 February, London-owned steamship; 1,451 tons; built at Whitby in 1882. Foundered after collision with the *Sovereign* off Lundy.

1890   *Ashdale*, 10 September, Glasgow-registered steamship; 117 tons gross; owned by the Clydesdale SS Co; Cardiff to Tralee with coal; master J. Brown. Foundered 10 miles north-west of Lundy. Crew saved.

1891   *Tasfield*, 22 November, Bristol-registered steamship; 416 tons, Cardiff to Havre with coal. Developed serious leak in her engine-room when 7 miles off Lundy. Attempted to reach the island but foundered offshore. Crew rescued by the ss *Rembridge*.

1892   *Tunisee*, 19 February, Bordeaux-registered steamship; stranded and wrecked on Sugar Loaf rock, Lundy. Crew saved by lighthouse keeper with a home-made breeches buoy.

1892   *Ackworth*, 22 April, British steamship, Cardiff to Port Said with coal. Stranded on Lundy in fog. Crew taken off by the Glasgow tug *Flying Elf*; vessel valued at £2,600.

1893   *Ismyr*, 1 December, North Shields-registered brigantine; 226 tons gross; built at Liverpool in 1850. Stranded on Rat Island, Lundy.

1895   *Marie Collier*, 19 September. Steamship owned by T. Pooter of
       Rotterdam; Cardiff to Naples, with 3,500 tons of coal.
       Stranded on the west side of Lundy.

1895   *Llanisley*, 2 October, Penzance-registered schooner; 131 tons
       gross; Neath to Penzance with coal; master Becherley.
       Foundered between Lundy and Hartland Point. All four crew
       reached Ilfracombe in the ship's punt, but capsized in the
       surf and all were drowned.

1896   *Dyfed*, 22 January, pilot cutter; foundered off Lundy during
       a gale.

1896   *Kate*, June, local sailing vessel, wrecked whilst unloading
       cement for the Lundy church.

1897   *Salado*, 21 March, London-registered steamship; 2,188 tons
       register; built in 1890; Newport to Buenos Aires with coal.
       Stranded and wrecked near the Granite Stone, Lundy. Four
       of her crew rowed to Ilfracombe to report wreck.

1897   *Millicent*, 1 April, Padstow-registered ketch; Cardiff to Pad-
       stow with coal. Foundered off Lundy.

1897   *Infanta*, 19 May, Padstow-registered sailing vessel. Wrecked on
       the north end of Lundy.

1897   *Ballydoon*, 1 November, Glasgow-registered steamship; in
       ballast. Stranded on west side of Lundy in a gale.

1897   *Labarrouere*, 25 November, French-owned steamship; 1,173
       tons gross; built in 1880; Cardiff to St Nazaire with coal.
       Foundered after collision with a schooner off Lundy. Master
       and four crew drowned.

1898   *Rover*, 31 August, barge; 146 tons register; master Grant.
       Loaded with machinery and boilers from the wreck of the
       Salado, sank in a gale, whilst moored over the site. Crew
       saved.

1898   *Earl of Jersey*, 28 November, Cardiff-registered, steam paddle
       tug; 147 tons gross; built in 1886; owned by H. B. Marquand
       & Co; master Halbert. Struck a submerged rock 300yd off
       the west coast of Lundy and sank. Crew saved by the tug
       Royal Briton and landed at Ilfracombe.

1899   *Escort*, 21 April, Milford Haven-registered ketch; 40 tons;
       owned by P. L. Hancock; master Pine. Sank after collision
       with the Brixham fishing ketch *Fish Girl*, west of Lundy;
       two crew drowned.

1900   *Bath City*, 24 February, British steamship; 2,431 tons gross;
       built by Thompsons in 1899; New York to Bristol with

grain and general cargo. Struck the Needle Rock, Lundy and foundered 2 miles offshore in 30 fathoms, south of the island.

1901   *Ruby*, 24 April, wooden fishing vessel, unregistered, sank near Lundy.

1904   *Fiona*, 6 May, Cowes-registered ketch; carrying coal from Cardiff. Wrecked on the east side of 'quarter wall', Lundy.

1906   HMS *Montagu*, 29 May, battleship, Duncan class. Launched at Devonport dockyard 5 March 1901 as the *Montague*, re-named the same year. 14,000 tons; 750 crew; 418 × 75·5 × 27·25ft. Carried a 7in belt of armour on the waterline; 11in on the top of her main turrets and 12in on the control tower.
   Armament, 4 × 12in guns; 12 × 6in; 12 × 12 pounders; 6 × 3 pounders; 2 × Maxim machine guns; 4 × 18in submerged torpedo tubes.
   Propulsion, 2 × 4 cyl, vertical inverted, triple expansion steam engines, developing 18,000hp; 24 Belville boilers, twin screws, giving a maximum speed of 19 knots (burning 15 tons of coal per hour).
   Went ashore on the Shutter Reef on the south-west corner of Lundy in fog and became a total loss.

During the afternoon of Tuesday, 29 May, the relatively new battleship *Montagu* anchored off Lundy in the course of fleet exercises. She attempted to communicate with the Isles of Scilly by means of the recently installed 'wireless telegraphic signalling apparatus', but found the distance was too great. These early radio trials were of considerable importance to the navy, and had it not been for the dense fog which quickly enveloped her, the *Montagu* would have reduced the distance until communication could be achieved. Anchored where she was, risk of collision with a merchant vessel was high, so it was decided to move in closer to Lundy. Soundings were taken at regular intervals and the lookouts warned to listen for the Lundy fog signals as the ship moved closer inshore. At 2 pm a depth of seventeen fathoms was reported, and at 2.12 pm, when the navigating officer had calculated that they were at least four miles from the island, the warship shuddered to a halt, having run ashore on the Shutter Rock on the south-western corner of Lundy. Attempts were made to get her off by putting her engines alternatively ahead and astern, but she remained fast and was leaking so badly that a landing party was detailed to scale the cliffs and report to the authorities.

On reaching the clifftops, the lieutenant in charge found a footpath which was, in fact, the north–south track which follows the western coastline. Unaware that less than half a mile to their right lay houses and the south lighthouse, the party turned left and walked the entire length of Lundy until they reached the north lighthouse at the opposite end. At first, the keeper was unable to understand what it was they wanted, until it dawned on him that his unexpected callers thought they were on the mainland, and that this was the Hartland light. The lieutenant was emphatic in his belief that the *Montagu* was stranded on the north Devon coast, and after some heated words on the subject the keeper turned his back with the irrefutable remark, 'Do you imagine I don't know *which* bloody light I'm keeping?'

With all the battleship's lower compartments flooded and the hull working badly on the rocks, and lacking any salvage equipment of its own, the navy called upon the assistance of the Liverpool Salvage Company and one of its most experienced salvage officers, Capt Young. This brought the famous salvage steamer *Ranger* to the scene, but instead of making the best use of Capt Young's experience by putting him in charge of the work he was seconded in an advisory capacity only to Admiral Sir A. K. Wilson RN, commander of the Channel Fleet, a brilliant naval officer and full of ideas, but completely out of his depth in dealing with a wrecked battleship. A whole fleet of vessels was ordered to the scene, battleships, cruisers, destroyers, with picket boats buzzing about between them like wasps. Working parties of seamen, hundreds strong, appeared on board the *Montagu* and succeeded in doing little else but get in each other's way. They did manage to remove some of the heavy armour plating in an attempt to reduce her weight, but wires parted, expensive gear was lost overboard, caissons lashed alongside the wreck to give additional buoyancy broke adrift, pumps fell down hatches, and all the time the warship was settling lower and lower in the sea until her upper deck was almost awash. The final straw came when the admiral seriously suggested to Capt Young that they fill the entire ship with sheets of cork and let the rising tide float her clear!

By now it was obvious that the *Montagu* was lost and Capt

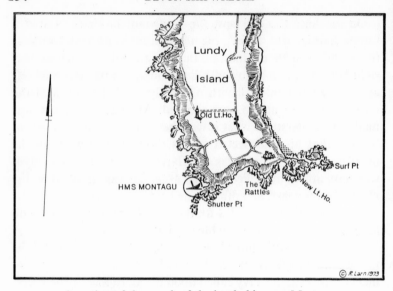

Location of the wreck of the battleship HMS *Montagu*

Young suggested that at least they could salvage the barrels of the 12in guns, described as being the latest Mk 10, wire wound, weighing 48 tons and costing £9,040 each. Apart from their value, the nation's reserve stock of such guns was then very low, following the need to replace defective ordnance in the *Majestic* and *Canopus* class vessels. Almost overnight the fleet of ships and its glittering staff disappeared, leaving the cloth-capped, overalled experts to complete the task in peace.

For technical purposes, it was necessary to blow out a portion of the ship's side, alongside the forward and after turrets, to allow the massive gun barrels to drop down into the hull, from which they were then lifted clear of the barbettes. It was here that Tommy Hyland, the foreman, and his Liverpool riggers came into their own, erecting 60ft high sheerlegs of 20in timber, to which were attached 100 ton lifting blocks. These same blocks, dug out from some half-forgotten hiding place, had previously lifted the boilers into the *Great Eastern*. Massive four-fold purchases were rigged with 10in manilla, and with only the assistance of a donkey engine rigged on an upper deck, clear of the waves, the first of the forward guns was lifted clear, placed in a waiting lighter, and taken to Pembroke dock. Three days later the second barrel was on its way to Wales, and to celebrate the successful salvaging of two guns in twenty-one days a concert was held aboard the wreck. Alf Gloyne, the chief diver, amazed everyone by giving a very creditable tap dance routine; Kearney, the fireman, played the concertina and Capt Young sang 'Blow the man down', by which time everyone was too drunk to appreciate fully the forty-verse poem specially written for the occasion which began, 'Midst the cheers of the spectators, the *Ranger* left the town . . .' Within days, both after guns were safely on their way to the naval dockyard and the salvage crew still aboard was joined by members of the Western Marine Co. Between them, they stripped the *Montagu* of her many condensers, pumps and tons of non-ferrous metals.

During the salvage work, serious allegations were made concerning the standard of workmanship in the construction of the *Montagu*. It was reported that rivets had been placed too far apart for watertightness, that joints and seams had been left uncaulked, that lead rivets had been used in places and, worst of all, that even some wooden 'rivets' had been found painted over. Strong denials followed from the Devonport officials, but no doubt some of the defects were genuine. A naval court-martial was ordered to be held aboard Nelson's old flagship, HMS *Victory*, at Portsmouth, at which Capt Adair and his chief navigating officer, Lt Dathan, were jointly charged with, 'having by negligence or default, did hazard, strand or lose HMS *Montagu*'. The arguments for the defence hinged on an unpredictable tidal set, which put the battleship out of its estimated position, and the fact that the Lundy fog signals were not heard, either before they went ashore, whilst on the rocks, or when the landing party reached the top of the cliffs. Certainly, had the signals been audible the landing party would not have walked the length of the island, away from the lighthouse, and it is perhaps significant that Trinity House later sent a vessel to the island to steam round and round at varying distances to establish the effectiveness of the signals. The court found the charges against both officers proven. Capt Adair being severely reprimanded and dismissed his ship, and Lt Dathan receiving an identical punishment, plus the loss of two years seniority in his rank. Six months after the incident the salvage men left the wreck to the sea and, weakened by explosives and dismantling, the remains of Lundy's largest and most dramatic incident was reduced by the first winter gales to a heap of rusting plates, scarcely visible at high tide (Pictures, pp 214–5).

1908   *Auricula*, 1 May, London-registered steamship; went aground on the west side of Lundy, close to the *Montagu*, but was later refloated and saved.

1912   *Augoustis*, 30 November, sailing vessel aground on Lundy, fate uncertain.

1915   *Childwall*, 1 April, British steamship; built in 1914; machinery aft; 593 tons register; Cherbourg to Swansea, in ballast. Foundered after collision with the ss *Trinculo* off Lundy.

1915   *Cottingham*, 26 December, British steamship; 513 tons register. Attacked by German submarine when 16 miles south-west of Lundy. Steamer finally sunk by gunfire, seven crew killed.

1916   *Edward Arthur*, 2 January, Caernarvon-registered schooner, three-masted; 151 tons gross; built at Portmadoc in 1877. Stranded in Jenny Cove, Lundy.

1916   *Sambo*, 26 March, British steamship; built in 1910; 144 tons gross; Swansea to Morlaix with patent fuel. Foundered 3 miles south-east of Lundy.

1916   *Balvenie*, 24 July, British steamship; built in 1911; 872 tons register; machinery aft; Clyde to St Nazaire with general cargo. Foundered after collision with the ss *Tagona* 4 miles south-west of Lundy.

1917   *Alice*, 20 January, French-registered schooner; built 1882; 299 tons gross; Granville to Swansea with pitwood. Foundered after collision with the Norwegian ss *Barnston* 5 miles south-east of the south light, Lundy.

1917   *Knatten*, 20 August, Norwegian-registered steamship; built in 1892; 532 tons gross; Swansea to St Malo with patent fuel. Foundered 1 mile north of Lundy after catching fire.

1917   *Gurly*, 26 November, Norwegian-registered steamship; built 1908; 578 tons gross; Swansea to Rouen with coal. Foundered when 2½ miles south-west of Lundy.

1917 *Courage*, 30 November, steam trawler, stranded on Lundy.

1917 *Gazelle*, 30 November, steam trawler, stranded on Lundy.

1918 *Northfield*, 3 March, British-registered steamship, 2,099 tons gross. Torpedoed and lost south-west of Lundy. Fourteen lives lost.

1918 *Enfield*, 5 December, steamer, ashore, refloated 1919.

1918 *Plover*, 11 May, British-registered steamship; built in 1888; 302 tons gross; Portreath to Saundersfoot, in ballast. Sank after collision with the ss *Lesseps* 5 miles east-north-east of Lundy.

1922 *Canterbury Bell*, 5 January, British-registered steamship; built in 1909; 703 tons gross; Llanelly to Carcubion with coal. Capsized and sank 14 miles north-west of Lundy.

1929 *Maria Kyriakides*, 25 March. Greek-registered steamship; 1,556 tons register, ran aground off the Quarries, Lundy. All eighteen crew were rescued, and eighteen months after the incident the vessel was refloated and saved (Picture, p 216).

1930 *Andros*, 27 March, steamer, stranded, saved.

1931 *Taxiarchis*, 28 March; Chios-registered steamship; 3,445 tons gross; stranded on east side of Lundy, under old quarries. Crew of twenty-four rescued, vessel refloated and saved in 1933.

1937 *Carmine Filomena*, 1 July, Genoese-registered steamship; Swansea to Genoa with coal. Stranded and lost on Mouse Island. Crew of twenty-four saved (Picture, p 213).

1937 *Nellie*, 13 July, Belgian-registered motor vessel; built in 1937; 479 tons register; Brussels to Llanelly with scrap iron. Struck a rock north of Stanley Bank, foundered 2 miles off Lundy. Crew of ten saved by ss *Ranger*.

1939 *Freckles*, 13 August, motor yacht; ex-RNLI lifeboat; stranded on wreckage of the *Carmine Filomena* and lost.

1940 *Halton*, 27 January, Liverpool-registered steamship. Stranded on Lundy, refloated.

1941 *Kestrel*, 28 March, steam trawler, attacked by German aircraft, beached at the north end of the island; later broken up.

1942 *Atlas*, 10 October, Dutch-registered motor coaster of Groningen; built in 1938; owned by J. Beck. Hayle to Newport in ballast. Stranded near the Shutters reef, Lundy. Only the mate survived from crew of nine.

1948 *Amstelstroom*, 18 July, Dutch-registered motor vessel; 398 tons gross; built by Van der Grissen & Zonnen in 1936. Stranded near the old battery, Lundy. Crew saved.

1952 *Cambria*, 9 August, launch; wrecked.

1952 *Devonia*, 9 September, lost after stranding.

SOURCE NOTES

CHAPTER ONE

1 Stowes 'Annals'
2 Ibid
3 *Observations on the Western Counties of England* (1794–6)
4 Chope, P. *Early tours in Devon and Cornwall* (Travels of Cosmo III—Count Magalotti, 1669), reprint 1967
5 *Journal of Edward Barlow*, vol 2, 1659–1703
6 *A Philosophical dissertation on the diving vessel projected by Mr Day, and sunk in Plymouth Sound*
7 *Naval Chronicles*, vol 37, p 135
8 *Gentleman's Magazine*, 1799, p 159
9 *Western Daily Mercury*, 20 January 1817
10 Larn, R. *Cornish Shipwrecks, the Isles of Scilly*, vol 3, pp 94–7
11 *Plymouth and Devonport in times of War and Peace*, p 159
12 Ibid, p 162
13 *Western Daily Mercury*, 22 February 1861

CHAPTER TWO

1 Laughton. *Defeat of the Spanish Armada*
2 Leyland. *Early Tours in Devon and Cornwall* (reprint 1967)
3 Fairweather. *Salcombe, Kingsbridge and neighbourhood*, p 25
4 Ibid, p 26
5 *Sherborne Mercury*
6 Ibid
7 *Gentleman's Magazine*, 1795, p 964
8 Larn, R. & Carter, C. *Cornish Shipwrecks, the South Coast*, vol 1, p 71

CHAPTER THREE

1 *Western Daily Mercury*, 14 December 1868, p 3
2 *Select Pleas in the Court of Admiralty* (Court of the West), vol 1, 1390–1404

CHAPTER FOUR

1 State Papers, Domestic. Elizabeth, v.i
2 Defoe, D. *A Tour through Britain*, 1724
3 State Papers, Domestic. 1657–8, vol CLVII, p 161
4 *Exeter Flying Post*, September 1771
5 *Gentleman's Magazine*, 1784, p 143
6 Ellis. *An Historical survey of Torquay*, 1930, p 407–8
7 *Naval Chronicles*, 1804, vol 12

239

CHAPTER FIVE

1 High Court of Admiralty, File 45, No 301 (1573), p 148
2 State Papers, Board of Trade enquiry, 1854
3 *Western Morning News*, 8 January 1867, p 3

CHAPTER SIX

1 Exeter City Library, reference Wreck—T&A, 34–432

CHAPTER SEVEN

1 Stowe. *Early Tours in Devon and Cornwall* (reprint 1967, p 6)
2 Campbell, A. Lord. *Armada Cannon*, 1899
3 *North Devon Journal*
4 State Papers, Domestic. Charles I, vol XLVII, 1627, p 7
5 *Naval Chronicles*, vol I, p 256
6 Tugwell. *North Devon Handbook*
7 Pages. *Coasts of Devon and Lundy*
8 Gosse, P. *A Naturalist's Rambles on the Devonshire Coast*
9 State Papers, Domestic, 1675
10 Farr, G. *Wreck and Rescue in the Bristol Channel*, p 112

CHAPTER EIGHT

1 Boquet, M. *Lundy Fields Society, 18th Annual Report*, 1967, p 19
2 Lock, W. *North West Devon*, 1963, p 58
3 Rieseberg, H. and Mikalow, A. *Sunken Treasure Ships of The World*, New York, 1965
4 L'Estrange, Rev. A. G. *Yachting Round the West of England*, 1865

ACKNOWLEDGEMENTS

My grateful appreciation and thanks are extended to John Behenna, of Brixham, for allowing me to reproduce photographs from his collection, for reading the manuscript, and for suggesting many changes; to Eric Collins, of Penzance, for Torbay wreck material, and other invaluable assistance; Alec Reynolds, of the Naval Hydrographic Section, for wreck information, also for drawing the wreck location charts and other maps. Clive Carter, of Sancreed, for his painting of the *Ramillies* and much useful information and photographs; G. E. Mills, of Redruth, and K. V. Burns, of Plymouth City Library.

To H. L. Douch and R. Penhallurick (Royal Institution of Cornwall, Truro); the Archivist, Mr O'Shee, and staff of H. M. Customs and Excise Library, London; and the Curators, staff, and Superintendents of St Austell (Cornwall) Public Library; Exeter City Library (Reference Section); Torquay Public Library; British Museum Reading Room and State Paper Room; National Maritime Museum Reading Room; Colindale, and the Public Records Office (London).

To F. E. Gibson (Isles of Scilly), *Torquay Times*; National Maritime Museum; Imperial War Museum; R. Rossiter (Paignton); A. R. Tucker (Dartmouth); B. Salmon (Wembury); L. Carlile Davis (Plymouth); G. Dunn (Torquay); J. Horsely (Brixham), and R. L. Knights (Barnstaple), for permission to reproduce photographs. To the Hydrographer of the Navy for permission to reproduce chart extracts and other information.

To the publishers, for their patience, Roy Davis and Peter McBride for their friendship and encouragement, and my wife, Maureen, for all her help.

St Austell, 1974   RICHARD LARN

BIBLIOGRAPHY

Andrews, K. R. *Elizabethan Privateering (1585–1603)*, Cambridge (1964)

Arber Newell, E. A. *The Coast Scenery of North Devon* (1911)

Baring-Gould, S. *Book of the West*, vols 1 & 2 (1899)

Barlow, V. & Etherton, P. T. *Tempestuous Isle* (1950)

Bickerseth, S. *Up and Down the Devon Coast*

Billing, M. *Directory and Gazetteer of the County of Devon* (1857)

Blackwell, A. E. *The Charm and History of Instow* (1946)

Boquet, M. *Lundy Shipwrecks*, 18th Annual Report of the Lundy Field Society (1967)

Bowring, W. D. *Ilfracombe Throughout the Ages*, Exeter (1931)

Boyle, V. C. & Payne, A. *Devon Harbours* (1952)

Burton, S. H. *The North Devon Coast* (1954)

Burton, S. H. *The South Devon Coast* (1954)

Campbell, A. *Armada Cannon* (1899)

Campbell, G. *My Mystery Ships* (1928)

Chanter, J. R. *Lundy Island* (1924)

Chatterton, E. K. *Q-Ships and Their Story* (1922)

Clowes, L. W. *A History of the Royal Navy*

Colledge, J. J. *Ships of the Royal Navy*, vols I & II, Newton Abbot (1969)

Coxhead, J. R. *Smuggling Days in Devon*

Dawson, A. J. *Britain's Lifeboats* (1923)

Delderfield, E. R. *Cradle of the Seadogs* (1951)

Delderfield, E. R. *North Devon Story* (1952)

Delderfield, E. R. *Torbay Story* (1951)

Domville-Fife, C. *Epics of the Square-rigged Ships* (1958)

Ellis, A. C. *An Historical Survey of Torquay*

Erikkson, P. *The Duchess* (1958)

Fairweather, J. *Salcombe, Kingsbridge and Neighbourhood*

Farr, G. *Wreck and Rescue in the Bristol Channel*, Truro (1966)

242

Farr, G. *Wreck and Rescue on the Coast of Devon*, Truro (1968)

Fiennes, C. *Through England on a Side-saddle*

Gardiner, W. F. *Barnstaple*, Barnstaple (1897)

Gordon, St Ledger, D. *Portrait of Devon* (1963)

Goudge, E. *Gentian Hill*

Grant, R. M. *U-Boats Destroyed* (1964)

Greenhill, B. *The Merchant Schooners*, vols I & II, Newton Abbot (1968)

Heath, S. *Devon and Dorset coasts* (1910)

Hocking, C. A. *A Dictionary of Disasters at Sea, in the Age of Steam, 1824–1962*, vols I & II (1969)

Hoskins, W. G. *Devon* (1954)

Hoskins, W. G. *Old Devon*, Newton Abbot (1966)

Hoskins, W. G. *Two Thousand Years in Exeter*, Exeter (1960)

Steelase. *Interesting Particulars Relating to That Great National Undertaking, the Plymouth Breakwater* (1821)

Jameson, W. *The Most Formidable Thing* (1965)

Jewitt, L. *A History of Plymouth*, Plymouth (1873)

Langham, A. & M. *Lundy, Bristol Channel*, Bradford (1960)

Langham, A. & M. *Lundy*, Newton Abbot (1970)

Laughton. *Defeat of the Spanish Armada*

Le Fleming, H. M. *Warships of World War I* (1965)

Lewis, R. W. *Lundy, its History, and Natural History* (1925)

Lindsay, W. S. *History of Merchant Shipping and Ancient Commerce* (1874)

Lubbock, B. *The Last of the Windjammers*, vols I & II, Glasgow (1929)

Lyson. *Magna Britannia, History of Devonshire* (1822)

Magalotti, L. *Travels of Cosmo, the 3rd Grand Duke of Tuscany, Through England and Wales, in the Reign of Charles II* (1821)

Majdalany, F. *The Red Rocks of Eddystone* (1959)

Mitchell, W. & Sawyer, L. *British Standard Ships of World War I* (1968)

Oppenheim, M. M. *The Maritime History of Devon*, Exeter (1908)

Page, W. *Victoria County History of Devon*, vols I & II

Page, W. J. *The Coasts of Devon and Lundy Island* (1875)

Parkes, O. *Ships of the Royal Navy* (1932)

Pearse, Chope, R. *Early Tours in Devon and Cornwall*, Newton Abbot (1969)

Pearse, Chope, R. *The Book of Hartland*, Torquay (1940)

Presland, J. *Lynton and Lynmouth* (1917)

Presland, J. *Torquay* (1920)

Rogers, I. *Ships and Shipyards of Bideford*, Bideford (1947)

Roskill, S. W. *The War at Sea*, vols I & II (1954)

Russel, P. *A History of Torquay*, Torquay (1960)

Russell, P. *Dartmouth* (1950)

Saville, M. *Come to Devon* (1969)

Sellman, R. R. *Illustrations of Devon's History* (1962)

Shaw, S. *A Tour of the West of England* (1788)

Steinman, S. G. *Some Account of the Island of Lundy*

Sutton, A. *A History of Sidmouth*, Exeter (1960)

Tugwell, G. L. *The North Devon Handbook* (1877)

Ward. *North-West Devon* (The Red Guide) (1851)

Ward, C. S. *South Devon and a Description of the Isles of Scilly* (1702)

Watkin, H. R. *Parochial Histories of Devonshire*, Dartmouth (1935)

Westcote, T. *A View of Devonshire*, Exeter (1845)

White, J. T. *History of Torquay*, Torquay (1878)

Whymper, F. *The Sea* (1890)

Worth, R. N. *History of Plymouth*, Plymouth (1890)

Young, D. *Ship Ashore* (1932)

NEWSPAPERS, JOURNALS, ETC

Gentleman's Magazine, various issues

Journal of the Royal United Services Institution, various issues

Lifeboat, Journal of the Royal National Lifeboat Institution

Lloyds' Universal Register, various issues 1764–1973

Mercantile Navy List and Maritime Directory

Naval Chronicles, various issues

Sea Breezes, various issues 1932–73

The Naval and Military Record

Transactions of the Devon Association

Alfred West of England Journal and General Advertiser, 1816–31

Daily Western Mercury, from 1860

Devon and Exeter Gazette, from 1896

Devon Express and Echo, from 1933

Devonport Independent and Plymouth and Stonehouse Gazette, from 1833

Devonshire Chronicle and Exeter News

Devon and Somerset News, from 1953

Exeter Gazette Telegraph, from 1873

Exeter and Plymouth Gazette, from 1814
Exeter Weekly Times and West of England Advertiser
Felix Farley's Bristol Journal, from 1714
Plymouth and Cornish Advertiser
Plymouth Times and South Hams Advertiser, from 1897
Pulman's Weekly News, from 1935
Richard's Topsham Herald, from 1864
Sherborne and Yeovil Mercury, from 1738
Taunton Courier, from 1824
The Plymouth and Devonport Weekly Journal, from 1823
The Plymouth and Plymouth Dock Weekly Journal, from 1821
The Weekly Times, from 1827
Torquay Times
Trewman's Exeter Flying Post, from 1763
West Devon Standard, from 1835
Western Independent
Western Luminary and Family Newspaper, from 1827
Western Morning News, from 1860
Western Times, from 1829
Woulmeis Exeter and Plymouth Gazette

INDEX OF SHIPS

Page references in italic denote illustrations. Ships without a page reference are Devon wrecks unmentioned in the text.

Abbreviations used to denote ship types:

SS	steamship	Tr	transport
Mv	motorvessel	Pt	privateer
S	sailing ship	Sn	snow
Frs	full-rigged ship	Tg	tug
Bq	barque	HMS/1	HM ship of 1st rate
Bqn	barquentine	HMS/2	HM ship of 2nd rate
Br	brig	HMS/3	HM ship of 3rd rate
Brn	brigantine	HMS/4	HM ship of 4th rate
Kt	ketch	HMS/5	HM ship of 5th rate
Yl	yawl	HMS/6	HM ship of 6th rate
Sk	smack	HMS/B	HM battleship
Sl	sloop	HMS/S	HM submarine
Sc	schooner	HMS/T	HMS trawler

246

Name	Type	Date	Location	Page reference
Eliza	Br	8.12.1872	Plymouth	52
Eliza	S	23.3.1873	Off Lundy	228
Eliza & Ann	Sc	14.11.1860	Plymouth	
Elizabeth	S	22.2.1767	Bigbury Bay	
Elizabeth	S	17.12.1833	Northam Sands	194
Elizabeth	Sk	8.12.1854	Barnstaple	
Elizabeth	S	25.4.1857	Off Clovelly	
Elizabeth	Sc	1.11.1859	Plymouth	
Elizabeth	Kt	29.3.1871	Off Start	
Elizabeth	Kt	7.7.1890	Plymouth	
Elizabeth Lass	Brn	25.10.1859	Dartmouth	
Elizabeth Lewis	Br	10.1.1866	Torbay	
Elizabeth Maria	S	31.10.1851	Topsham	
Elizabeth Mary Ann	Sc	11.1.1887	Sidmouth	
Eliza Jones	Sc	16.12.1889	Lundy	230
Elk	SS		Plymouth	
Ellen Edwards	S	10.1.1866	Torbay	
Elsa Kuehlke	Sc	24.10.1926	Westward Ho!	200
Elsie	SS	30.1.1888	Lundy	
Elsie	Kt	27.2.1900	Eddystone	
Emile	Br	10.3.1891	Berry Head	150
Emilie	Bq	29.5.1870	Prawle Point	99
Emilie & Charles	Brn	10.1.1866	Torbay	
Emily	Sk	11.5.1897	Clovelly	176
Emily	Kt	14.1.1881	Eddystone	
Emma	S	22.11.1889	Plymouth	
Emmanuel	Br	–.1.1863	Plymouth	
Emmeline	Bq	31.12.1872	Sidmouth	
Empire Alfred	Tg	17.12.1944	Torbay	
Empire Grove	Mv	18.10.1941	Longpeak	183
Empire Harry	Tg	6.6.1945	Bolt Tail	
Empire Otter	SS	16.2.1941	Hartland	
Encourage	Mv	5.10.1940	Plymouth	65
Encouragement	Sk	14.3.1862	Start Bay	
Endeavour	Kt	19.12.1890	Ilfracombe	
English Trader	SS	23.1.1937	Dartmouth	107, 126–7
Ensign	Sc	30.1.1915	Salcombe	93
Erin	S	5.3.1850	Teignmouth	
Erin	S	3.6.1862	Ilfracombe	
Erin	Br	–.3.1833	Plymouth	
Erna	Sc	21.2.1914	Plymouth	59
Ernest	Kt	10.1.1866	Torbay	
Escort	Kt	21.4.1899	Off Lundy	231
Esperance	Sc	18.9.1879	Off Start	
Espoir	Br	22.11.1865	Plymouth	50
Estrella de Mar	Sc	1811	Lundy	222
Ethel	SS	3.2.1877	Off Lundy	228
Ethiope	SS	28.5.1915	Off Start	
Eureka	Br	6.2.1870	Dartmouth	127
Exeter	HMS/3	12.9.1691	Plymouth	
Fair City	Sc	8.1.1919	Plymouth	59–60
Faith	Sc	6.9.1851	Eddystone	44

P

Name	Type	Date	Location	Page reference
M.I	HMS/Sm	12.11.1925	Off Start	122–3
Millicent	Kt	1.4.1897	Off Lundy	231
Minesweeper No *382*	HMS	7.5.1945	Off Berry Head	
Minnie	Kt	14.4.1874	Clovelly	
Minnie	S	1.12.1882	Berry Head	
Mischief	Sc	22.11.1865	Plymouth	50
Miura	Sl	2.1.1867	Plymouth	
Mizpah	S	4.2.1899	Plymouth	
ML. 160	HMS	6.5.1942	Brixham	
Moliere	SS	27.5.1918	Hartland	181
Monarch	Kt	22.2.1917	Eddystone	
Monda	Brn	10.1.1866	Torbay	142
Montagu	HMS/B	29.5.1906	Lundy	*214–15*, 232–6
Monte Gurugu	SS	12.11.1949	Hartland/Lundy	
Monte Moro	Sc	4.8.1876	Ilfracombe	217
Moon	S	20.2.1817	Exmouth	156
Moor	HMS/4	7.3.1716	Plymouth	23
Morning Star	Kt	14.10.1910	Dartmouth	
Morrison	Brn	1823	Off Lundy	222
Moulin	Frs	7.8.1862	Off Start	109
Mountpark	SS	21.8.1917	Off Bull Point	208
Mousse Le Moyec	SS	6.12.1940	Hartland	182–3
Muse	Brn	20.2.1877	Barnstaple	190
Myra	S	8.9.1886	Plymouth	
Mystery	S	9.3.1891	Plymouth	54
Nahant	S	18.3.1846	Berry Head	140
Nancy	S	22.1.1861	Start Bay	
Nancy	Sc	18.3.1869	Hartland	174
Nancy & Betty	S	–.2.1793	Off Lundy	221
Naphtalie	Sc	22.11.1886	Eddystone	
Native	Sc	1841	Torquay	
Nebraska	Sk	1.2.1895	Plymouth	
Neches	SS	15.5.1918	Off Start	122
Nellie	Mv	13.7.1937	Off Lundy	237
Nellie Bywater		28.12.1951	Bolt Tail	
Nelly	Br	30.11.1804	Berry Head	133
Nelly	Sk	27.7.1852	Bolt Head	85
Nepaul	SS	10.12.1890	Plymouth	47
Nepenthe	Bq	16.11.1863	Hartland	
Neptune	S	31.1.1881	Salcombe	92
Nera	S	–.12.1885	Eddystone	
Nettleton	SS	11.2.1916	Hartland	180
Newholm	SS	8.9.1917	Start Point	121
Newhouse	S	5.9.1872	Lundy	228
New Prosperous	S	14.2.1888	Lundy	230
Newton	SS	21.3.1886	Hartland	
Newton	SS	7.1.1916	Barnstaple	207
Nimble	HMS	20.2.1847	Off Berry Head	140
Nimble	Kt	6.1.1888	Off Start	
Nora	S	6.10.1907	Bull Point	
Nora Roas	Sc	10.5.1883	Plymouth	53
Norbiton	SS	13.8.1887	Off Start	

270 INDEX OF SHIPS

ADDITIONAL DEVON SHIPWRECKS

GENERAL INDEX

Page numbers in italics refer to illustrations

271